THE GUIDE TO
MYSTERIOUS
PERTHSHIRE

THE GUIDE TO
MYSTERIOUS
PERTHSHIRE

GEOFF HOLDER

The
History
Press

To Mum and Dad

Frontispiece: The Pass of Killiecrankie, where many a Highland ghost has been seen.

First published in 2006 by Tempus Publishing
Reprinted 2007

Reprinted in 2010 by
The History Press
The Mill, Brimscombe Port,
Stroud, Gloucestershire, GL5 2QG
www.thehistorypress.co.uk

British Library Cataloguing in Publication Data.
A catalogue record for this book is available from the British Library.

ISBN 978 07524 4140 5

Typesetting and origination by
Tempus Publishing
Printed and bound in Great Britain.

CONTENTS

ACKNOWLEDGEMENTS

To all the people who let me poke around their property; the staff of the Local Studies section of A.K. Bell Library, Perth; the staff of Perth and Kinross Heritage Trust; West Stormont Historical Society; Charles Fort; Dave Walker, Ségolène.

Soundtrack: Stuart Maconie's Freak Zone, BBC Radio 6, www.bbc.co.uk/6music/shows/freakzone.

The photographs on pages 14, 17 (top left), 18 (top), 19, 42, 91, 95 (centre and bottom), 97, 107 (bottom), 166 and 173 are by Ségolène Dupuy; all other photographs are by the author.

INTRODUCTION

WHAT'S IN THE BOOK?

Encounters with non-human entities – ghosts, demons, fairies, angels, loch monsters and dragons.

Death and the afterlife – graveyards, tombstones and prehistoric burial sites.

Religious phenomena – miracles, holy wells and superhuman saints, as well as prehistoric ritual monuments (stone circles, standing stones and the like).

Legendary characters like King Arthur and Fingal.

Strange nature, such as out-of-place animals or disappearing lochs.

Aerial phenomena, from meteorites to UFOs.

Witchcraft and all kinds of magic.

Folklore – defined as broadly as you wish.

Gargoyles, Pictish stones and other strange and marvellous sculpture.

Bizarre behaviour, from bodysnatching to training pigs for showbusiness.

The book is organised geographically. You can find everything mysterious and weird about one location in the same place and the places flow logically with the traveller in mind. The book starts with Perth and proceeds in a more-or-less widdershins (anti-clockwise) route around the county. Cross-references to other locations are shown in SMALL CAPS. Things worth seeing are rated, from ★ to ★★★.

KEY CONCEPTS:

Apotropaic – Protective against evil.

BVM – The Blessed Virgin Mary.

Christianisation – 1. The process by which the sanctuaries (and powers) of the pagan deities were transferred to the Christian cult of the blessed dead, hence widespread saints' holy wells (formerly shrines of water divinities). 2. The de-fanging of the pagan power of standing stones by carving them with a cross.

Deus loci (or *genius loci*) – 'Spirit of the place': a pagan spirit inhabiting a river, spring, valley or other natural place. Often converted into Christian saints.

Druids – Earlier generations of antiquarians loved Druids so much they scattered their names (and their supposedly bloody sacrifices) willy-nilly across ancient sites.

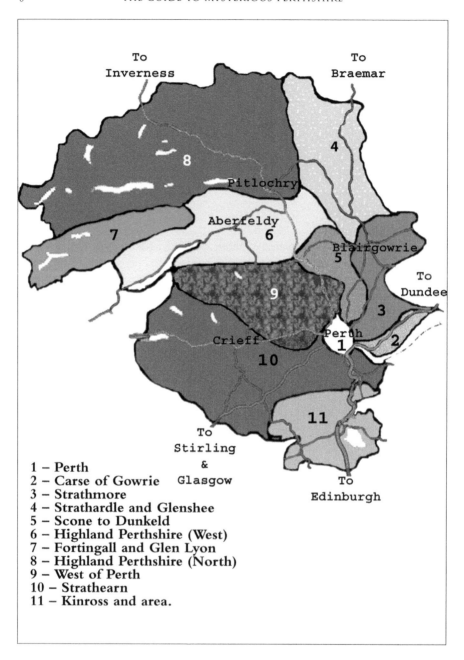

1 – Perth
2 – Carse of Gowrie
3 – Strathmore
4 – Strathardle and Glenshee
5 – Scone to Dunkeld
6 – Highland Perthshire (West)
7 – Fortingall and Glen Lyon
8 – Highland Perthshire (North)
9 – West of Perth
10 – Strathearn
11 – Kinross and area.

Above: Map of Perthshire showing chapter areas. (Map by Ségolène Dupuy)

Opposite: 'Where the blood and the oil of the sacrifices flowed'; *NSA.* Cupmark on standing stone, Fowlis Wester (not Druidic).

Druids did not actually appear until at least 1,000 years after the stone circles were erected. However, the myth has percolated down into modern popular use and now not only do standing stones get given Druid names but also the neighbouring housing development.

Fairies – Placenames featuring the Gaelic word 'sith' (pronounced 'shee', hence Glenshee) are generally taken to mark an association with the fairies. 'Sithean' and 'Sidhean' ('shee-an') usually indicate fairy knolls or hills but this is not absolute. Some sitheans were burial grounds for unbaptised infants.

Fingal and The Fingalians – Fingal (Finn MacCool) and his war band the Fianna are the Irish equivalent of King Arthur and the Knights of the Round Table. Magic, monsters and battles fill their stories. In the 1760s James MacPherson published 'authentic' (= fake) poems attributed to Fingal's son Ossian, but even before then Gaelic storytellers had transposed the original Irish stories to Scotland and there is a swathe of Fingalian placenames across Highland Perthshire.

Liminality – That which is betwixt and between, a transition, a threshold. This is very important in magic, when encountering the supernatural, and burying suicides. Liminality can apply to places (caves, bogs, rivers, parish boundaries) or times (Hallowe'en, Hogmanay and Beltane on 1 May).

Magical Thinking – 1. Certain things (a saint's relics, water from a special source, an unusual stone) have power. 2. This power can be accessed through proximity to the source so rich people paid large sums to be buried in church, the closer to the altar – the power source – the better. 3. Things which have been connected once are

Above: Statue of Ossian, Fingask Castle. Probably not sculpted from life.

Opposite: Dunsinnan Iron Age Hillfort. Macbeth was not here!

connected for ever ('sympathetic magic'); for example, illness can be transferred to clothing which is then discarded – as the clothing decays so does the illness.

The Piper in the Tunnel (PIT) – A story told all over Scotland. A piper (or drummer) enters a tunnel or cave and his companions hear the music for some time (often following it overground) but then the sound stops and the man is mysteriously never seen again. There are several local variations on this theme.

Placename Disinformation – Just because a place references a religious, mythological or famous name doesn't mean there is any actual connection between place and name, no matter what 'tradition' says. The most common placename-colonising celebrities in Perthshire are Macbeth (Shakespeare's, not history's), various saints, Bonnie Dundee, Pontius Pilate and the Romans, the Druids, and Fingal. Placename spelling corresponds to that used on the (highly recommended, nay essential) Ordnance Survey 1:25000 Explorer maps.

Simulacra – Natural formations in trees and rocks which we, pattern-seeking apes that we are, interpret as faces, animals and 'Signs from God'.

Storytelling – Our species is misnamed: *Homo sapiens* (wise human) should be *Pan narrans*, the storytelling ape. It is in our nature to take a chaotic series of events and turn it into a story; we do it all the time in our daily lives. Paranormal events are often random and confusing, but they quickly become transformed into a ghost *story*. Moral: don't depend on stories if you're looking for truth.

'Tradition' – Also known as 'it is said that', 'they say that', and other get-outs used by writers to bring a spurious gravitas to tall tales. Treat with caution.

Truth – Just because a respected chronicler from a previous age has written something down, doesn't make it true, and I'm often reporting the words of storytellers, fantasists, liars and journalists in this book; *caveat lector*.

'Roman Bridge', Glen Lyon. Not Roman.

TERMINOLOGY

Neolithic – *c.* 4,000 – 2,500 BC } The periods of the stone circles, standing stones
Bronze Age – c. 2,500 – 800 BC } and cupmarked stones

Cupmarks – prehistoric art carved into boulders, rock outcrops and standing stones, sometimes elaborated with rings, channels and more. Utterly mysterious – there are as many theories as there are experts.

Iron Age – *c.* 800 BC – early centuries AD. The actual period of the Druids.

Romans – in this part of Scotland on and off from the first to the third centuries.

Picts – Dark Age people, generally assumed to have lived from the third to tenth centuries.

Scots – Gaelic-speaking Celtic peoples from Ireland, arriving in Perthshire from the eighth century.

Pre-Reformation – before 1560.

Jacobites – supporters of the Stuart claim to the throne 1689-1746, from *Jacobus*, Latin for James (James II of England/VII of Scotland). James' son James Edward Stuart led the 1715 Rebellion and his son Charles Edward Stuart, 'Bonnie Prince Charlie', the '45 (which ended in disaster at the Battle of Culloden).

HS – sites in the care of Historic Scotland (www.historic-scotland.gov.uk).

There are many interesting graveyards to see, often with gravestones carved with symbols for death. These are indicated by the shorthand GRAVESTONES. There are also many gargoyles, grotesques, Classical figures, Green Men and other similar carvings

Typical eighteenth-century carved gravestone: winged soul, sexton's tools, *memento mori* banner, hourglass, skull and crossed bones.

worth viewing; these are shown by the shorthand GARGOYLES. When they are not discussed in the main text, these, and other things to see in the surrounding area – such as the archaeological curiosities – are listed in each location.

SOURCES

Many references come from *The Statistical Account of Scotland*, usually called the 'Old', hence the abbreviation *OSA*. Published in the 1790s by Sir John Sinclair, each parish was described by its Church of Scotland minister. The similarly compiled *New Statistical Account* (*NSA*) was published between 1834 and 1845. Both accounts are incomparable resources (www.edina.ac.uk/stat-acc-scot), although allowances have to be made for the ministers' prejudices. The *Third Statistical Account for Perthshire and Kinross-shire* was published in 1980.

Much of the witchcraft material here is taken from the *Survey of Scottish Witchcraft* database at www.arts.ed.ac.uk/witches.

Much archaeological detail on standing stones and related phenomena can be found at the online 'Canmore' database of the Royal Commission on the Ancient and Historical Monuments of Scotland, www.rcahms.gov.uk. Other recommended internet sites are Andy Sweet's megalith-tastic www.stravaiging.com/history/ancient/stones and www.themodernantiquarian.com, based on Julian Cope's epic guidebook of the same name.

Carved foliate animal face, High Street, Perth.

THE SCOTTISH OUTDOOR ACCESS CODE

Everyone has the right to be on most land and inland water providing they act responsibly. Your access rights and responsibilities are explained fully in the *Scottish Outdoor Access Code*. Find out more by visiting www.outdooraccess-scotland.com or phoning your local Scottish Natural Heritage office.

The key things to remember when you are out are:

- *take responsibility for your own actions*
- *respect the interests of other people*
- *care for the environment*

Access rights can be exercised over most of Scotland, from urban parks and path networks to our hills and forests, and from farmland and field margins to our beaches, lochs and rivers. However, access rights don't apply everywhere, such as in buildings or their immediate surroundings, or in houses or their gardens, or most land in which crops are growing.

Many sites in this book are near houses and other private property; always ask permission – it's good manners. Don't disturb animals – wild or domestic. Respect the sites – don't scrape away lichen, leave offerings, do any damage or drop litter (even better, pick litter up – it's good karma).

PERTH

MYTHOLOGICAL ORIGINS

King Lear's second daughter Regan had a son who governed the whole of Britain long before the Christian era. He built three temples, to Apollo in Cornwall, Mercury at Bangor and Mars in Perth. Later the Romans turned up and, delighted at finding a temple to their favourite god of war already in place, built the city-grid of Bertha around the holy precinct. In the eighteenth century the Kirk or House in the Green, on the site of the temple, was regarded as the omphalos, the focal point of Roman Perth. Even the double-headed eagle of the current arms of Perth – seen everywhere on buildings and signs –refers back to the Romans. But the entire story is fabulation. Perth wasn't founded until at least 500 years after the Romans left. The fort of Bertha (two miles north) was purely a military camp and there was no city attached (in fact there were no Roman urban developments in this part of Scotland at all). 'Perth' actually means brake, bush or copse, but whatever vegetation inspired this pre-urban name is unknown. King Lear and Regan didn't exist. There were no early Britons making sacrifices to Mars, a tale that comes solely from Geoffrey of Monmouth, an eleventh-century chronicler who was never one to let the facts get in the way of a good story. Geoffrey invented an entire politically-motivated royal mythology to bolster the supposed ancient ancestry of the rulers of his era. Historians like Holinshed took Geoffrey at his word and provided the spurious British mythological source material which Shakespeare reworked into *King Lear* and *Cymbeline*.

TAY STREET

Greyfriars Burial Ground★★★ on site of former Greyfriars monastery, destroyed at the Reformation. GRAVESTONES★★★ A place capable of bringing out anyone's inner goth.

Above: Tombstone detail, Greyfriars graveyard.

Left: Tombstone with angels of the resurrection, Greyfriars graveyard.

Left: Tombstone detail, Greyfriars graveyard.

Below: Tombstone, Greyfriars graveyard.

Above left: Tombstone detail, Greyfriars graveyard.

Above right: Face simulacrum in a tree, Greyfriars graveyard.

Below: Skull and hourglasses over entrance, Greyfriars graveyard.

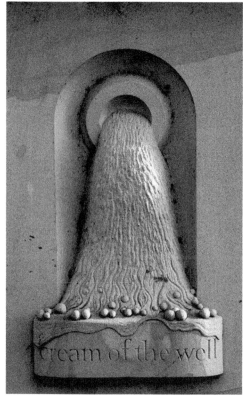

Above left: Flood defences, Tay Street, *Ecce Tiber* (Behold the Tiber) – as not said by the Romans.

Above right: Flood defences, Tay Street. The 'cream' is water from a holy well on 1 May.

Left: Flood defences, Tay Street. King Snake.

Flood defences, Tay Street.

Pseudo-creatures and symbolic sculptures on new flood walls,★★ Gargoyles on Nos 2-68,★★ Perth and Kinross Council Buildings, 2 High Street,★★★ St Matthew's Church,★ The Capital Asset and former Middle Kirk.★

In 1600 James VI turned up unexpectedly at Gowrie House, home of the power-ful Ruthven family in pursuit of a cock-and-bull story about mysterious gold. He ended up alone in a tower room for several hours with the teenaged and good-look-ing Master of Ruthven, possibly having sex, or at least trying to persuade the young lad to do so. According to the only testimony ever released – that of James himself – the Master and his older brother, the 22-year-old Earl of Gowrie, then attempted to assassinate him. James managed to get to a window and shout treason. His men burst through the door and stabbed the two 'conspirators'. A man in armour who was also in the locked room somehow managed to disappear without anyone other than the king seeing him. What actually happened has exercised historians ever since, with several conflicting theories. Whatever the truth of the Gowrie Conspiracy, it's undeniable that James was conveniently relieved of a £80,000 debt he owed the Earl. James was generous to those who had saved him, and so the confiscated palace

No. 2 High Street, Perth and Kinross Council buildings, formerly headquarters of General Accident.

and lands of SCONE were transferred to the Murrays, who still hold them today. In a move that would have gladdened the black heart of anyone involved in modern spin and 'reality management', much was made of the Earl of Gowrie's addiction to magic, based on a magical parchment found in a pouch on his body. On it was written the Tetragrammaton, the four Hebrew letters that make up the holy name of God, a charm to stop a wound bleeding. The charm may well have been real, but then all his contemporaries would have either used similar magical protection or at least believed in it. To damn the Earl for his beliefs in this area was to ignore the general credulity of the age. The people of Perth were deeply sceptical about the whole affair, which soon generated a supernatural aspect. Observers claimed to see re-runs of the events, with dopplegängers of James leaning out of the window shouting treason, and a whole host of ghostly shouts and screams. Sadly, there is nothing left of 'Perth's Dealey Plaza', having been replaced by the County Buildings and Sheriff's Court.

PERTH MUSEUM AND ART GALLERY★★

78, George Street. Open 10–5 Mon-Sat. Free entry. 01738 632488. www.pkc.gov.uk/ah.

It's a good rule of thumb that any local collection will include a number of items with a ritual, religious, magical or just plain weird association, and Perth Museum is no exception. Although there are no big signs saying so there are tidbits all over the place if you look hard enough. Highlights include:

The St Madoes Stone, large Pictish cross-slab.
A bronze cauldron deposited in a bog at Abercairney. The size and quality of this Celtic ritual deposit makes it the Iron Age equivalent of sacrificing a BMW.
Six Neolithic carved stone balls. These beautiful ritual objects, laboriously fashioned out of hard rock, have no obvious practical function. One suggestion from comparative anthropology is that they are 'talking stones' – you can only talk at a tribal

No. 2 High Street.

gathering if you hold the stone. Other possibilities are symbols of chiefship or priestship.
A Celtic stone head (ritual function?) found in a garden in Beech Hill Place, Coupar
Angus.

A rough boulder with four carved heads. One head has such deep circular eyes it
appears to be wearing spectacles.

A Roman altar stone to the (divine) emperor from the fort at Bertha.

St Fillan's Bell, formerly kept at STRUAN church. In *Church and Social History of
Atholl*, historian John Kerr relates how a Rannoch man stole it and placed it on a rock
at the top of Bohespic Hill, where it miraculously remained stuck. It was only when
he resolved to return it and faced the right direction that it unstuck itself.

A replica brass death collar, inscribed 'Alex. Stewart sentenced to death for theft at
Perth 5th Dec 1701'. In a kind of extreme community service, Stewart had his death
sentence commuted to lifetime servitude with one of the local nobles, who effectively
had him as a slave for the rest of his life. Stewart had to wear the collar at all times. If
he misbehaved he could be returned to the authorities and executed.

A Tahitian mourner's costume, worn by a priest when patrolling the area around a
corpse to protect the spirit of the dead person. He and his followers were permitted
to injure or even kill anyone they met.

On 3rd December 1917 Perthshire was bombarded from space. At 1.15pm a brilliant
fireball was seen. Detonations followed, meaning the meteor exploded in mid-air.
All four pieces of the Strathmore Meteorite are on display. At 12.30pm on 17 May
1830 a small meteorite 17cm across hit the North Inch during a thunderstorm.

A small section on Witchcraft and Magic, with information on Kate McNiven (see
CRIEFF), the Maggie Wall witch memorial (see DUNNING), the trial of Isabell
Haldane (see p. 28) and Inchadney healing well.

A cupmarked and cross-incised stone from near WEEM.

Three Pictish stones; the main sculpture on the Pittensorn stone shows two men
whose genitals are being bitten by interlaced serpents. As the text on the case dryly
puts it, 'This is an image of hell'.

The four concealed shoes are not normally on display. Concealed shoes turn up only when old buildings are renovated so no one really knows who deposited them or how many still exist *in situ*. In *The Archaeology of Ritual and Magic* Ralph Merrifield notes that builders deposited the items under conditions of great secrecy, usually not telling the householder. It is possible that many of the items represent a folk belief among the building trade – a way of ensuring the houses they built were 'lucky'. Apotropaic items found concealed in houses include gloves, spoons, clay tobacco pipes, animal bones and skulls, candlesticks, glassware and live, dead or deliberately smoked or mummified animals such as chickens, cats, birds, mice and rats. The idea was that any evil entering the house is trapped in the concealed object. Boots and shoes are by far the most common concealed items. Very occasionally the shoe is cut with a cross, presumably to invoke official as well as unofficial protection. Deliberately mutilated shoes represent malevolent magic – not only is the 'luck' removed but the damaged shoe is actually an invitation to an evil spirit. To find out more about concealed shoes in your area, see www.concealed.garments. org. Also not usually on display but in the collection are an 'elf shot' (a Bronze Age flint arrowhead), a curing stone, and a really strange Romano-Celtic stone head.

NORTH PORT

The Fair Maid's House at North Port is lacklustre, but there is a gruesome story to cheer us up. In 1863 workmen laying a new floor discovered the skeleton of a tall, well-built man. The bones were not just under the surface but below two earlier stone floors. As medieval peoples were not given to burying their relatives under the floorboards, this looks like a deliberately hidden body. The room had been the meeting hall of the Glovers guild. If anyone wants to speculate on professional jealousy in the world of glove making and subsequent murder with scissors, be my guest. The original report (*Perthshire Advertiser*, 8 January 1863) said that some of the bones were thrown out with the rubbish but others were replaced in the position they were found. This sounds like they might still be there. Another murder victim was found in a shallow pit under the floor of a building during the 2003 excavations in advance of the construction of the Horse Cross concert hall.

BLACKFRIARS STREET

On 20 February 1437 James I was murdered at the Dominican Friary here. As described in a 1440 account 'The Dethe and False Murdure of James Stewarde, Kyng of Scotys', James was travelling from Edinburgh to Perth when he was stopped at the Water of Leith by a woman who prophesied his death. Described as Irish, but probably a Gaelic-speaking Highlander, she stood in the middle of the road and said, 'My Lord King, and ye pass this water, ye shall never return again alive'. Her message came from 'Huthart' (presumably a supernatural advisor or, as he would nowadays be styled, a spirit guide). Huthart may also be the same as 'Ethart', the spirit familiar of a West Highland witch in the seventeenth century. James had already heard of an old prophecy that foretold the death of a Scottish king that year, so he sent one of his knights to question the soothsayer. The knight dismissed her as a drunken fool and the royal party continued to Perth. During a feast the woman again appeared to warn the king. James told her to return the following day, but that meeting never took place. That night the plotters burst into the royal apartments and stabbed James. The king was hiding in the very cludgie whose drain he had previously ordered blocked up because he kept losing his tennis balls down it.

Another prophecy had also encouraged the regicides. Walter, Earl of Atholl had been told by a witch that he would 'wear a crown before he died'. During his later torture a red-hot crown was placed on his head. In *The Magic Arts in Celtic Britain*, the great folklore scholar Lewis Spence argues that Huthart may be etymologically linked with the Gaelic words for crow or raven, creatures whose shapes were sometimes taken by the Irish spirit called the banshee. Spence sees the Irish woman who warned James not as an actual human being but as a banshee, an ancestral spirit who is tied to the royal Stuart line and appears to warn of impending death. Another mysterious figure warned James IV not to fight at the Battle of Flodden Field; like James I, he ignored the prophecy and was killed.

HIGH STREET, KING EDWARD STREET AND ST JOHN'S PLACE
Perth Theatre has been haunted by the Grey Lady since a fire in 1924. GARGOYLES★ on the corner with King Edward Street and on the Market Cross. St John's Kirk★★ had a relic of the fictional blacksmith saint St Eloy (possibly to appease or get money out of the powerful Hammermen Guild) and over forty altars to various other saints. The numerous monasteries and chapels of the city – and the magnificent Augustinian abbey at SCONE – were annihilated by the Reformation mob following John Knox's famous rabble-rousing sermon in the Kirk. A combination of religious hatred and naked avarice ensured that not a single stone of the religious houses survives above ground.

SOUTH STREET
There are GARGOYLES★ on Café Royalle, Royal Bar and Dickens Bar. Near the junction with Princes Street see carving of axe, cleaver, bone saw and two long cutting blades. In *No Common Task,* ghosthunter extraordinary, Peter Underwood relates the experience of Jack and Gwen Mott, who were staying in the oldest part of the Salutation Hotel on 13 August 1975. About one o'clock, on a hot and oppressive night, Jack, who was lying on his side, woke with a feeling of great cold on his back. Turning over he saw an immaculately turned out Scottish soldier wearing green tartan and white spats. The man was solid and appeared real in every way; his face was fierce but not menacing. Jack somehow knew he meant him no harm and went back to sleep. When he woke again the soldier was still there, but this time gradually faded away. The door was locked and the key was still on the table.

Around the 1745 rebellion an English traveller, along with his horse and valise, disappeared from a house in South Street, the second above the Meal Vennel.

No. 15 High Street.
Marriage lintel. The
head is James Graham,
Marquess of Montrose.

St John's Kirk.

St John's Kirk, detail.

Above: Lloyd's Pharmacy.

One of numerous Green Men on McCash & Hunter, South Methven Street. This one bears a striking resemblance to Joseph Stalin.

The landlord became suspiciously rich but the crime was never investigated. Popular opinion believed divine justice caused all the landlord's children to be born mad. Around 1808, when the house was pulled down and rebuilt, a skeleton was discovered under the hearthstone of the former kitchen. Meal Vennel was also the home of Black Jean. In the early part of the nineteenth century lassies would come thirty miles to seek the old fortune-teller's advice on a choice of husband.

See GARGOYLES★★ on York Place, Caledonian Road Primary School,★★ Morrisons supermarket (modern),★ No. 59, Pizza Express,★ and McCash & Hunter,★★ both North Methven Street. Fabulous winged sphinx on corner of Mill Street and Scott Street, near two owls★ and the words 'Light' and 'Wisdom' on former Sandeman Library, now Sandeman 'superpub'. Oh the irony.

INVASION OF THE BODYSNATCHERS

In the eighteenth century medical apprentices had to provide at least one body for dissection as part of the terms of their studies. The easiest and cheapest source was recently buried corpses. The garden at Atholl House, a doctors' mansion formerly on Watergate, sloped down to the river where Tay Street now stands. Corpses stolen at night from the graveyards at Kinfauns and Kinnoull on the opposite bank were delivered via boat to a secret staircase down to the basement dissecting room next to the river. A bye-law against the 'raising and abusing' of dead bodies was passed by the council, although this did little to limit the predations. In *Traditions of Perth* George Penny describes how on one occasion a couple of 'resurrectionists' parked a body in a wheelbarrow while visiting a drinking den. A group of boatmen saw this, removed the corpse and one of them took its place in the barrow. When the bodysnatchers returned one asked the other if they should take South Street. The boatman promptly roared out, 'No, by God, you'd better take the Watergate!' Cue hasty exit of two grave robbers.

WATERGATE

At No. 24, John Queen & Son plumbers, is the site of a long-term haunting reported in the *Perthshire Advertiser* 1 September 1995. During winter the staff would turn off the water and drain the cistern before leaving, in case the pipes burst overnight. But each morning the water would be back on. This had been going on for twelve years. In April 1994 clairvoyant Mairie Wares from Methven made contact with a spirit called John during an overnight vigil. He is reported to have said, 'I was a merchant who ran a small but thriving business here in Watergate. My family and myself worked hard, selling ham and cheese among other things, but I was very proud of my collection of ales which were very popular amongst the gentry… I think it was around October 1808, when Gillespie accused me and my family of conspiracy against the Crown. He was a very jealous man and his trade was not doing well at all. When the soldiers came to arrest us we all hid in the basement. We could hear them bursting their way into the premises and there was a lot of noise – we feared for our lives. We decided to wait for several hours until dark then slip away. But when we tried to emerge from our hiding place, we couldn't get out. My son and myself wrestled with the doorway until our fingers bled. As time passed we tried again and again – to no avail. One by one my family died and I could do nothing.' Who 'Gillespie' was, and why John kept turning the water back on, are equally obscure.

Oliver Cromwell built a great fortification on the South Inch. Lachlan Buchanan, in *Stories From Perth's History*, describes how the Restoration of 1660 was marked by two omens – a thistle grew over the Commonwealth arms on the front of the Citadel, and a small fish called the Cherry of Tay, which had vanished during Cromwell's time, reappeared in abundance. Thus nature confirmed that the world was once more in its proper kingly balance. Cromwell had offered a reward for the best lines on the death of a trooper named Monday. A Perth shoemaker suggested:

Blessed be the Sabbath Day,
And cursed be worldly pelf;
Tuesday will begin the week,
Since Monday's hanged himself.

Cromwell thought this was a so chortlesome he decreed that shoemakers should be allowed to enjoy a holiday called 'Cobblers' Monday'.

On Fridays and Saturdays in summer Gary Knight runs History and Horror Tours in the city centre. In the persona of John Larg, a violent criminal who was hanged in Perth in 1817, Knight tells everyday stories of cannibalism, ghosts, murders, clan feuds, witchcraft, execution and plague.

WITCHCRAFT IN PERTH

The North Inch was the main execution ground for convicted witches. After the Reformation local kirk sessions became responsible for 'moral discipline'. Daily life became subject to the obsessions of a grim fundamentalist local theocracy and witches and their supposed Satanic master soon figured large in some disturbed imaginations. 'Thou shalt not suffer a witch to live' (Exodus 22:18) was taken literally (the accurate translation is in fact 'poisoner', not 'witch'). Witches often confessed, but this cannot be taken at face value. Unlike in England, torture was legal in Scotland, and accused people would say anything under torture, such as naming their friends and neighbours as fellow witches. The kirk session extracted a confession, then obtained a local commission to prosecute from the civil authorities. Once the witch's guilt had been established in the civil court, she could be sentenced, strangled and burnt. Some witches didn't even get that far, dying in custody of abuse or simple neglect, cold and starvation. Witchcraft became a capital crime in the 1570s. Perth's catalogue of shame starts on 29 December 1572, when Janet Boyman was convicted and burnt. The following gives an impression:

1580. 20 December. An unnamed witch banished.

1582. 12 February. A suspected witch was living in the Meal Vennel. 1 April. A witch was incarcerated in the Tolbooth.

1589. 2 November. John Watson and his daughter Helen Watson accused Guddal, the elderly wife of Richard Watson of Tirsappie, of witchcraft. Neighbours testified she was a poor honest woman and certainly not a witch. The Kirk Session decided the accusation was brought out of personal spite, dismissed the case and charged John and Helen Watson with slander. The shared surnames of the accused and accusers may mean this was a family dispute, a malign soap opera with added malefica.

1 December. Violet Brown was investigated for 'divining', using a sieve to magically discover the location of some lost gold, possibly as part of a fraud.

1596. 27 November. Christian Stewart of Nokwalter was executed in Edinburgh for causing the death of Patrick Ruthven at Gowrie House (see TAY STREET). Patrick must have been a relative of the Earl of Gowrie. The murder weapon was an enchanted black clout (a rag or piece of cloth) containing a piece of iron, produced by Katherine Stewart. Christian left the clout near a gate where her victim often walked, after which she gave it to the Devil. When it became obvious she was going to be tried she tried to cure Patrick with a herb bath. But he still died.

1598. 9 September. Janet Robertson, Agnes Macause and Bessie Ireland were burned on the South Inch. The few snippets we have of this case are intriguing. Bessie and Agnes had somehow previously convinced the Earl and Countess of Atholl of their innocence, and the Duke had refused to hand them over. There then followed a complaint from two other accused witches, Margaret Stewart and Issobel Douglas, that their arrests were based on false accusations by Bessie and Agnes. The latter therefore had their trial processes suspended while both sets of accused witches confronted each other in front of the Privy Council, the highest court in the land. We are not told what took place other than that the first three were executed.

1601. A strange and vicious case of failed witchcraft took place at Balhousie Castle, on the west side of the North Inch. Roy, the castle's cook, lusted after Elizabeth, daughter of Lord Colin Eviot. First he consulted Walter Lauder, bookbinder and burgess of Perth. This pillar of the community gave Roy an aphrodisiac, the notorious Spanish Fly; it almost killed Elizabeth. Roy's next ploy was to hollow out part of an apple, fill it with his semen, and give it to the girl to eat. (This may be a masculine echo of the still-current spell in which women include their menstrual blood in food to keep a man faithful.) This too failed to win the maiden's heart, so to satisfy 'his filthie and beastlie appetyte' he used a potion of daffodil roots supplied by a witch; it made the poor girl vomit copiously. Finally the young cook gave up on magic altogether. He was tried for raping Elizabeth on 21 February but despite his confession was declared innocent. A complaint was made to the Privy Council who, when they learned of the witchcraft, reversed the decision (clearly witch-consulting counted for more than rape). But this was three months later and in the interval Roy had fled the area, and he does not appear on any judicial record thereafter. James VI prosecuted the jury for wilful error.

1612. 22 December. Janet Campbell and a woman called Robertson were held in the Tolbooth for witchcraft.

1615. 30 May. Marion Murdoch imprisoned awaiting trial for witchcraft. No further news.

1620. December 18. James Stewart imprisoned on suspicion of witchcraft.

1623. 18 July. Execution of Isabel Haldane, Margaret Hormscleugh and Janet Trall (see p. 30).

1628. 30 July. John Bog investigated for using 'devilish means' to divine the location of his stolen purse. Anyone who has ever lost their car keys may have some sympathy for him. In 1626 Bessie Wright had been repeatedly brought before the Kirk Session of Scone and had promised to stop plying her cures, but two years later she was back in the dock. The main accusations appear to relate to healing rituals and advice that did not work (i.e. the patients died). The herbs and other ingredients that she used in salves included rippell grasse (ripple grass or robwort plantain), finglie (possibly finkle or fennel), and hyssop, plus the obscure waffron leaf and plantain feather. (Don't try any of these at home.) She denied she had used foxtree leaves (foxglove), the source of digitalis, a noted poison. Her skill, she said, came from a book which had been handed down from her grandfather to her father to her, and was a thousand years old, but as she was illiterate her son, Adam Bell, would read out parts to her. The book was taken from her by the minister of Perth around 1611, so clearly she had been well-known as a witch for many years. Her ultimate fate is unknown. What the minister did with the grimoire is not recorded.

1632. 21 May. Laurence Boik and his wife Janet Black confessed to using an incantation to heal sores:

> The sores are risen through God's work,
> And must be laid through God's help;
> The mother Mary, and her dear son,
> Lay the sores that are begun.

Again, there is no further entry so we do not know the result of the case. Note the couple were prosecuted for trying to help people.

1634. 30 December. Robert Thomson, maltman, was punished for placing his child in the water race between the parts of the wheel at Mill of Balhousie, 'a lesson of Satan'. Using a mill in healing was common practice.

1643. 30 November. Agnes Stoddart, Thomas Rob and Jean Rob executed for witchcraft in Perth.

1649. 'Many witches' executed in Perth, Fife, Stirling, Linlithgow, Edinburgh and Haddington.

From 1651 to 1660 Scotland was ruled by Oliver Cromwell and there was not a single witch trial during these years, while there were 120 across Scotland in a single month in 1661.

1662. There was a major witch-hunt in Perth with fifty-five cases. As before, however, the details are sketchy; not all would have been brought to trial.

1715. Margaret Ogilvy and Sarah Johnson burnt on the North Inch. These appear to be the last people executed for witchcraft in Perth; the last witchcraft execution in Scotland took place at Dornoch, Sutherland in 1727. Witchcraft ceased to be a capital offence in 1736.

Perth's legacy of magic continues into modern times. Raymond Buckland is one of the best-known modern practitioners of witchcraft, his Seax-Wica group having a high profile in America. Buckland acknowledges his debt to Gerald Gardner, an eccentric and controversial man who became the first publicly known witch when witchcraft was taken off the statute books as a crime in 1951. The historian Ronald Hutton called Gardner the originator of a countercultural religion that united paganism with the figure of the witch. Gardner is credited with inventing the whole notion of modern witchcraft – every witch 'self-help book' that talks about covens, athames (ritual knives), cleansing rituals, the horned god, and the nature goddess owes something to Gardner's powers of invention, no matter how much an attempt is made to claim a continuity with historical witchcraft. Buckland was initiated into Gardnerian witchcraft by Gardner's then High Priestess, Monique Wilson, also known by her Gardnerian magical name of Lady Olwen. This took place in autumn 1963 at an unidentified house in Perth, where Wilson was then living.

In June 2004, forty-two year-old Mary Stewart caused a drunken disturbance at Perth Royal Infirmary. She shouted at the police who had been called to the incident, 'I have got gypsy blood in me and I'll put a curse on you'. (*Perthshire Advertiser* 29 October 2004.)

THE WITCH TRIAL OF 1623

The trial of Isabel Haldane, Margaret Hormscleugh and Janet Trall is well-known case, because unusually, much of the trial documentation has survived. The three women were first examined by the kirk session court in May and June. They were clearly tortured, as there is a note that the 'punishment should not endanger life nor limb'.

Margaret Hormscleuch of Perth, to cure Alexander Mason's wife, ordered a member of the household to collect south running water from the Tay, not to speak coming or going, and to hold the mouth of the pig (vessel) to the north. She washed the sick woman with this water, then made a bath of oatmeal. The woman was instantly cured, got up, and ate with Margaret.

She cured Marjory Lamb, sick by an 'ill wind', in the Muirton. She washed her with south running water and rubbed her arms with fresh butter. She learned these cures from Oliver Rattray's wife in Pittmudyne. She restored milk to the cow of Robert Christie from Ruthven by ordering a peck of draff (a measure of grain) to be carried home to the cow in the name of the Father, the Son and the Holy Ghost.

She restored milk to the cow of Andrew Louraine in Muirside, by mumbling some words over a firlot of draff (another measure of grain), which he bought by her directions. She sent him home with it, he cut the cow's ear, mixed the blood with the draff and the cow gave milk.

Patrick Auchinleck became sick as he was working at the plough, so she washed him in south running water and bathed him in black wool and butter.

She bewitched Patrick Ruthven, a skinner from Perth.

Issobell Haldane of Perth, ten years previously, was taken from her bed and was carried to a hillside which opened into Fairyland. She stayed there three days, from Thursday to noon on Sunday, then a grey-bearded man took her out again. The hint is that she acquired her powers from this period in the Otherworld.

The greybeard told her things from the future. With this information she told the carpenter James Christie that there was no hurry in making a cradle for one of his customers, as the child would not be born for five weeks and it would die before it could use the cradle. She also told Margaret Buchanan that she would perish in a few days' time; the perfectly healthy woman duly wasted away and died.

She cured Andrew Duncan's child by taking water from the burn at the Turret Port (while not speaking), and on her knees washed the child in the name of the Trinity.

Then with Alexander Lockheart she took the water and the child's sark (shirt or night-dress) and cast both into the burn. On the way she spilt some of the water and it was said that if anyone had walked over it they would have received the child's sickness.

She made 'three several cakes' every one of them made of nine curns (grains) of meal, which had been gotten from nine women that were 'married maidens'; she made a hole in the crown of every cake and put a child through every cake three times in the name of the Trinity. There were women present who put the children three times backwards through the same cakes, using the same words. These references to cakes made of just a few grains, but large enough to pass a child through, have resisted interpretation.

She went silent to the well of Ruthven and returned silent, bringing water to wash John Gow's child and she deposited part of the child's sark at the well, and did the same for John Powery's child.

She unwitched Patrick Ruthven, the skinner who had been bewitched by Margaret Hormscleuch. To do this she lay on top of him on his bed, muttered a few strange words then got up, telling him he was now free of the spell.

Three years earlier Stephen Ray from Muirton had tried to stop her stealing some beer from Balhoussie Hall. Isabell had clapped him on the shoulder and said, 'Go thy way! Thou shalt not win thyself a morsel of bread for a year and a day!' Ray claimed he then wasted away due to a terrible disease. Haldane admitted she had stolen the beer but had only said to Ray, 'He that delivered me from the fairy folk shall take amends on thee!' Presumably this would be the grey-bearded spirit.

She made a brew from star-grass leaves gathered by her son, and used it as a drink to cure many sick children. The wife of David Morrice of Perth consulted her about her child, whom she feared was a changeling (a sick fairy substituted for her stolen real child). Haldane confirmed the diagnosis and prescribed a certain drink with magical powers, but the child died after taking it. Another interpretation is that she deliberately administered a lethal dose to quickly bring about the death of the changeling.

Janet Trall of Blackruthven was taken from her childbirth bed to a dub (a pond) near her house door in Dunning, and was 'puddled and troubled' by the fairy folks, some red, some grey, and riding horses. Their leader, a bonny white man riding on a grey horse told her to speak of God and help poor folks through washing, bathing, speaking words, putting sick persons through hasps of yarn and the like.

She cured Janet Burry's child who was sick 'by dint of an evil wind'. She told two people to get south running water silently, wash the child, then take the water and the sark and cast both into the place where the water was taken. The child was then bathed with black wool and butter. She 'got a shot star at the burnside, and sent it in with black wool, and after the cure was used the child was healed'. A shot star was the jelly fungus Tremella mesenterica, better known as witch's butter, which is found on dead wood; it was thought to be most in evidence after rain and was supposed to be the substance of a fallen shooting star. [It has no known curative or hallucinogenic properties].

Duncan Tewis and Isabell Haldane came to her house in Black Ruthven because Duncan's child was paralysed, possibly being near death. She took the child on her knee in front of the fire, and 'drew the fingers of its hands and every toe of its feet, mumbling all the while some words that could not be heard, and immediately the child was cured'.

A great deal of information can be gleaned from the above on folk beliefs and folk magic. There is an emphasis on south running water, the importance of silence and holy words, and the sympathetic magic of transferring illness to clothing and water. There is the use of plants, grain, black wool, butter and oatmeal – commonly available materials to the peasant population. It was undoubtedly not a good idea to cross any of the three women, but on the other hand most of their activities were aimed at healing and, most interestingly, there is the involvement of the fairies. Perhaps by emphasising the fairy aspect they hoped to show they had nothing to do with the devil or powers of evil. If this was the case, their hopes were sadly misplaced; to the seventeenth-century élite, fairies appear to have been every bit as demonic as Satan's hordes.

Having heard these confessions, the kirk session obtained a commission, which inevitably found the women guilty. They were strangled at the stake and burned on Friday 18 July 1623, probably in a hollow in the North Inch. The kirk session then censured the people who had sought the cures, forcing them to make public repentance on a Sunday before noon, dressed in black cloth, and standing under the bell ropes, the latter being a particular mark of disgrace.

The details are variously from: George F. Black, *A Calendar of Cases of Witchcraft in Scotland*, David Pickering, *Dictionary of Witchcraft*, the *NSA,* and webdb.ucs.ed.ac.uk/witches. Dalyell, in *The Darker Superstitions of Scotland*, wrongly gives Isabell Haldane's name as Isabell Wall; this may just possibly be a link to the case of Maggie Wall (see DUNNING).

THE TAY

Ron Halliday (*UFO Scotland*) records how Angela Humphreys was crossing one of the Tay bridges in 1985 when she was suddenly enclosed in complete silence. Then she saw a translucent circular craft near her. It was about 30 to 40ft long and through a window she could see several small beings, one of whom was manoeuvring the ship with a set of levers. It vanished, or moved out of sight, then reappeared again moving alongside the river. When it finally could no longer be seen the world of sound returned around Angela. It was clear to her that no-one else had seen anything.

The Ravenna Cosmography – a list of all the important places throughout the Roman Empire compiled in the seventh century by an unknown monk in the Italian monastery at Ravenna - contains a haphazard list of Roman Britain. Among the places mentioned are several *loca*, which appear to be tribal meeting or holy places. One, *Locus Taba*, has been interpreted as *Tava*, the Tay. Celtic expert Anne Ross (*Pagan Celtic Britain*) says the loca may be places where Iron Age religious cults held ritual gatherings, possibly at simple shrines. Many rivers had their own *genius loci*, usually female. Tava, (or Taus) and Tatha, may have referred to a goddess, Talitha, 'the silent one'. Like all good goddesses, Talitha required to be kept sweet with gifts, or she could retaliate with flooding or drowning. Many valuable Bronze and Iron Age objects – swords, cauldrons, shields and axes – were deposited in the Tay and its tributaries. At the start of the fishing season whisky is still ceremoniously emptied into the Tay, accompanied by the skirl of the pipes.

In the seventeenth century a well-known prophecy ran:

Says the Shochie to the Ordie
Where shall we twa meet?
At the Cross o' bonny St Johnstoun
When a' men are fast asleep.

Bridges across the Tay were frequently destroyed by floodwaters. When John Mylne's new bridge was finally completed in 1616 after several years of construction, an urban legend grew up that the Cross of Perth was taken down and built into the central arch of the bridge as a means of protecting the city against the prophecy (but this was not true). Coincidentally in 1621 a three-day storm swept away the bridge and flooded the city so perhaps the prophecy came true after all.

Crawford Smith, in *The Historians of Perth*, tells how a religious fanatic publicly announced he would walk on the Tay. He first ordered sawdust to be thickly sprinkled on the river, to prevent water from dazzling his eyes, then stepped out, stopping only when the water was up to his neck, saying 'O Lord! Ye'll surely no drown poor Peter Mackie this way, gaun ye'r ain errands'. [loosely translated as 'I won't do your work for you, Big Man'.] The crowd loved it.

Some time before the Reformation a very large bell was on its way to Perth for installation in St John's Kirk. Unfortunately the men unloading it at Friarton Pier dropped the bell and it sank to the bottom of the deep Friarton Hole. Many years later a diver tried to recover the bell. At the very earliest this must have been in the late seventeenth century, the period which saw the first successful diving contraptions. The diver returned to the surface empty-handed and terrified. He claimed he had seen 'the devil and his dam' (wife) using the bell for making porridge. There is no record of the bell being disturbed thereafter, so presumably it is still down there, being used as the underwater porridge pot of Mr and Mrs Satan.

A different kind of Tay monster was encountered by Irish Johnny, a well-known fisherman. As reported in the *Perthshire Courier* (1 October 1889) he was out very early above Woody Island (NO105265) when through the mist he saw a terrible beast approaching. It had a white top and a big crest of feathers 15ft high, and was moving slowly but surely through the water. Johnny was at first petrified, but as it got nearer he found his legs and headed for the bank. It was only then that he recognized 'the Otter', another fisherman, who, because of the cold, had wound a large handkerchief around his head, leaving only the eyes visible. The 'feathers' were the bushy leaves of the long branch he had been carrying to steady himself as he crossed the ford.

EAST OF THE RIVER

Somewhere in Bridgend, in an old tenement, a very noisy ghost made an incessant racket day and night, with an audience of 'gaping petrified listeners'. An exorcism made no impact. There is no record of what eventually happened, or even when this was, but it must have been before 1836, when George Penny wrote about it in *Traditions of Perth*. Apart from the noise there were no other ghostly phenomena and Penny put the whole thing down to sound pollution transmitted by shared floor-boards from the neighbouring tenements.

Kinnoull Aisle and Monument★, off Dundee Road. Open 10-5 April – September (not weekends). Admission free. Monument to George Hay, 1st Earl of Kinnoull, within the former North aisle of the medieval church of Kinnoull. Amid the Baroque clutter, angels reveal the privy purse to Hay, dressed for his day job as Chancellor of Scotland. Another beneficiary of the GOWRIE CONSPIRACY, he was granted the Perth estates of the Earl of Gowrie. Kinnoull Burial ground has interesting grave-stones★. In the 1980s the gendarmes investigated the discovery of a sheep's head, dead rats and a ritual knife hidden in a box beneath one of the horizontal table-shaped tombstones in the cemetery. The collection of strange objects suggested that 'black magic' rituals were being carried out among the gravestones. The investigation petered out and no-one was ever implicated. Perhaps it was just teenagers obsessing over Clive Barker and lame heavy metal.

St Mary's Monastery★, Hatton Road is a Redemptorist Monastery built 1868-70, now used as a religious retreat. The splendid Victorian chapel has angel corbels. Originally there was no water on the property. Prayers to the Blessed Virgin Mary caused a well to be discovered. Our Lady's Well, still with statue of the BVM, supplied the house with fresh water until a regular supply was brought up from Perth.

Kinnoull Hill has a tower, a deliberately distressed folly, built by one of the local aristocrats to mimic the cliff top castles on the Rhine seen during a Grand Tour in the late eighteenth century.

THE WESTERN SUBURBS

In a story of 1911 (*The Grey Piper and the Heavy Coach of Donaldgowerie House, Perth*) Elliott O'Donnell described a phantom piper who haunted an upper middle class family in Donaldgowerie House on the outskirts of Perth. The renowned 'gentleman ghost-hunter' published dozens of books; sometimes he was not averse to mixing fact and fiction. The anthology in which the story appeared, *Scottish Ghost Stories*, seems to be one of those occasions; although it has been included among many examples of 'Perth hauntings', it is actually a fictional story.

One haunting that O'Donnell claimed was true (in *Casebook of Ghosts*) took place in a house called 'Bocarthe', somewhere on the outskirts of Perth. Sometime before the First World War a Mr and Mrs Rowlandson were haunted by an ugly hyperactive ghost. It even followed them when they temporarily escaped to Edinburgh. O'Donnell visited the new residence and at midnight, with the Rowlandsons and another couple, Colonel and

Mrs Rushworth, encountered a glowing cylindrical column which transformed into a spectacularly monstrous man. His misshapen red fingers identified him as Ernest Dekon, an occultist and failed suitor of Mrs Rowlandson. He had attended the Rowlandsons' wedding and three months later shot himself. Effectively, his spirit was stalking Mrs Rowlandson. Colonel Rushworth, clearly an old Empire hand, suggested the answer might be cremation – the solution employed by the hill tribes of northern India against a haunting. Dekon had died somewhere in Africa. The Colonel noted the officials there 'are, as a rule, open to bribery' and that exhumation should be attempted. This took place, Dekon's corpse was exhumed and burnt and the hauntings promptly stopped.

Cluny Terrace, Letham (NO09052434). Near here was the Hole of Ruthven, a holy well much visited for its healing virtues. The accused witch Isabell Haldane ritualistically used its water for healing and left the patients' clothes behind as sympathetic magic. By the early nineteenth century the well had vanished.

The *Perthshire Advertiser* (29 December 1973) reported a bright bluish-green fireball over Abernyte, Pitlochry, Longforgan and Madderty about 9 p.m. on 27 December. One witness said: 'A bright burning object like a huge firework descended from the sky. Streamers of fire licked from it, and it was brighter than my car headlights. It filtered itself out and appeared to drop over the Crieff Road area'. As there have been no reports of alien bodies or crashed flying saucers in the west of the city, I think we can assume this was a meteor.

Before it became a residential area there were permanent gallows on the moor of Burghmuir. Executions created strange mood swings in their audiences. The prisoner would be brought in a cart from the prison and followed by a large crowd in a carnival mood. If the body was to be hung in chains after death, the hangman would lay the corpse out on the scaffold, cut out the bowels, hold them up for the crowd to see (to cheers and applause), then bury them at the foot of the gibbet. On the way out to the gallows the hangman and any accompanying troops or officials were unmolested (any abuse being directed at the prisoner), but on the way back to Perth all those involved in the execution had to run a gauntlet of thrown stones, rubbish, mud and curses.

The notion that pregnant women experiencing dramatic events would see effects on their unborn children was once very common. George Penny tells of a man called McEwan, executed on the Burgh Muir for a double murder – a young woman he had got pregnant and a small boy. First his right hand was cut off and then he was hanged. The severed hand was stuck on top of the gibbet and the body hung in chains. A tradesman's pregnant wife in the crowd subsequently gave birth to a boy who was minus a hand, 'just by the same place where the murderer's hand had been amputated'.

The Hangman's Well is a spring-fed rectangular stone-lined well covered with a stone vault in the back garden of 30 Burghmuir Road (NO09882387). It may have been the place where the hangman washed himself after an execution on the Burgh Muir. By 1932 the name had changed to the King's Well, possibly because of the unfortunate associations of the original name and, who knows, its effect on property values. A story grew up that the well supplied water to the castle in central Perth (swept away by floodwater in 1209). This suggestion is ludicrous given the distance between the two, and probably derives from the glamour of a royal name.

A large house called Belfield used to stand near Bellfield Avenue. In January 1915 Col. J. Everard Rae of Aberdeen was in command of the army unit quartered at Belfield, the 2nd/1st Highland Artillery Brigade. About midnight he returned to the billet and heard a disturbance, which he put down to the young subalterns lark-ing about. But at 8 a.m., Rae found that – contrary to the usual formal procedures – the servants had not prepared breakfast. The adjutant told him the men were upset because they had seen a ghost. The sceptical colonel interviewed the head mess waiter, who told him that for several nights the forty or so officers' servants had been dis-turbed by knocking at the windows, so the previous night they had decided to catch the culprit. One half of the men were to pull up the blinds when the knocking began, and the other half would wait at the doors and rush out to catch whoever was there. At midnight the knocking began as usual, the blinds were pulled up and they all saw a naked figure flitting across the lawn and into the woods. The colonel pressed this point: was the man running or walking? Neither, said the waiter, he was flitting; and he left no footprints in the snow. Some young officers sat up for a couple of nights afterwards with revolvers at the ready, but saw nothing. Twelve servants asked for transfers to another posting, even though the work was much harder there. A week later Col. Rae was approached in a Perth club by a lawyer who told him that the ghost's tendency to knock at the windows had meant the house, prior to the army commandeering it, had been virtually impossible to let for several years. (Source: R. MacDonald Robertson, *Selected Highland Folk Tales*.)

In the early part of the nineteenth century, Anne Simpson was repeatedly haunted by the ghost of a woman she had known called Mrs Molloy. The ghost had only one thing to say – she owed three shillings and ten pence and Anne Simpson had to tell a priest about this. Despite not being a Catholic herself, Anne sought out Father McKay and repeated the message. Mrs Molloy had worked in the laundry at the army barracks, so the priest went there first, but had no luck. He then tried the local shops – and the grocer's pro-duced a 'tab' which showed Mrs Molloy owed him three shillings and ten pence when she died. The priest paid the amount and the ghost ceased to trouble Anne Simpson.

The following episode should probably be treated with caution: the original published source (Ron Halliday, *Evil Scotland*) gives no dates, place names or any other details that could be corroborated. A young woman living in Perth was attacked by some kind of parasitic invisible entity. It started when 'Teri' was 16, when she experienced what she described as 'some sort of energy coming over me'. Poltergeist activity ensued, and Teri felt the invisible presence trying to speak through her. She started to sing songs she had no idea she knew and wrote letters to people she had never heard of. In later years Teri kept seeing people invisible to everyone else. Physical symptoms developed – severe stomach pains that had no medical cause. Eventually the entity was expelled by a medium, who put his hands on Teri's head and drew the spirit from her. The action caused Teri to jump up, thrash her arms and run around the room 'as the entity left her body'.

LEARNED PIGS AND SINGING CATS

Samuel Bisset, born in Perth around 1721, was a shoemaker by trade, but found the horizons of his hometown too restrictive and set off, in the approved manner, to make his fortune in London. Soon he had married a wealthy woman and was running a successful business as a broker. All seemed right with the world. But Bisset's restless energy was not content with material success. He wanted a challenge. Eighteenth-century Europe was awash with animal shows. To our eyes they would appear grotesque and cruel, with animals dressing up, performing tricks and engaging in shams of human behaviour, all 'encouraged' by the whip, heated floors and the like. However, at the time, they were all the rage, and the paying public was particularly keen on what were called 'prodigies' – animal acts which were strange and unusual. Bisset started with a dancing dog, a performing horse and a couple of musical monkeys. But he aspired to something greater, and eventually taught three cats to read music, play the dulcimer and sing in harmony. Now, anyone who has ever tried to persuade a cat to do anything it doesn't want to do will regard this as far-fetched. However, when The Cats' Opera opened at the Haymarket Theatre in London, it was a huge success. Thereafter Bisset taught a hare to drum, canaries, linnets and sparrows to tell the time, turkeys to dance and a turtle to spell. But all was not well. His brokering business had suffered neglect and soon his thunder was stolen by other, even more elaborate and bizarre animal acts. Eventually Bisset retired and opened a pub in Belfast. But old habits die hard and soon he was again training a dog and cat, although his experiments with a goldfish were less successful.

His greatest moment, however, came with his 'learned pig'. This boar could spell names, tell the time, distinguish between married and unmarried spectators, perform sums and even read minds. Truly, Bisset, master of animal prodigies, was back on track. But his nemesis was on hand – in the form of a petty official in Dublin. On the pretext that Bisset did not have the necessary paperwork, this man destroyed the show's props, assaulted Bisset and killed the pig with his sword. Bisset never recovered from the incident and died shortly afterwards in Chester on his way back to London. Such was the sad end of one of the more original and unusual sons of Perth.

THE CARSE OF GOWRIE

Meares' milk, and deers' milk,
And every beast that bears milk,
Between St Johnston and Dundee,
Come a' to me, come a' to me.

Old rhyme used by witches in the Carse

THE DRAGON'S HOLE is a cave on the upper slopes of Kinnoull Hill. A report from 1559 described the Festival of the Dragon. By the cave there was 'a figure fantastically dressed, and adorned with garlands of flowers'. The huge crowd (including clergymen) were dressed in their May Day holiday best. In 1580 the spoilsports of the Kirk Session banned the festivities, handing out substantial fines. But up until the nineteenth century local girls would still go to Kinnoull Hill on May morning, hail the rising sun, and wash their faces in the dew.

The Muses' Threnodie (Henry Adamson, 1638) and *Northern Memoirs* (Richard Franck, 1694, written 1658) both describe the cave's Stone of Invisibility. The fact that this stone is itself described as invisible didn't alert certain individuals that this was a jest designed to gull the credulous, and quests for the stone were duly undertaken. One of the search parties was organised by the 'Lady of Kennule', who, along with her female attendants, quartered the hill, picking up stones at random (remember, the stone was meant to be invisible...) and asking 'I see ye, see ye me?' Soon the sight of a crowd of ladies engaged in eccentric behaviour attracted the wrong sort of attention, and the party disbanded to pursue other pursuits in private. This left the field open to one Jamie Keddie, tailor of this parish, and his foolish mates, who 'day after day so hounded these hills as hitherto no churchyard has been haunted with goblins'. Came the day, a Dundee man joined in with the farrago. Jamie picked up a stone and – miracle! – the stranger said, 'Where are you sir, I can no see ye?' The tailor had found the stone of invisibility! Immediately he entertained the usual fantasies: theft, pranks, voyeurism. He decided to go naked through Perth and one can imagine the consequences – children threw stones, adults beat him, everyone mocked him. This a well-known folklore motif found in many cultures, a discourse on vanity and self-delusion. However, if anyone has found the stone of invisibility, I would be delighted to take possession of it for safe-keeping.

The face of Kinnoull Rock also hid a great diamond, which shone every night but was invisible by day, until one man fired a ball of chalk at it and claimed it. In the early nineteenth century a poor elderly lady, driven by a vision, spent many days fruitlessly searching for both Keddie's stone and the diamond and was plagued with voices who claimed the magic stones were indeed there, but would never be found by a living human. These stories may be connected to the common legend of the gem lodged in a dragon's head and the occasional finds of agates, onyx and carnelians on the slopes.

Then there is a story of a robber who preyed on travellers from the cave. One dark night he bit off more than he could chew and was killed in the cave by his intended victim – who then discovered the thief was his long-lost brother. The traveller fell down the slope in shock, lived long enough to confess to his companions what he had done, and then died. And finally, just as with nearly every other cave and hidey-hole in the area, 'William Wallace took refuge here'.

With this catalogue of legendary and supernatural lore, you'd expect the Dragon's Hole (NO13192244) to be a truly amazing place. But it isn't. The trek up is dangerous and from personal experience I do not recommend doing it.

The Dragon's Hole. At
just 3m deep it could
not have sheltered any
brigand, monster or hero.

In the nineteenth century it was said a dozen men could live in it but these days just two is a squeeze. Apart from some rather mundane graffiti there is nothing to see.

KINNOULL HILL

At about 11.30 p.m. on September 30 1965 Maureen Ford and several friends were driving on the A85 below Kinnoull Hill when Maureen saw a big creature on the side of the road. 'The animal was long and gray', she said. 'It had no legs, but I'm sure I saw long pointed ears'. About ninety minutes later Robert Swankie was on the same road heading to Dundee when he saw a similar creature. On 5 October 1965 he was reported in the *Scottish Daily Express*: 'The head was more than two feet long. It seemed to have pointed ears. The body, which was about 20ft long, was humped like a giant caterpillar. It was moving very slowly and made a noise like someone dragging a heavy weight through the grass'. Swankie reported it to the police the next morning but they found nothing at the spot. Later on, Ford drew a picture of what she saw – a narrow, cigar-shaped thing with a long neck and a cow-like head with long ears or horns on top. The case has been discussed by two discerning writers on the paranormal, F.W. Holiday (*The Goblin Universe*) and Karl Shuker (*In Search of Prehistoric Survivors*). Could the witnesses have simply mistaken something common-or-garden flashing past in the headlights for a monster? The fact that they both saw something within the same timeframe suggests there may indeed have been a creature near the A85 that night. A seal moving slowly and awkwardly over the ground? An otter carrying a large fish, or a big eel? (Both have been mistaken for 'water monsters' in the past.) Did the car headlights cast shadows larger than the animals? Perhaps it was Kinnoull's resident dragon, returning to his comfy Dragon's Hole after an evening hunting in the river.

KINFAUNS

There's a story set at an unspecified date that the earth once swallowed up the Manse of Kinfauns and the minister with it, the chasm so created being filled by inrushing water: when the people of the Kirkton of Kinfauns later set about draining Loch Kaitre to recover the minister's golden rocking cradle, the whole of the Kirkton suddenly caught fire. They rushed to save their homes – but found the conflagration was an illusion. Back at the loch, all trace of the digging and drainage ditches had vanished. This was considered a powerful hint and all attempts to locate the cradle were abandoned. In 1880 the tenant at Burnfoot did actually drain Loch Kaitre, and ploughed the land. There was no supernatural comeback, despite the inevitable dire warnings.

A different version of this story can be found in The Priest of Kinfauns, a poem by a nineteenth century local writer, David Millar. The eponymous priest was pious but not liked, a day-sleeping curmudgeon who indulged in astrology after dark. One night he was praying to the Virgin to reveal the whereabouts of a nun missing from the nunnery at Elcho, when the BVM appeared before him and Told Him Secrets. But this is an ambiguous visitation: the priest spent the next day laughing maniacally in the church, and as evening drew in, strange lights and the figure of a woman were seen. That night, the entire human and animal population could not sleep but lay awake, terrified of they knew not what. When the morning dawned, the priest, church and churchyard had all disappeared under a small loch.

Balthayock, stone circle, three-stone row and cupmarks (NO17502484)

KILSPINDIE

Lady's Brig, on the Kilspindie road west to Balmyre, is haunted by a White Lady, who, apparently conversant with the Highway Code ('Rule 2 for Pedestrians: walk facing the traffic'), travels down Smithy Brae on one side of the road and back uphill on the other. In his poem 'A Legend of Kilspindie Castle' Charles Spence relates how Lord Huston became estranged from his wife through jealousy. He went hunting on Gascon Hill but his horse refused to move no matter how much he whipped it. His wife appeared, dressed in fairy green – 'a green no man can dye' – criticised his cruelty, then prophesised that he would die ignominiously in combat and that the castle would decay. Both came true. Lady Huston was only ever seen again playing the Fairy Game on the hills with her children.

Kilspindie church, GRAVESTONES.★

RAIT

A ploughman had a mistress who was a witch. She had ridden him to Italy but he slipped his head out of the halter and regained his human shape. On the witch's return he slipped the halter over her head and repeated the words she had said to him. The witch turned into a fine mare; he rode her home again and in the morning he sold her to her own son. The son took her to the smith in Rait to have her shod; when he removed the halter his own mother was there with horseshoes on her hands and feet. The son's children were always known as the 'shod-wife's oyes' (grandchildren). The Mill of Rait could, reputedly, be heard after dark, grinding meal for the fairies.

In 1982 a real mystery was discovered on a large boulder near the front entrance of Ladywell House (NO210276). Three, difficult to see, pecked out circles on the same axis contain a variety of Christian symbols. Some or all of the letters may have been added after the original designs, which are stylistically similar to those found near the fifth-century Christian community at Whithorn (Dumfries and Galloway). The spring was either dedicated to the BVM ('Ladywell'), thus explaining the symbols, or we could be looking at de-paganisation in action, the well's *deus loci* being Christianised through the carvings and the subsequent re-dedication to the Virgin.

Old church and burial-ground GRAVESTONES★ (NO22742685).
Cupmarked boulder★★ (NO22752677).

FINGASK CASTLE★★ (NO22802745), home to the Thriepland family for centuries, is private but the beautiful grounds are occasionally open. It is a superb testament to aristocratic eccentricity and architectural scavenging. The grounds are filled with statues, GARGOYLES and GRAVESTONES. Underground passages (still partly open in 1766) may have connected the castle with Kinnaird Castle, 2km away. Certainly a footpath linked the two castles, and a triple-arched Gothick folly, The Monument, marks the halfway resting point above Flawcraig Farm (NO235278). There is a standing stone★ at NO22922715.

KINNAIRD

At the north-west end of KINNAIRD stands the impressive tower of Kinnaird Castle, restored in 1855. One night the Lord of Kinnaird returned home around midnight to hear a song drifting through the windows:

> *Mak' it neat and mak' it sma'*
> *Like the lady of the ha'*
> *Mak' it neat and mak' it tidy*
> *Just like Lord Kinnaird's lady*

He rushed into the bedroom, rescued his enchanted and helpless spouse, and scattered the fairies with words they hated. The fairies were so startled they left behind the

Above left: Gargoyle at Fingask Castle.

Above right: Fingask Castle. 'Drink weary pilgrim, drink and pray and bless St Peter's Well. Which springs unscath'd by scorching ray or frost or thawing swell'. Recently reconsecrated.

Below: Fingask Castle. The grounds are sprinkled with characters from Walter Scott and Robert Burns.

stock, the effigy they were making 'neat and tidy' to replace the human woman. The stock could still be seen in the eighteenth century, but like every other artefact from fairyland has long vanished. William Wallace also makes his legendary presence felt here, lifting the iron yett.

Church and burial ground, GRAVESTONES* (NO24292862)
Westown medieval chapel GRAVESTONES* (NO249274)

PITMIDDLE
Two cases from this now deserted village show the way accusations of witchcraft grew out of small-minded arguments between neighbours. On 1 December 1649, Margaret Lowsone (of Craigdallie) complained that Johne Gourlaw (of Kinnaird) had slandered her as possessed by – and having sex with – Satan. Gourlaw confessed his accusation was baseless, but he was 'distracted of his wittes at that tyme', and got off with a plea of diminished responsibility. Eight years later, on 25 July 1658 Elisabet Anderson was charged with 'charming' (using spells). Witnesses said they saw her coming out of byres and the cows then gave no milk, that she had borrowed a buttermaker which would never after churn and that she had fed grass to cattle which made them rush around in a frenzy. Note none of the witnesses actually heard her using spells - she just happened to be around when unfortunate things happened. Presumably Elisabet decided to follow the path of least resistance: she made public repentance on three Sundays, when she was 'sharplie rebuked and promised never to use such sinfull and scandalous wayes herafter'. This was a relatively light sentence; both women were lucky not to have been much more severely punished, and merely on the say so of their neighbours. (source: Perthshire Society of Natural Science, *Pitmiddle Village and Elcho Nunnery*.)

ABERNYTE
The *OSA* noted that in the eighteenth century, 'Belief in the power of spells and charms still prevails here in a great degree…. a knowledge of them is confined to a few families'. The healing cures were always performed without direct payment. Parish church, GRAVESTONES**. Witches Dub, a small muddy pond used for witch-ducking, was at North Pitkindie farm (NO254323). Some taboo obviously adhered to the natural hillock called Gallows Knowe (NO25173373) - the road-makers deliberately left the site undisturbed, and an offer from the laird of Lochton to grant some land so the dangerous road bend could be removed was turned down by the Council. Near Littleton (NO266337) the road passes the deep Bogle Den ('haunted den'; bogle, a spirit or ghost).

ROSSIE
The village of Rossie was cleared by Lord Kinnaird in 1795 as part of the improvements to the Rossie Priory estate (Rossie Priory is not and never was a priory, just a vast castellated gothic fantasy, built 1807-15.) The old church of Rossie (NO29153080)

has GRAVESTONES, and is now a private mausoleum for the Kinnaird family, housing a very impressive eighth-century Pictish cross slab★★ carved with a veritable bestiary of monsters.

LONGFORGAN

The semi-legendary St Modwenna founded seven churches in Scotland, the last being Longforgan. Here she immersed herself in cold water while singing hymns, and received visions of angels. One day Modwenna and her fellow nuns tried to ford a shallow river, but it immediately rose in flood. Modwenna knew this must have been caused by an unexpiated sin among the group. Sure enough, one of the sisters confessed she had stolen a handful of leeks, at which point the river fell and they were able to cross. When told by an ardent suitor that the things he found most beautiful about her were her eyes, Modwenna promptly plucked them out. She died in 660 at Longforgan at the ripe old age of 130. Some of her relics were preserved here, others being sent to Burton-on-Trent and Cill-tsliebhe in Ireland. Parish church★, Main Street, GRAVESTONES (NO309300). Archaeological bits and pieces have turned up locally, including a carved sandstone head, possibly Celtic but probably Victorian. North of the village is the very ruined twelfth-century chapel of Dron (NO29553240), on a road which linked Coupar Angus Abbey and its properties around Longforgan. The old track is reputedly haunted by one of the monks. A boulder in the gully beside Dron Chapel has an unusual runic inscription, 'MCBRIDE LIWED HERE FROM OCTOBER 1970'.

CASTLE HUNTLY (NO30192910), is haunted by the spirit of a daughter of the Strathmore family who, imprisoned in a small upper room, either fell to her death while attempting to escape or was pushed; after all, she was pregnant with a serving-man's child. The ghost turned up at one spot so often it was renamed Bogle Bridge. One April afternoon she was also seen flitting among the trees along one of the drives. Manifestations (or expectations) in the haunted chamber, now called the Waterloo Room, have scared reluctant servants and thrill-seeking visitors alike. The castle is now an open prison; I have no record of what the current occupants think of the White Lady.

INVERGOWRIE

The church★, Station Road, (NO35063015, GRAVESTONES), is claimed to be the first church built north of the Tay, and this peeved the Devil. He stood on the hills of Fife and threw two stones at the church, but one fell into the river and the other, the Paddock Stone or De'il's Stone, overshot by a kilometre and is in the grounds of Greystane Lodge (near the Swallow Hotel, northwest of the Kingsway, Dundee). It turns round three times every morning when the cock crows at Balgartno. Near the churchyard are two large stones, the Yowes of Gowrie. Thomas the Rhymer is supposed to have predicted that:

When the Yowes o' Gowrie come to land,
The Day o' Judgment's near at hand.

Around 1800 the Yowes were within the high-water mark, but since then the Tay has receded, and by 1826 the stones were said to be moving nearer to the shore by an inch a year, much to the consternation of people haunted by the Book of Revelation. The Yowes are now between the railway line and the village, so have definitely 'come to land'. The iron-rich waters of the chalybeate well at the ruined medieval church of Benvie (NO328314) were used for healing up to the eighteenth century.

INCHTURE

A woman dreamt that her son had fallen into the village well. Going to the well, she found two children – her son, and the minister's boy. The latter, saved as it seemed by a miracle, became the distinguished Dr Thomas Randall Davidson (b. 1747).

Parish church – GRAVESTONES*
Standing stone* (NO26152758)
Carving of a cow plus other stones, Castlehill (NO276304)

CARSE GRANGE

Patrick Matthew, the laird of now-demolished Gourdiehill, seems to have been one of those eccentric well-travelled Victorian intellectuals whose reclusiveness tended to prompt suspicions among the peasantry. He was reportedly a believer in the transmigration of souls and because a female friend or relative had returned to him as a blackbird, he banned the shooting of the birds, despite them eating all his fruit.

MEGGINCH CASTLE

During the 1745 Jacobite rising Captain Drummond entrusted a young guest to hide some papers in a secret room in Megginch Castle. In classic style, she descended staircases and negotiated several passages before entering the secret chamber, only to be imprisoned by a trapdoor. The young lady fainted twice in the darkness, but luckily Drummond returned and saved her. This sounds like an episode from an adventure novel, but Megginch did have a network of secret passages and rooms, unfortunately obliterated by Admiral Sir Adam Drummond in the early nineteenth century. A long underground passage curving around the east side of the house is blocked up where it enters the house. The castle, which is privately owned, is allegedly haunted by the ghosts of two talkative old women.

ERROL

A hairy Brownie lived at the Mains of Errol (NO241219) in the eighteenth century. Despite his ability to thresh more crops in a night than eight men could in a month, the farm workers were always complaining about the brownie's appetite. When they accused him of eating some of their sowens (a poor-quality food made from oat husks and water), he cried out from a corner, 'You needna blame me, for I only got twa slags and a harl'. (Roughly, two and a bit helpings). He promptly departed when, on a cold day, the goodwife laid out a cloak and hood for him in the barn.

A mermaid was netted as she combed her golden hair on the banks of the Tay near Daleally (NO256219). The unfortunate creature was imprisoned in the nearest dwelling. She watched the servant of the house go about her cooking, then sang a song flattering the lass's beauty. Enchanted, the maiden cut the ropes, and the mermaid found her way back to the Tay (how does a mermaid operate on land?). Once in the water, she sang another song about never coming back to the area. And indeed she never has. As a child, Robert Curr, the miller of Trotack Mill, had often seen the fairies work his father's mill at night. One Monday morning he was in the Mill of Errol. Something was holding up the water in the tail lade, and on investigating outside, he found a kelpie whose seaweed-like hair and cloak 'the colour o' tangle' were keeping back the water. Robbie hit the kelpie with a large stone; it plunged into the water and cried:

Auld man Madison,
This you shall rue;
Some misty morning
I'll meet wi' you.

The kelpie had mistaken him for Madison the dryster (the man who worked on the mill's kiln). The next Sunday, a very misty day, Madison disappeared by the riverside.

The imposing Errol Park House was mentioned in Sir James George Frazer's monumental work of anthropology and comparative mythology, *The Golden Bough*. Although much discredited since, Frazer's classic remains hugely influential on the world of magic and myths. The fate of the Hay family, the Earls of Errol, was bound up with that of a nearby ancient oak. If on Hallowe'en a Hay walked round the tree three times in a sunwise direction, said a certain spell, and used a new dirk to cut some of the tree's mistletoe, the sprig would protect the wearer against enchantment, witchcraft and death in battle. If placed in an infant's bed it kept away child-stealing fairies. There was a great taboo on a family member either damaging the tree or killing a white falcon. There was clearly an air of awe surrounding this huge old tree, possibly connected to its proximity to the Falcon Stone which legitimised the clan's landholdings (see LUNCARTY for the falcon's part in the Hay creation myth). A legend of mutually entwined fate foretold the end of the Hays (the prophecy, like so many others in Scotland, is attributed to Thomas the Rhymer):

While the mistletoe bats on Errol's aik,
And that aik stands fast,
The Hays shall flourish, and their good grey hawk
Shall nocht flinch before the blast.

But when the root of the aik decays,
And the mistletoe dwines on its withered breast,

The grass shall grow on Errol's hearthstane,
And the corbie roup in the falcon's nest.

It is not known when the tree finally fell, but as Frazer notes, 'The estate has been sold out of the family of Hay, and of course it is said that the fatal oak was cut down a short time before'.

Old kirkyard behind School Wynd GRAVESTONES.★★★
'Grey Stone' standing stone (NO222213).

ST MADOES

A well-known but bizarre tradition claims the St Madoes area was once joined to Rhynd (on the south side of the Tay). The *Annual Register* of 1760 says 'The inhabitants of the country have a tradition that the course of the Tay in former ages was by the foot of the hills to the north of Errol and to this day show the very holes in rocks to which the ships' cables were fastened'. An old ballad claims:

The stannin' stones o' Semmiedores,   [St Madoes]
Be sou' the river Tay

When the river changed its course the parishioners of Rhynd were forced to row to church at St Madoes, until one Sunday the boat overturned in a storm and everyone drowned. A related story tells of a subterranean passage under the Tay between the hospital of Seggieden and the nunnery at Elcho. Needless to say there is no evidence for any of these traditions.

The Hawk Stone★, inscribed with 'CALEDONIA' sometime before 1779, supposedly where the Hay super-falcon landed (NO20462121) (See LUNCARTY)
Three-stone row, with cupmarks★ (NO19722098).

STRATHMORE

THE MACBETH MYTH

The mention of Dunsinane in Shakespeare's *Macbeth* creates much of the associated folklore of this area. In the play Dunsinane is Macbeth's fortress where the tyrant finally comes to grief when the witches' prophecy comes true – the attacking army disguise themselves with foliage and 'Birnam Wood comes to Dunsinane'. Shakespeare's troubled murderer is a brilliant creation, but is basically Anglophile propaganda, and a far cry from the historical Macbeth, who, by the admittedly brutal standards of medieval kings, seems to have been a reasonably decent chap. But the power of Shakespeare's fiction has mythologised the landscape; by the pricking of my thumbs, fantasy Macbeth toponymy this way comes:

Cairnbeddie, Macbeth's first castle (NO14983082).

Macbeth's Law, a Bronze Age tumulus (NO20153446).

Lang Man's Grave★ (NO223316), Macbeth's grave. Or, the grave of a very tall man, a traveller from Dundee who was murdered or committed suicide on his way home from Scone fair. The stone was formerly a favourite camping ground for travelling people, which may account for this story.

King's Seat (NO 233333), with a really strange carving on a large boulder - a saltire with feet! Nearby is a spring called the King's Well, marking the route MacBeth took when travelling north.

The Witch's Stone★★ (NO159316) where Macbeth met the two most celebrated witches in the country. Exactly the same story is claimed for the Knock of Alves in Moray. You can see how this boulder got its name – it has a really odd shape, worn away in the middle as if by a chain.

 Some of this lore can be laid at the door of Sir John Sinclair, the redoubtable editor of the first *Statistical Account of Scotland*, who visited the area in 1772 with the express purpose of finding evidence for Macbeth. The local people pointed out the blasted heath where the witches met (near St Martins), and Sinclair's plan of the area clearly marks two 'Witches Houses' to the west of Dunsinnan. Nineteenth-century writers also convinced themselves Shakespeare had actually set foot on Dunsinane on a visit to Perth in 1598 as a member of a company of players sent by Elizabeth I to amuse James VI – another example of how Macbeth's story colonises everything around it.

DUNSINANE★★★ is these days called Dunsinnan Hill (NO213316). This is still a visit to cherish, with much to see and speculate about. The wettest part of the path is Macbeth's Well. Dunsinnan is an Iron Age fort in two phases: the older, larger fort whose walls are much robbed, possibly to build the newer inner citadel, the ramparts of which can be easily seen. The bumps on the summit are the soil tips from the 1854 excavations, which revealed an underground corbelled stone structure containing the skeletons of two adults and one child. The bodies may have been buried after the site was abandoned, a way of tapping in to the 'specialness' of the place, or they may have been a foundation sacrifice. Like many of the local forts, Dunsinnan was vitrified, the stones fused by great heat. Experimental archaeologists have tried to see how this could be done and discovered it was very difficult to set a rampart alight – they needed petrol. The vitrification therefore could not have been done during a siege. So it was fired: 1. by the enemy after conquest; 2. by the inhabitants to strengthen the rampart, although this is doubtful; or 3. when the site was abandoned, as a cleansing ritual. There are two small, difficult to find, cupmarked rock outcrops in the south-west corner of the inner citadel at NO21333166. Just like Fingal and Wallace, Macbeth is sometimes made into a giant. In the eighteenth century Dunsinnan was the Giant's House, and Macbeth threw the huge Giant's Putting Stone half a mile from the hill. Dunsinnan also holds the real Stone of Destiny (see SCONE). The story goes that Edward I was palmed off with a fake and the authentic Stone was secreted in a cave here. The Stone was accidentally discovered in the nineteenth century but the exact location was lost. The story is an example of two locally powerful myths – the Stone of Destiny and Macbeth – feeding off each other's glamour (of all the hills in the area, it is of course Dunsinnan that the Stone has to be buried within).

BALBEGGIE, ST MARTINS AND KINROSSIE

When the predecessor of the current church (GRAVESTONES*) was put up in 1773 John Donald, the builder, thought it was not quite where he wanted it, and supervised the locals in a big push against the walls to straighten it out. The fact that this took place during the completion celebration, and that alcohol may possibly have been taken, is I'm sure neither here nor there. (The same story is told of MEIGLE a century later.) The minister of St Martins encountered the ghost of the laird's wife from Cairnbeddie in the churchyard. When, with due pastoral concern even for the dead, he asked her why she was not in her grave, she confessed that during her lifetime she had used false weights and measures to cheat the poor spinners she had employed – the flax she had given them was overweighted, and the oatmeal payment underweighted. The accidentally lexilinked 'Fixed home hath none' (actually in Latin, Nulli Certa Domus), is carved over the front door of the 1792 manse. The source is Virgil's The Aeneid (VI: 673), which describes the journey of Aeneas in the world of the dead. The full text is 'Fixed home hath none. We dwell in shady groves, and live on cushioned river-banks, the meadows fresh with streams'. It is spoken by one of the spirits in the lands of the blessed. A 'Law' mound near the manse at NO153301 is for some reason called Glengarry's Bonnet. Kinrossie has a well named after someone called Harry.

Bandirran Stone circle** (NO20903099).
Stone circle* (?) (NO21053105).

COLLACE

The Devil apparently would meet the minister in the Manse garden every twilight – Satan tempted and the minister resisted. The fairies abducted a two-year old child from a family in nearby Saucher (NO197332) and gave it as a gift to a farming couple, Charles and Jenny Grant, at the Quilky, on the other side of the hills in the Carse of Gowrie. When the baby was deposited Charles heard a sound overhead like wild geese. Fortunately the Grants were able to trace the original parents and return their child, who had returned from fairyland with a preternatural gift for spinning. Fairies lived on Kinpurnie Hill and Dunsinnan, and danced on summer nights at Fairygreen (NO219332). In Victorian times the Revd Andrew Bonar campaigned against the 'superstition' of Collace farmers nailing horseshoes on their byres to keep the witches out. He was partially successful – the farmers took the horseshoes down and simply re-erected them inside.

Collace Parish Church, GRAVESTONES* (NO197320).
Pitcur I Souterrain (site of) (NO247365).
Pitcur II Souterrain, with cup-and ring-marked stones* (NO25293738). See COUPAR ANGUS for folklore.
Pictish Stone with bear (wolf?), double disc and Z-rod* (NO27323975).
Kettins Parish Church, eroded Pictish stone, GRAVESTONES* (NO238390).

COUPAR ANGUS

During the nineteenth century some workmen found the Secret Tunnel of Coupar Angus Abbey near the entrance of the Abbey churchyard. One of them went in but was never seen again (PIT-story). In 1982 a stonemason told local author Martha Jane Sievwright that he and some other men went into it one day and travelled quite a distance until they came to a cave-in, suggesting this is what killed the earlier explorer. The mason confidently asserted that the tunnel goes right through to the souterrain at Pitcur, two and a half miles away, although if the passage was blocked, how did he know this?

Three times in 2004 and 2005 the Paranormal Investigation Scotland team conducted investigations at the Victorian Royal Hotel. They used a combination of psychics and recording technology to catalogue the apparent legions of ghosts that inhabit the now boarded-up building. Their extraordinary claims (see www.paranormalextra.co.uk) include the psychics detecting the presence of over seventy-five spirits from medieval times through to the 1970s. Other reported phenomena included physical contact with invisible hands, a water droplet appearing from nowhere, cold and hot spots, other temperature variations and possible minor poltergeist activity. A visit by one of the mediums to the Abbey produced a series of vague impressions including the notion that treasure was (or had been?) buried beneath the ruins.

Cistercian Abbey, ruined, with parish church, GRAVESTONES** (NO22343972).
Bendochy Parish Kirk, GRAVESTONES (NO21844145).

Two eighteenth-century accounts record strange aerial phenomena. *The Annual Register: A View of the History, Politics, and Literature for the Year*, was a digest of all things of interest to the Georgian gentleman. Its 1767 edition published the following letter from Edinburgh, dated 8 September, which deserves to be quoted in full: 'We hear from Perthshire, that an uncommon phenomenon was observed on the water of Isla, near Cupor Angus, preceded by a thick dark smoke, which soon dispelled, and discovered a large luminous body, like a house on fire, but presently after took a form something pyramidal, and rolled forwards with impetuosity till it came to the water of Erick [Ericht], up which river it took its direction, with great rapidity, and disappeared a little above Blairgowrie. The effects were as extraordinary as the appearance. In its passage, it carried a large cart many yards over a field of grass; a man riding along the high road was carried from his horse, and so stunned with the fall, as to remain senseless a considerable time. It destroyed one half of a house, and left the other behind, undermined and destroyed an arch of the new bridge building at Blairgowrie, immediately after which it disappeared.'

Note the (anonymous) writer did not actually witness the event, but is reporting what he has heard, so it is possible that some parts have been altered in the telling. The vivid description gives us smoke and a bright, fiery, fast-moving object creating wind effects in its wake and smashing through structures before disappearing. Put it all together and it sounds like a large meteorite – the impact with the house and bridge arch effectively vaporises it, with any minute remnants disappearing into the waters of the River Ericht. A once-in-a-lifetime sight; I wish I'd been there to witness it.

The second account is from about thirty years later, when the Revd James Playfair, compiler of the Bendothy [Bendochy] chapter of the *OSA*, saw something strange in the sky: 'One night I observed in the air a long narrow stripe of a whitish cloud, one end of which was near me; its position was horizontal. The end next to me, as it advanced, became more red, bent into a curve; then revolved upon itself with a very quick spiral motion, and the appearance of intense fire; and though it was quite calm where I stood, the phenomenon was attended with the sound of a whirlwind, which I would have perceived it to have been, had it been daylight, and a cloud of dust to make it visible.' Once again, this was probably a meteor.

BLAIRGOWRIE

The Welton Road, on the west side of the River Ericht south of Blairgowrie, passes a farm called The Welton (NO196442), where, on the north side of the road once stood a house famed in fairy lore. The lintel stone had a carving of a blacksmith, his anvil and two brownies, with a crown above, along with the inscription 'We amongst mechanics have rendered our hands our arms and our crown' . The tale is told in Lewis Spence's *The Fairy Tradition in Britain*. About 1730 blacksmith Abram Low was walking along the river one evening when he encountered a group of fairies. 'Welcome, welcome, Abram, forever and for aye!', they cried. Abram knew that to accept the invitation on these terms would mean he would live the rest of his life in Fairyland, so he replied, 'Never a bit, quoth Abram, but for a night and a day'. And so he only spent twenty-four hours with the fairies and then went home. This visitation provoked two major changes: Abram seemed to become wiser and more reflective, as if he had access to secret knowledge; and two brownies turned up at his forge and, each day, worked harder and faster than ten men. One of the brownies wore a red cap and the other a blue. Abram knew better than to speak to them, as the creatures were notoriously quick to take offence at acknowledgement or any display of kindness, so he showed them what work he would like completed, and they did it without a word. Inevitably, with such skilled and efficient workers, Abram's smithy business prospered.

Then one day a journeyman assistant (or Abram himself) forgot the prohibition on talking and called out, 'Well struck, Red Cap, better still, Blue'. The brownies turned round and cried, 'Well struck or ill struck, we strike no more for you', (or, 'Strike here, strike there, we'll strike no more for you',) and they vanished. Abram saw Blue Cap one more time, when passing a small loch at night (at NO193437, to the east of the A923 in Rosemount). Unfortunately he said, 'Hello, Blue Cap'. The brownie was furious at being recognised and spoken to, and stormed off, saying 'Blue Cap or Red Cap, whoever I may be, Red Cap or Blue Cap, you'll see no more of me!' This story has many aspects that distinguish it from the usual fairy legend. Firstly, there is documentary evidence to show that Abram Low was a blacksmith in the area at the time. Secondly, the Low family were still living in Welltown (Welton) in the 1840s, and Abram's great-grandson, Alexander, published a book in 1841 in which he reiterated the family tradition of the story, as well as setting out the family tree, attested by members still alive. Then there is the lintel. It was said to have been carved by Abram himself; the house was built in 1770, so this seems plausible. The story was well known locally in the nineteenth century. Of course, it may have arisen to explain Abram's business success and high level of skill in his job (rather like the 1930s bluesman Robert Johnson was supposed to have learnt his astonishing guitar playing from the Devil) but it is still a story with more roots in reality than most. The lintel was still in good condition in the 1930s, but a few decades later it was badly mutilated and when the house was demolished it was in too poor a condition to preserve. One aspect of the story that is never commented upon is that the names of Abram Low and his descendants – Isaac, Jacob, David and so on – suggest the family was Jewish showing that it wasn't just Christians who had encounters with the fairies.

Near where the A93 crosses the Lunan Burn (NO172416) is the Witches' Pool, allegedly where witches were tried by ducking. Ardblair Castle (private) (NO164446) is a focus of high strangeness, as recorded variously by Peter Underwood (*The Ghosthunters Almanac*), Roddy Martine (*Supernatural Scotland*) and Ron Halliday (*UFO Scotland*). The Blairs were constantly feuding with their neighbours the Drummonds, so when Lady Jane Drummond fell in love with a Blair the marriage was forbidden and she drowned herself. Her ghost appears infrequently – she is silent as she passes through rooms and along corridors but she always opens and closes doors as she goes. The current family is Laurence Blair Oliphant, his wife Jenny, son Charles and daughters Amelia and Philippa. Charles and Amelia have seen Jean Drummond, watched door handles turn, and heard her footsteps. Most of the sightings are in the narrow passageway leading into the Long Gallery, and usually take place between 5 and 6 p.m. on a sunny evening. When very young, Charles saw small people dancing on the lawn – and the dogs were frozen in position, their heads moving backwards and forwards looking at something only they and the boy could see. When a life-size portrait of Margaret Oliphant was returned to the house from storage, old family documents, previously thought lost, turned up, a very old musical clock started up on its own, and there was a sense that everything – paintings etc. – was fitting into place with Margaret's approval. In the 1970s broadcaster Jimmy Black came to the house to make a TV programme about the religious content of Lady Carolina Nairne's work (Carolina Oliphant of Gask, writer of 'Charlie is My Darling' and other popular Jacobite songs). The room they chose was filled with Carolina memorabilia; but filming was impossible because lights would fuse or sound equipment pack up whenever there was no member of the family in the room. Eventually baby Charles was left in the room and all was well, but not until Jimmy had shouted, 'Carolina, would you no let me get on with it!' In the freezing winter of 1981/82, when temperatures dropped to -17°C, Laurence was alone in the castle when a voice woke him at 4a.m. shouting, 'Get up to the top of the house!' He arrived just in time to prevent a thawed pipe flooding the castle. On a summer afternoon in 1951, Laurence saw a huge Irish elk silently cross his path on the edge of a wood by the castle. Thirty years later, Jenny also saw the elk in the same wood. Just as in the earlier encounter, it crossed from right to left. The Irish elk, *Megaloceros*, was actually a deer, about the size of the modern moose, and had the largest antlers of any deer known — up to 4m across. It has been extinct for at least 2,500 years. In the eighteenth century a marl pit nearby yielded up a specimen. Laurence is chieftain of the Blairgowrie Highland Games, held in the Bogle Field at Ardblair. Possibly in the mid-1980s, yellow and white lights were seen several times moving across the water of Loch of Rae, just to the west. There is a suggestion the lights may have been seen since the 1960s. And in June 1990 a crop circle formation appeared nearby, in a field of grass bordering the A923. GARGOYLES.

Newton Castle (private), a castellated late sixteenth-century Z-plan chateau on an impressive elevated site on Newton Street on the northwest edge of the town (NO172453), is supposed to be linked to Ardblair by an underground tunnel. Under the Scottish Haunted Castles (Compulsory) Act of 1828, the castle was allocated the ghost of Lady Jean Drummond, who, to regain the lover who had jilted her, consulted a witch. On the hag's instructions, she made a charm from graveyard grass and a branch from a rowan recently used as a hanging tree on the Gallows Knowe. She then sat all night with her eyes closed on the Corbie's Stane at the Coble Pool in the Ericht. In the dark she heard an unearthly voice chanting:

Warlocks, wabsters, ane and aa,
Weave the witchin claith;
Warp o'grass an' weft o'rash-
Weave the wab o' death!

Warlocks, weavers, one and all,
Weave the witching cloth;
Warp of grass and weft of rush-
Weave the web of death!

In the morning she found her dress had been transformed into fairy green, and she proved irresistible to the man of her dreams. They were married straight away but she died that evening and her body was laid out on her bridal bed. At midnight on Hallowe'en her gravestone (which may be somewhere on the hill above Newton) turns three times and she walks through the rooms of the castle, singing sad love songs and searching for her missing bridegroom. In another version of the story, those who taught her the magical arts came and actually abducted Jean on the wedding night. Mrs Don, who lived at Newton for about ten years following the First Word War, claimed to have seen her several times, although she has not been spotted by the current owners, the Macpherson family. There is also a report of a second ghost, Janet Drummond, the wife of a George Drummond murdered by the laird of Drumlochy in 1554. When one of Drumlochy's sons later fell in love with her daughter, the widow Drummond brandished her husband's bloody shirt from a window as a warning to offski. In the early 1900s a researcher from the Psychical Society spent time at Newton at Hallowe'en, hoping to spot Green Lady Jean. Jean didn't turn up, possibly due, he thought, to the irritating presence of a servant woman waving a red duster. It was only later that the man learnt the 'servant' must have been Janet Drummond with the bloodied shirt.

Former holy wells include St Ninian's in the Wellmeadow, where the saint drank while on a camping trip to the area, and St Margaret's. For a still-existing holy well, you could try Rory's Well, which springs from the slope of Terminus Street below Gas Brae, but given that it is a patch of wet and muddy ground which has been used as a de facto rubbish dump, it's the least holy, holy well I've seen. Rory is an incredibly obscure early Celtic saint. In 1870 a music-loving ghost visited the Blairgowrie choral society during evening rehearsals in the former First Free Church schoolroom (the site is now St Andrew's church on James Street). She was heavily veiled, came and left without a sound during the piece, and may have turned the lights blue during her visit. A ghost of a soaking wet woman was seen on two separate occasions in the early 1950s around West Mill, near Haugh Road. She was wearing a green cape and a hat hanging down the back of her head.

According to Ron Halliday in *UFO Scotland*, Blairgowrie has been something of a UFO hot spot. The first report is from October 1957, when, at around 7 a.m., a nurse cycling over the Ericht Bridge saw a metal disc over the road next to the east bank of the river. Halliday gives this as Riverside Drive, although that's a small side road off Riverside Road, which actually borders the river. The disc was about 30ft across and emitted a soft humming. It hovered for a while then moved north, following the River Ericht. And at 9.30 p.m. on 25 June 1984 four people saw a tennis ball-sized light in the sky. It had a red tail and a beam of light occasionally flashed from the edge of the object. Through binoculars a V-shaped object was seen to leave and return to the ball several times. This sounds like the misidentification of an aircraft.

Newton Castle, Blairgowrie.

A series of apparently UFO-related incidents on Riverside Road commenced on 25 April 1984. In the morning two people saw twelve men and children dressed in orthodox Jewish attire – complete with black coats and hats, and long pigtails – walking in single file with a regular space between them. They entered the next-door bungalow without knocking, and then came out a few minutes later. All this while maintaining the same distance between each other and not saying a word. When asked, however, the neighbour had seen no-one come into her house. That afternoon, at 5.30, Gwen Freeman, one of the two witnesses, noticed the family dog cowering and running into the kitchen with its tail between its legs. Then she was enveloped (and briefly blinded) by a strange cloud of light. She had a warm sensation all over, centred on her abdomen. A forsythia bush shimmered with sparkling lights, caused by a beam of light coming from a silvery 'spaceship' that looked like a giant Yale key. The ship then vanished in a bright flash. About a week later Gwen was visited by two strange looking individuals dressed like characters from a 1920s film and uttering vague threats about not speaking about what she had seen, otherwise a 'great evil' would come her way. Several days later, Gwen found she had the ability to heal her friend's arthritic fingers simply by massaging them. In early 1990 Sid Freeman, Gwen's son, saw a huge ball of fire moving fast across the night sky. He was convinced it was going to crash into the Sidlaw Hills, but there was no impact. Now, the last event could easily have been a meteor (and most meteors do burn up before actually hitting the ground), but what are we to make of the other experiences? Many UFO witnesses are allegedly visited by 'Men In Black' wearing old-fashioned clothing, urging silence and making threats (the meme is so well known it has inspired two enjoyable Hollywood films), and bright lights, floating craft and unusual post-contact abilities are also commonly reported. But the line of orthodox Jews is unique in UFO contactee literature. I have no idea what to make of it all, and we cannot ask Gwen, as she died in November 1987.

RATTRAY

The famous Covenanter minister Donald Cargill was born in Rattray in 1610. When he was finally captured in Lanarkshire, he correctly predicted the soon-to-come demise of his captor in the same place (the man was run through with a sword by one of his own colleagues). The Archbishop's factor insulted him as he lay in prison. Cargill replied, 'Mock not, lest your bands be made strong; the day is coming when you shall not have one word to say though you would'. A few days later the factor's tongue swelled up, he became unable to speak, and died in agony. And when he was threatened with torture and execution by Chancellor Rothes, Cargill's response was, 'My Lord Rothes, forbear to threaten me, for die what death I will, your eyes shall not see it'. Rothes died several hours before Cargill was executed. Most writers have seen all this as proof of Cargill's divinely-given gift of prophecy, but to me it sounds more like the power of cursing.

AROUND BLAIRGOWRIE

Lucifer built the Deil's [Devil's] Brig (a peculiar stretch of columnar basalt that looks man-made) to get across the Ericht from Rattray (where he had landed when he was ejected from Heaven; the exact spot is supposed to be 150 yards northwest of Bramble Bank). He then tried to climb the steep Heughs of Mause in an attempt to return to Heaven's Gate. The soil was so soft his claws gouged deep gullies, which can still be seen today. He reached the top, realised he was not a jot nearer his destination, burst into very unSatanic tears (which formed a spring) and thrust his angelic sword deep into the earth (which is why the chalybeate water is 'rusty'). The Heugh Well is still there (NO172472) but there is no sign of the Devil's sword. The Lornty Burn was the home of a particularly foul-tempered kelpie, and just past Craighall Bridge on the Ericht are the Witch's Pool and Samuel's Pool. Then, about three miles north of Blairgowrie the river runs through a chasm. On the west side is Craig Liach, the Eagle's Craig, a large rock 300ft high. On the very edge of the precipice are the scant ruins of a circular tower, Lady Lindsay's Castle (NO177488). The setting is spectacular and you just know that there has to be some legend connected with this place – and so there is. Of course, it comes in different variants, and of course there is no evidence at all linking the characters of the story with the castle. Lady Janet Gordon (who died in 1489 or 1491), the daughter of the second Earl of Huntly and granddaughter of King James I, had four husbands. The first, Alexander Lindsay, the Master of Crawford, was a brute and a brigand; when he was wounded in a fight with his younger brother, Janet, having endured years of abuse, decided not to nurse him back to health but to smother him with a pillow. The Master of Gray was husband number two, but the marriage was dissolved very quickly. Then came Patrick Butter of Cormack, and finally Halkerston of Southwood. Then what happened depends on the version being told. In one story she was confined to the tower for life by order of the Pope, as penance for killing her husband. Every day she had to earn her food by spinning a thread long enough to reach the river below. When she finally died at the age of one hundred her fingers were almost worn away. But this was not the end of her misery. Her ghost continued to spin a thread, and both it and she were often seen by men fishing in the gorge below. In 1746 the thread saved the life of Niall Mor nam Breac, a Jacobite fugitive from the slaughter at Culloden. He was in danger of being swept away by the raging torrent, but the thread was strong enough to help him climb his way to the safety of the bank. Lady Lindsay immediately gave a cry of relief, threw the spindle into the river, and vanished. Her redemption was only possible because she had saved the life of a supporter of the Stuarts, her noble lineage (remember, she was the granddaughter of James I). In version two of the story, her ghost haunted Inverqueich Castle, the Lindsay family home on the banks of the Isla, east of Alyth. Here she constantly implored Alexander's spirit to forgive her for murdering him – even though he may have deserved it. Eventually Alexander got so fed up with Janet moping around that he banished her to the tower at Craig Liach. Her penance was to spin a thread long enough to get her to heaven. The visible remains of Lady Lindsay's castle are of a medieval earthwork with a defensive ditch and bank and the remains of a rectangular building.

The Mause, the area west of the main road, used to be peppered with burial mounds, most long gone. This is the haunt of the famous phantom dog discussed in detail by Maurice Fleming in his highly recommended book *The Ghost o' Mause*. The dog haunted William Soutar, who lived at Middle Mause. It spoke to him, claiming to be David Soutar, William's uncle. He had, said the dog, murdered a man thirty-five years ago; unless William dug the body up and gave it a good Christian burial, the spirit of the murderer could have no rest. The grave was in the Isle (a piece of low-lying land near the river southeast of Bridge of Cally NO c.152515). On the second attempt William and other local men did find some bones, they were indeed re-buried in Blairgowrie kirkyard, and the ghost padded no more. What makes this story remarkable is that immediately after the funeral Thomas Rattray, the local bishop, took down the events as related to him by William Soutar in front of witnesses. Rattray's letters describing the deposition, from December 1730, are still in existence.

The policies of Glenericht estate (north of Mause) were planted with trees showing the formations of the troops at the Battle of Waterloo, but felling has now removed the shape. I'd like to know what sort of tree represented Napoleon. A 'Roman spearhead' was found in the great Moss of Cochrage, northwest of Mause (approx NO1449), and another near the bed of the river Ericht. These may have been misidentified Iron Age weapons, ritually deposited in liminal watery environments. There was also a story that a 'Roman soldier in full armour' was found buried in an upright position in the Moss. There is no verification of this, and it sounds preposterous anyway, so it probably is either an exaggeration of the spearhead discovery mentioned above, or a garbled description of a 'bog body', such as the famous Lindow Man.

Left: Former church, Kirk Wynd, Blairgowrie. The bones of the Ghost o'Mause murder victim are supposedly buried in this litter-strewn wilderness.

Opposite: Old Rattray church. Two thirds Angel of the Resurrection, one third mermaid.

Craighall House (NO17504817) (private) has a Grey Lady who manifests as a great weight on top of people sleeping. Other ghostly phenomena include knockings, phantom footsteps, a sense of being watched, and, in the North Room, the lingering influence of a servant girl thrown out of the window by Cromwell's troops. Around 1900 a cist was discovered somewhere in the area below Strageith Wood and rebuilt in Craighall's garden. GARGOYLES.

Essendy Stone Circle★★ is possibly the most dangerous stone circle in the country (a fast road goes right through it); there have been recent reports of a dog and a horse refusing to go near the stones (NO15994388).
Craighall stone circle★ (NO18424807).
Standing stone★★ (NO18524826).
Woodside stone circle and Horse Stone (NO18485005).
Church and graveyard, GRAVESTONES★ (NO190457).
Standing stone★ (NO20184582).
Old Mains of Rattray, ruinous, GRAVESTONES★ (NO20654526).
Burial ground from former chapel dedicated to St Findeach (or St Fincana?), GRAVESTONES (NO21464722).

ALYTH

'An Escape…(A True Story)', adapted by PL Hartley, appeared in the *Scots Year Book* of 1959. In the 1820s/30s many travelling people and other itinerants lived in fear of the Resurrection Men, who made their living selling corpses to doctors for anatomy practice. The belief was that the 'Burkers' (from the Edinburgh duo Burke and Hare) preferred simple murder to graverobbing because it was less hassle and the body was guaranteed fresh. Betty Abbot, a widow from Alyth who traded in eggs and butter, was walking on a lonely road near Kirriemuir one dark, wet November night, when a gig drawn by a single horse approached from behind. 'That's a dirty night', said a voice from within. 'It is that', she replied, in her rough, very masculine voice (Betty was a large, muscled woman). The gig drove off, only to return a while later. 'That's a dark night', said a different voice. 'Very dark', Betty muttered. She then heard the two men debating over whether she was a woman or not. She realised they were Burkers and knew they planned to kill her. She fled into a nearby wood, where a fortuitous sprawl cast her into the undergrowth and hid her from her pursuers, who after much searching and swearing eventually gave up. She stayed in her hiding place all night and in the morning, having found her basket where she had abandoned it, picked it up and went on her way.

The lintel over the south doorway of the walled garden at Balhary (NO26304659) reads, 'I shall overcome Invy with God's help; to God be al Prais, Honour and Glorie'. The associated story has the hunch-backed laird of Balhary seeing the inscription in a dream, and realising his envy and jealousy were preventing the happiness of a young couple. A well-worn tale has Bamff (NO222515) home to a magical white serpent. Sir James Ramsay's political intrigues had cost him the estate and he was wandering in exile on the continent when he was taken under the wing of a renowned wise man and doctor, who told him the most wonderful medicine in the world could be made from a certain white Scottish serpent. Ramsay recognised the description of its lair as being on his own estate, and despite still being an outlaw for plotting against the King, he returned to Scotland in disguise and travelled to Bamff. For two nights under the full moon he failed to capture the serpent, but on the traditional third try he killed it. On returning to his safe European home the laird was instructed by the good doctor to cook the great snake, but to do so in secret, to avoid food before the task was complete, and on no account to taste the reptile's oil, which was a fatal poison. Ramsay accidentally splashed oil on his fingers, sucked it off without thinking, and, instead of dying, found he now had the ability to see through walls and into people's bodies. Realising the old man had lied to him and was probably up to no good, the honest Scot snuck away, and proceeded to make a good living doctoring. Eventually he decided to return to Scotland, where he found the city of Edinburgh aghast at the King's terrible illness. Ramsay looked into the King and saw a huge hairball in his stomach ('trinchobezoars' were themselves prized magical items). You can probably guess the rest. In quick order, Ramsay saved the King's life, revealed his true identity, was pardoned, regained his estate and married the King's daughter. A surgeon, Neis de Ramsay, did, it seems, actually cut a hairball out of Alexander II, enabling the king to live for another seventeen years. This was the earliest recorded abdominal operation (at least in the West). In 1232 he got his reward with the grant of the Bamff estate. The real 'miraculous' operation has been folklorised and transmuted into what is clearly a version of the 'hero accidentally gains secret knowledge' trope. Fingal, to choose one hero from many, learned a thousand things in a second when he sucked his burned finger while cooking the Salmon of Wisdom. More locally, the same story is told about a laird in GLENSHEE.

Alyth Parish church, Kirk Brae, with Pictish Stone★.
Burial ground, GRAVESTONES★ (NO24484879).
Burnside standing stone★ (NO25544886).
Shealwalls stone circle (NO23965149).
Lady Well (NO263462).
St Ninian's (?) Well, enclosed by a dry-stone wall (NO24994730).

KING ARTHUR AND GUINEVERE: THE SCOTTISH CONNECTION

Alyth, Meigle and Barry Hill share an unusual variant on the tales of King Arthur. Normally, Guinevere falls in love with Lancelot. But in Strathmore, the 'other man' is Mordred – Arthur's illegitimate son with Morgan le Fay in the 'classic' version, and his eventual nemesis. There are several variants to the core story, but they all agree that Guinevere spent time at the 'castle' on Barry Hill (actually an Iron Age fort); she had (willing or unwilling) carnal knowledge of Mordred and she met a terrible end, killed by vicious animals. In these Scottish versions Guinevere is variously called Guinevar, Gwenhwyvar, Guanora, Vanora, Vyonar, Venera, Wanor, Wander, Wandor, or Helena. The variants of the story are: Modred, son of Loftus, King of the Picts and Arthur's nephew, usurped both the kingdom and the queen when Arthur went on a pilgrimage to Rome. Mordred and Arthur killed each other at the battle of Camlann, Guinevere was imprisoned on Barry Hill and later torn to pieces by wild beasts. Or, Guinevere was a rape abductee who managed to escape from Barry Hill, then called Dunbarve, but was hunted down by Mordred's wolfhounds; or, she was brought to the castle after the death of Arthur to live out the rest of her life there; or was abducted by Mordred and got fed up fending him off; or fell in love with Mordred from the start, and marriage counselling being unknown in the Dark Ages, it was then Arthur who had the poor woman torn apart by wild animals. Another version has Mordred and Guinevere dallying not on Barry Hill, but at Dumbarrow, in Angus and in a final version Mordred is not a Pict and was killed when the fort was overrun by the Picts and Scots.

Stone No. 2 in MEIGLE Museum, a finely-carved Pictish cross-slab, preserves the principal story in stone. Supposedly. The back has a scene of a robed figure flanked by four beasts – a representation of Daniel in the lions' den. Alternatively it shows the execution of Queen Guinevere. The story originates with the fabulist Hector Boece (see LUNCARTY), and his fictions echo down the centuries and into the lives of local people. Before it was brought into the museum at the end of the nineteenth century the cross-slab stood to the north of the church in front of a grassy mound known as Vanora's Grave. The Queen was said to be barren, and any young woman walking over the mound was at risk of infertility. The back of the stone – the face resting against Vanora's Grave - is well preserved, but the front is much more worn. This suggests some form of habitual activity which rubbed against the stone. My suggestion is women kneeled in prayer in front of it, quite possibly asking for Gwennie's help in conceiving. Here, Guinevere can be seen as an avatar of the BVM, or one of the martyred female saints. Some of the other Pictish stones found at Meigle were trimmed and re-used to ornament Vanora's Grave in the sixteenth and seventeenth centuries. One of them was the stone where her servants were buried. Further Arthurisation can be found in the names of Arthurstone House (NO262429), a 1789 castellated tower folly with an antiquarian corner of carved fragments, and Arthur's Stone, a large boulder built into nearby Arthurbank Farm in 1791.

The 1979 *Third Statistical Account* relates how in 1926 the Meigle Women's Rural Institute embroidered a banner showing Gwennie as she is allegedly depicted on Stone 2. (The banner is in the KINLOCH Memorial Hall.) But here the story has changed again. Arthur is on horseback, but no longer is the Queen being savaged by dogs/wolves; she is one of the angels hovering nearby.

BARRY HILL★★ Iron Age hillfort (NO262503) had a large well or cistern which, as well as supplying drinking water, may have functioned as a watery route to the Celtic underworld, a ritual practice well-attested elsewhere. The well may explain the tradition of an underground passage connecting Barry Hill to another structure (marked 'enclosure' on the OS 1:25000 map) a quarter of a mile east. Anything Arthurian (or Guineverian) is, however, down to our imagination.

A very small area around Brucetown farmhouse has a high concentration of prehistoric sites. At least one standing stone, a probable stone circle (both Neolithic/Bronze Age), a burial mound (probably Bronze Age), at least eight cists (Neolithic? Bronze Age? later?), a souterrain (probably Iron Age, in a hollow called Hell Hole or Holy Howe) and a superb Pictish stone★★ (NO28985039). Was this a ritual landscape used for centuries or even millennia?

MEIGLE

The unmissable Meigle Museum of sculptured Pictish stones★★★ (HS) has excellent interpretation of its hundreds of carved figures, so here's just a few extra folkloric highlights. The numbers used are the same as the museum displays.

Stone 1. The strangest carving is a winged angel-like figure, which some experts identify as the Persian god Ahura-Mazda. The scattering of pits are from rifle target practice.

Stone 2. This is the 'Guinevere' stone. The *NSA* claimed this was a monument set up by the Knights Templar, with the arms of Jerusalem at the top and the Daniel/Guinevere figure actually an allegory of the Holy Land rescued by the Crusaders.

Stone 11. This has one of the most intriguing and suggestive carvings in the entire body of Pictish carving – a dancing Shamanic figure with a beast's head grasping two intertwined snakes, one of which has its head in the figure's mouth.

Stone 22. In *Pagan Celtic Britain* Anne Ross sees the seated 'deity' on this stone as the horned Celtic nature god Cernunnos. Cernunnos is first known from rock carvings in Val Camonica, Italy, dated 400-250BC and he, or a similar horned god, was worshipped throughout the Romano-British period; he is famously depicted as a stag-god on the Gundestrup cauldron.

Nick Brazil (author of *A Journey with Ghosts*) and Hilary Wilding encountered a couple of dowsers at the museum in September 1996. The horizontal stones caused the rods to cross over each other, while Stone 1, the centrepiece of the museum, pushed a single rod away as if by an invisible force. The dowser, who was in his late fifties, explained that 'all these stones have energy trapped inside' and encouraged Hilary, Nick and the curator to use the rods; they all achieved the same reactions. Hilary and Nick returned the next day, armed with dowsing rods borrowed from friends. At first Nick had no success with Stone 1, but then realised the area he was dowsing was a later concrete repair. When he tried a single rod about half an inch from the upper part of the stone, it swung away from the surface in the same way as the previous day. The recumbent stones also caused the two rods to cross over, just as before. Then when he held one of the divining rods between two of the stones, it began to rotate through 360° like a helicopter rotor. The pair then had a similar set of experiences with the Pictish stones at FOWLIS WESTER.

Next to the museum is 'Vanora's grave' and the church and burial ground, GRAVE-STONES★★. The church was rebuilt in 1870. At the completion ceremony the elders decided it was a little too far to the west, and so trooped out of the shebeen and put their shoulders to the walls to push the church into its right place. Then they returned bar-wards, probably wondering whose round it was. The same story is told about the church in BALBEGGIE.

The following episode, taken from Ron Halliday's *UFO Scotland* and *Evil Scotland*, has no checkable references, and presumably 'Karen' is a pseudonym. In the summer of 1976 a ten-year-old girl set out from her family's farm cottage near Meigle to go for a picnic in the nearby wood. Unusually, no birds were singing. In a clearing she encountered four very short blue-skinned beings. What followed was a classic 'alien abduction' experience – a medical examination and other indignities on board a ship; when she returned home she had 'lost' six hours. Two years later she was abducted again from the same place. In 1995, now living in Paisley and bringing up a small child, Karen experienced missing time episodes, bright lights, and a visitation from a dog-faced entity. An X-ray apparently revealed an unknown metal object in the roof of her mouth – an implant from the first abduction. The medical recommendation was an operation, but Karen declined. Such stories never result in tangible evidence; why is that, we wonder? If you are inclined to make an aliens and fairies link, then note *Our Meigle Book* (1932) relates the local belief that fairy men from the Sidlaw Hills would steal newborn children and young girls and 'carry them off to their caverns or underground houses', and *Meigle, Past and Present* (1870s) says that human men from the area had 'cohabited with females of the fairy race'.

William Marshall, in *Historic Scenes in Perthshire*, relates two witchcraft stories. To fast-track his inheritance, young George Nairne of Drumkilbo House, east of Meigle (NO30394488) accused an older female relative of witchcraft.

His word was apparently enough, and she was put into a tar barrel and burnt without benefit of a trial. This may possibly have taken place as late as 1704. A witch named Jean lived at Cardean, north of Meigle (NO290457). Like all good witches, her house was solitary, by the edge of a wood. She was clearly a successful self-employed hag, being in great demand for curing animals and settling disputes, her fee for which was five shillings per person. At night, Jean used to fight with the Devil in the wood next to her house; in the morning her bruises and scratches were plain to see (there are other possible explanations for this.) But one morning her body was found close to the wood, floating in Dean Water.

The Bridge of Craithies (NO279454) crosses by the Boat Hole, home to a vicious kelpie which overturned the ferry one stormy night, drowning two men, a woman and a horse. The kelpie was later captured and put to farm work on nearby Balmyre (now Balmyle) Farm (NO273448). Its unhappiness at a life in harness is recorded in an old rhyme: Sair back and sair bones, Carryin' auld Balmyre's stanes.

Belmont Castle standing stone (NO286436)
Belliduff cairn, Macbeth's (or Macduff's) grave (NO28904421).
Macbeth's Stone, cupmarked, grave of one of his generals (or enemies)★★ (NO280435). Nearby is Duff's Knowe.

STRATHARDLE AND GLENSHEE

BLACKCRAIG CASTLE★★ (NO108535), fantasy-medieval from 1856, wonderful mock-fortified bridge, Gothic gatepiers. Mr Hogg, a later owner, one day fell into conversation with a stranger at the sundial. He finally recognised him as Patrick Alan Fraser, the rich artist who built Blackcraig. His dog then walked right through the visitor. The castle is open for B&B July–September.

BALLINTUIM
Woodhill, in Ballintuim, was a substantial eighteenth-century mansion near the current house of the same name (NO098544). A.G. Reid's mother met a little old lady in an old-fashioned dress rushing along a corridor. This was Mrs Trotter, who had been killed while hurrying to get to the chapel. Reid's grandmother had also seen her. In 1962 Woodhill was to be demolished, so Reid's soon-to-be wife attended the sale of the contents, looking for a bargain among the antiques. She returned early, shaken and white-faced. She had been looking into a room at the far end of the house, when the atmosphere turned icy cold and she saw a little old lady in a long, flowing, old-fashioned dress. Reid's fiancée knew nothing about Mrs Trotter before making the visit.

Steps of Cally burial ground, GRAVESTONES (NO128516).
'Standing stones' which are actually gateposts (NO120519).
'Druidstone', a modern fake (NO117520).
Hill of Cally kerb-cairn (NO133521).
Parkneuk stone circle★ (NO19535145).
Cupmarked rocks (NO19655114 and NO19755156)

BALNABROICH
Two stone row and standing stone★ (NO092566 and NO092568).
Cairns with boulder kerbs (NO066566, NO063564 and NO068564).
Cupmarked rock★ (NO062562).
Grey Cairn, 'built for Druidic sacrifices' (*OSA*) (NO101570).
Balnabroich stone circle (NO102570).
Ring cairn (NO101571).
Cairns (NO103568, NO102571 and NO105571).

One of the cairns on the west side of the road is the grave of a troublemaking mermaid killed by Fingal's' dog Bran. He had chased her from her home in Loch Mharaich (Loch of the Mermaid, NO118568). During a hunt in 1317 Robert the Bruce's favourite hound disappeared down a deep hole somewhere on the moors of Pitcarmick. About a week or so later the dog emerged from a cave at Craighall, emaciated and wounded, but alive. The hole was eventually filled in by a laird after too many of his sheep disappeared. A rocking stone a mile northeast of the Grey Cairn was a Druidic treason or guilt stone – an innocent man could move it with a finger, but it would not budge for a traitor.

DOUNIE
Robert Wallace, the son of a crofter, fell in love with the beautiful Christina, of the prominent Rattray family of Kirkmichael. Christina's cousin Jessie Cameron also wanted Robert, and the jealous lass had powers gifted from a Glenshee witch. She made a Corp Chreadh, a clay image like a Voodoo doll, and stuck pins in it, accompanied by incantations. She placed the image in the Dounie Burn (NO0859) by the usual lover's spot, near a small waterfall – a place still called the Witches' Pool. As the image eroded so Christina weakened, but a shepherd found the Corp and destroyed it. Jessie made another image but was caught and bound hand and foot, chained to an iron ring in the garnet rock by the Witches' Pool, and left immersed overnight. As she sank, Jessie chanted a plea to the Witch of Glenshee, who turned up in the form of a raven and a great storm – the fiercest on record, with one peal of thunder lasting for over an hour. In the morning the garnet stone had been smashed by lightning, and the body gone. Perhaps the Witch had rescued her protégé and taken her to the top of Mount Blair. 'The Witches' Garnet Stone of Strathardle', a fragment of the rock, was presented by local man Jock Fell

('The Sailor') to R. MacDonald Robertson. 'Robbie Wallace's Brae' is the hill road leading down to the Dounie Burn. One November night a farmer and his three daughters saw two lights coming from a lonely cottage on the hillside near the croft of Dounie. The lights moved down the narrow winding brae-side path in the direction of the Blairgowrie road. Two weeks later two children in the cottage died of diphtheria and their coffins were carried on the same route to Kirkmichael churchyard. Cultalonie Pool on the River Ardle (NO0859) was home to a tarbh-uisge, a water-bull, with a jet-black coat and no ears. The otherwise gentle fairy creature became 'The Demon Bull of Cultalonie' after a fisherman accidentally attacked it with a gaff or landing-net. Thereafter it lurked among the waterside reeds and boulders looking for victims. The tarbh-uisge's offspring could be identified by their short ears, and their large, fierce descendants were still being pointed out in the twentieth century.

KIRKMICHAEL

Bargains were struck at the livestock market by passing money (siller) over the running water of the Siller Burn (between Balnakilly and the council houses). The Old Manse (private) is haunted by a classic druid figure – long white flowing robes, flowers on his head, and carrying a golden sickle. He was seen by an English maid 'a good many years ago'. The encounter was dismissed as the half-awake view of morning mist. She also heard a 'sudden cry of anguish, which rose to a crescendo and then died shudderingly away'. This was explained away as a barn owl which had become trapped in one of the chimneys. Then further investigation revealed....the house was built on Druidic stones! Inevitably, the screams were reinterpreted as echoes of the blood sacrifices. In 1970, when the manse was a youth hostel, a young man in the upstairs left corner front bedroom felt the nape of his neck becoming very cold, and 'his hair seemed to rise and he was overcome by a feeling of abject terror in a matter of seconds'. As soon as he left the house he was fine. Another traveller swore he would never go back to Kirkmichael because of the feeling of terror (on the same floor but in a different room to the first experience). So bad was it that, despite the lateness of the hour, he cycled a further thirty miles to the next hostel (Andrew Green, *Our Haunted Kingdom*). A Victorian clergyman was returning home from a late meeting of the Presbytery (and the customary associated dinner) when he was seized by the fairies and carried high into sky (apparently to convince this sceptical man they did exist) and then deposited at his manse door. He often related this wonderful tale, but many suspected a different kind of spirits were at work. Plague victims were buried in the east corner of the churchyard (NO08066009) and no burials have taken place there since. GRAVESTONES.

Kirkmichael was troubled by a malignant invisible spirit called the Boabh (pronounced 'Buve') who tormented people and killed cattle. An old tailor accidentally discovered he could see her by looking through the finger-holes of his scissors. The priest took the scissors and, with the village folk in hot pursuit, chased the Boabh for a long time until she rested on a rock. He encircled her with holy water and had the people pile up stones upon her – 'one for every cow she killed'. She cried for mercy and promised to turn all the stones into gold, but the villagers carried on until she was completely buried. The 'Carn-na-baiodh' remained at Dalnagairn (NO0760) until the 1890s when the laird dismantled it for drain-stones. Contrary to local expectation, there was no supernatural comeback. 'Boabh' is very likely a derivative of Badb or Badhbh, an Irish war goddess who often assumed the form of a raven or carrion-crow. She feasted on the corpses of the slain and caused confusion among warriors with her magic. The Boabh's invisibility and her goads and pinches, designed to sow social discord, may be an echo of this.

Lachlan and George Rattray of Kirkmichael, having allegedly committed 'many mal-efices', were charged with charming and necromancy in December 1704. It took a year to bring them to trial. The sentence was execution, but after two reprieves and another year, it was commuted to life banishment. The backstory of the case is very revealing: Lachlan Rattray was a neighbour of the aggressive Spaldings of Ashintully Castle. It was the Spalding laird who accused Lachlan, and who obtained a Privy Council commission to imprison him (which he did in the dungeon of Ashintully). Presumably Lachlan was in Spalding's way. One of the other accusers was the minister, John Piersone, who just happened to be married to Spalding's sister. The Privy Council, the highest court in the land, took a proprietary interest in the conduct of the case; this, combined with the late date and the rise of disbelief in supernatural witchcraft, may have contributed to the relatively lenient sentence. Lachlan managed to escape and fled to Flanders, returning to the glen five years later.

ASHINTULLY CASTLE, private (NO102612) has a motto above the doorway, 'The Lord Defend This Hovs' and indeed it needs all the divine protection it can get, being haunted by at least three ghosts from its bloody past. The first is a tinker from the Robertson clan, who was hanged by one of the Spaldings of Ashintully for trespassing. The second, Crooked Davie, a hunchback also known as Fleet Davie, was a very fast runner. The laird sent Davie to deliver an urgent despatch to Edinburgh, normally a two-way journey of two days, but Davie did it in one day to return before a ball at Ashintully. The poor servant collapsed with exhaustion on his return and was found by Spalding under the table in front of the fire in the great hall. Assuming Davie had not even left, Spalding stabbed him. Finally in the Spalding ghost-list of infamy there is Green Jean, her throat cut by an uncle who wanted the property for himself. He also murdered her maid and pushed the body up the chimney before dragging Jean down the stairs. Muffled footsteps are still heard. Jean's green-clad ghost haunts the small, walled-in private burial ground beside the castle, standing beside the headstone the uncle hypocritically erected to her memory. R. MacDonald Robertson's dog refused to enter this 'weird, uncanny place'. Secret Passages link Ashintully with its predecessor, Whitefield Castle, a now-ruinous tower-house 1.2km west-southwest (NO090717).

A large boulder at BALVARRAN (NO074623) has four enormous cupmarks*: three, 25cm across and 14cm deep, in a line, and a smaller one 20cm diameter by 10cm deep. The story is that water was placed in the holes to baptize the children of the Barons Ruadh or Reid. The last Baron is said to have died without a son because the stone was not used at his christening. In 1644-1646 the Marquis of Montrose devastated the glen, concentrating on the property of the Ruadhs, who had refused to join him at the Battle of Tibbermore. Montrose was a Graham, and in the Jacobite uprising of 1689 Baron Ruadh held Blair Castle against the Jacobite Bonnie Dundee (another Graham) with just a small force of Strathardle men. The Baron was worried that Dundee would wreak the same kind of vengeance that had occurred over fifty years earlier, but then his wife dreamt of a dragon whose chain prevented it from damaging its target. The very next day, Dundee was killed at KILLIECRANKIE. The junction of the Altchroskie burn with the River Ardle, between Balvarran and Ardchroskie house, is haunted by a group of seventeenth-century cattle thieves lured into a trap and picked off by the one-eyed archer Cam Ruadh.

ENOCHDU's 'Giant's Grave'* (NO063628) is attributed to Ardle, name-giver to Strathardle. Prince Ard-fhuil (high, noble blood) fell with two of his men in a battle against the Danes in 903. The three were buried head to foot in a line, a creative expla-nation for the length of the long, low burial mound (which doubles as a flower bed). Its standing stone may or may not be prehistoric. The Vikings were buried in a mass grave called Grey Hollow. In the seventeenth century Donal Mor and his eight daughters built an underground kitchen where they secretly slaughtered and cooked the cattle that had been mysteriously disappearing from their neighbours' herds. The family was banished and the house burnt down (the site is covered by the front lawn of Kindrogan Field Centre, NO053629). Donal hid in a cave in Kindrogan rock, was discovered, and hanged himself on Cnoc Dhimhnuill Mhor – Donal Mhor's Knowe, 50m west of the burn.

Enochdhu standing stone (NO060630).
Croft House standing stone* (NO057633).
Cupmarked boulder* (NO053634).
Faire na Paitig stone circle (NO075661).
Cupmarked rock (NO077662).
Standing stone, modern fake? (NO069642).

STRALOCH. The Witch's Stone or Clach Mhor ('the big stone'), a huge natural boulder (NO045643) was being lifted from the Isle of Man to the Cummings' castle in Badenoch by a witch, but she dropped it when a hunter saw her flying overhead and said 'God preserve me!' The fertility-giving Saddle Stone is somewhere between

Dalnacarn and Glen Loch far to the north. In 729 McFergus and Drost, Kings of the southern and northern Picts respectively, battled at Loch Broom (NO580010). Drost lost. The slain were thrown into the tiny (20m x 3m) Lochan Dubh, the Black Loch (NO024607) and haunt it still. In the 1389 Raid of Angus the Robertsons and Stewarts invaded Glenisla and Glenesk and killed many of the Ogilvies and Lindsays. The barons of Angus unsuccessfully counter-attacked at Dalnacarn, 'the field or haugh of the cairns' (NO c.0063); said cairns were still visible in the nineteenth century. The dead of the losing side were thrown into (and haunt) the Black Loch of the Dun.

Standing stone★ (NO038637).
Cupmarked rocks (NO009636★ and NN996625).

GLENSHEE
In *The Fairy Faith in Celtic Countries*, Evans-Wentz asserted that Glenshee ('Fairy Glen') was once full of fairies, but that they were driven underground by the steam-whistle. Unfortunately for this attractive idea, there never was a railway anywhere near here. In 1965 four students from Loughborough College spent a week skiing in the area. Their rather unconventional transport was a small black 1932 Austin Seven (with the front seat removed) which they would carry over any inconvenient snowdrifts. They were often the only skiers on really snowy days because the roads were blocked to all other vehicles. Later a television programme was broadcast about a 1932 black Austin Seven which had been seen travelling in Glenshee in conditions that no car could travel in; it never arrived anywhere, disappeared en route, and had no driver or passengers… Belle Stewart of the famous Stewart travelling family tells a tale called 'The Shearer of Glenshee', about an old tramp who worked on a farm and died there of fever. He had been popular and people came to the wake from all over Glenshee and Glen Isla. A great deal of drink was consumed and when the coffin was being carried on the rough road to the graveyard, a fight broke out between the men from the two glens about where the dead man should be buried. Suddenly darkness fell. Then just as suddenly, it became bright daylight again and there were now two coffins lying next to each other. So the men from Glen Isla took one coffin and the Glenshee folk took the other. Exactly the same story is told about the eponymous saint at ST FILLANS.

Cairn Gleamnach★ (NO159554).
Ring cairn(?) (NO184528).
Cupmarks, Craighead (NO19565498), Drumderg 1★ (NO18525497), Drumderg 2 (NO18395451), Mains of Soliarzie (NO12375863).
Standing stone★ (NO171545).
Stone circle (NO12346246)
Borland standing stone★ (NO1535 6067).
Drumfork chapel, GRAVESTONES★ (O148595).
'Font Stone' (NO121554); nearby was a healing chalybeate spring.

The Cock's Stone.
Here McComie Mor
beat the Earl of Atholl's
tax-gatherers for
robbing an old widow.

The cairn on the summit of MOUNT BLAIR (NO168629) marks the grave of
Alexander Robertson, a suicide from Blackwater. He could not be buried in consecrated ground; the remote location was probably chosen because the county
boundary, a liminal space, passes through the summit. Colly Camb the giant lived in
a cave on the south side of Mount Blair. He liked to throw large rocks around, which
still litter the landscape. When he stole oatmeal from the mill the locals, complete
with traditional pitchforks and flaming torches, marched on his cave and killed him.
Many years later two men ventured into the cave; their voices were heard coming
from underground two miles east of the entrance, but they were 'Never Seen Again'
(see p.11). Colly's giantess wife Smoutachanty was just as dangerous and occupied a
cave on the Isla at Auchintaple. Mount Blair was also home to the Glenshee witch.

The folklore of the next part of the glen favours the heroic figure of McComie
Mor, laird of FINEGAND in the seventeenth century and master swordsman.

A man drowning in the Shee, near the ford just north of Finegand, cried out to
McComie for help by name, but when the laird extended his staff to the 'victim', he
found himself wrestling with a water kelpie, who tried to pull him into the floodwaters.
An ordinary man would certainly have been drowned, but McComie was stronger than
anyone in the glen and he almost lifted the kelpie onto the shore. Realising he had met
his match, the malignant creature gave a cry of rage and frustration and disappeared
into the darkness. One day in McComie's absence a travelling ceard (pedlar) insulted
the women of the Finegand household. McComie pursued him to a place opposite
Broughdearg and offered the man a choice of swords. It was an unequal contest and the
pedlar was buried where he fell. In the twentieth century the great uncle of Alexander
Mackenzie Smith (author of *Glenshee* and a source for much of this section) built a new
summerhouse, Corrydon Cottage (NO133667) in Imir-a-Chaird, the Ceard's Field.
This of course was much against local advice. A skeleton was uncovered, but the uncle

The Cock's Stone. When
McComie liberated
the widow's chickens a
cockerel gave a great cry
from the stone.

ordered it to be reburied in its original spot. Mackenzie Smith reported an 'uneasy atmosphere' about the house when he lived there for two months and several of his family have seen a Highlander dressed in an old ragged plaid walking in the garden.

Clach a Mhoid, the Stone of Judgement (NO14656400).

The story of the healing white serpent (see BAMFF) is transposed 500 years later to the laird of BROUGHDEARG. Here the magus is Cagliostro, a famous occultist-charlatan and the laird's royal patron is Bonnie Prince Charlie. Mackenzie Smith sees a pair of standing stones (NO13746704) as the remains of a circle, with remnants visible in the limekiln and stackyard wall. One stone is grooved as if to hold an iron chain, and the foot is blackened and firecracked. Druids! Blood! Sacrifice! Smith also identifies a second circle a few metres to the northeast in a small wood, with several fallen and semi-visible stones.

Remote LOCH BEANIE has a small artificial island about 100m from its south shore (NO16016867), the occasional dwelling of the chief of Glenshee in the 1600s. On steep rocky ground 670m northeast of the loch is Clach-na-Nathraiche (or Clach-na-marriche), the Serpent's Stone★, a large granite boulder with six cupmarks and an unusual pear-shaped hollow. Here the laird cornered a witch he blamed for the death of his infant son. The witch 'shape shifted' into a snake and slid into the hole in the rock, which the laird attacked with his claymore, leaving the still-visible marks. Another version of the story has the serpent as the laird's familiar spirit.

The floor of the original chapel at SPITTAL OF GLENSHEE,★ (NO109702) was paved with human bones, many of which had been gnawed by the dogs that attended

Spittal of Glenshee. Standing stone on a knoll next to the church. The graveyard has carved eighteenth-century gravestones.

the service. A new church was to be built at Runavey, as this was more central to the glen (c. NO130690) but the fairies did not approve and the stones laid each day were removed at night. This continued for some time until the committee submitted and in 1822 the new church was built on the site of the old one.

A midwife had travelled the several miles to one of the hill shielings in GLEN TAITNEACH on a neighbour's pony. She alighted on a stone and asked him how she could repay him. The man, who obviously knew that midwives were 'special' in the second sight way, asked her to warn him when a death was about to occur in his family. She told him the sign would be the squealing of a pig – and just then a little pig ran squealing under the stone, which was therefore called Clach-na-Meickle-breac (Stone of the Little Spotted Pig). In the nineteenth century the farmer at Old Spittal used the stone to build the foundation of a dyke, but an outbreak of murrain among his cattle persuaded him to replace it.

Fingal's nephew Diarmid (pron. 'deer-mutch') eloped with the old king's young wife Grainne (pron. 'gran-yeh'). Eventually the couple and Fingal were apparently reconciled, but the king set Diarmid the task of ridding Glenshee of a fierce boar which was terrorising the district. To Fingal's chagrin Diarmid killed the boar, so the wily king invited the young man to measure the size of the dead boar with his bare foot. Some of the bristles from the boar's back penetrated his skin and Diarmid was fatally poisoned. He could have been saved by a drink from Fingal's magical life-giving cup, but Fingal contemptuously threw the cup away and Diarmid died in agony. Grainne killed herself with an arrow and the unhappy couple were buried together under the GRAVE OF DIARMID★ stone circle (NO11717017) along with Diarmid's white hounds. The landscape is heavily Fingalised. The four stones form the shape of a spearhead which points to where the boar died. Fingal tossed the magic cup into the small lochan on rising ground across the river from Old Spittal Farm. 2km up Glenbeg to the north and 20m right of the road is Tobar-na-Feinne, Fingal's Well, a wishing well – if you walk around it three times holding a cup of water your dearest wish will be granted. Tobar-na-Ossian, Ossian's Well, is on the opposite side of the road (neither well is marked on the 1:25000 map). A steep rugged gulley on Ben Gulabin is the Boar's Bed although I have been unable to locate either it or Loch an Tuirc, the Boar's Loch. Diarmid, it is claimed, is also buried in Kintyre, Loch Nell (Argyll) and Ireland, which just goes to show how much you can trust place names. The power of the myth may have prompted the enthusiasm of the 1894 excavation, which dug down an incredible 6.7m without discovering a single find or structural feature in the natural glacial mound. As a result of this excavation the stones are probably not in their original positions; is it even a genuine prehistoric monument?

Glenshee has a variant on the 'Princess of Morocco' story (see MUTHILL). In the early 1700s the beautiful daughter of Alexander Ramsay, a tenant farmer, was wooed by the son of a landowner in Strathardle. His father was none too happy about this low class lassie, so he lured her to Dundee on the pretext of buying her wedding clothes and home furnishings, and tricked her into staying on board a ship as it sailed off. She was sold as a slave in Morocco, joined the royal harem and eventually became the Emperor's favourite wife and Empress. Years later the laird was enslaved by Moorish pirates and the Empress set him free. Some years on two of her sons, Princes of Morocco, arrived in Dundee intending to search for their mother's family in Glen Beg, but it was the '45 and it was considered too dangerous for foreigners to travel, and so they left, mission unaccomplished. Note this version is set earlier than the Muthill story.

Standing stones (remains of stone circle?) (NO12127318).

SCONE TO DUNKELD

SCONE PALACE★★★. Open daily 9.30am-5.30pm from end of March to end of October. This nineteenth-century country house is a must-see because of its association with the Stone of Destiny, although round here they like to call it the Stone of Scone. The story (or at least the most prevalent legend) goes that when the Scots under Kenneth Mac Alpin gained ascendancy over the Picts in the ninth century, they brought with them a sacred stone upon which, with the right ceremony, men became kings. Later Edward I of England ('Hammer of the Scots') and 10,000 troops turned up and took the Stone away as war booty, installing it under the throne in Westminster Abbey. Where, with one brief exception, it remained until 1996 when, with devolutionary politics in the air, the Conservative Government in London returned the Stone to…Edinburgh. A copy now stands on the low mound of Moot Hill.

The Stone, however, exists both in the real world and in 'idea space', the realm where fantasy, fiction and speculation are just as important as mundane fact. A full discussion of the mysteries and mumbo-jumbo associated with the Stone could take up an entire book, but here are a few of the main themes.

Origins:

The Stone was originally Jacob's Pillow. When the Hebrew patriarch fell asleep at Luz, God showed him a ladder to Heaven. Jacob subsequently consecrated his stone pillow to Jehovah. (Genesis 28:1-22).

The Stone came from ancient Egypt, brought thither by those pesky ancients who kept turning up from the great Mediterranean civilisations and founding parts of Britain. The usual suspect is the son of Cecrops, who brought it from Syria to Egypt and thence to Spain; then his son took it with him when he invaded Ireland.

The Scots themselves had brought it from Egypt. When Alexander III was crowned on the Stone a Gaelic greybeard intoned a long family tree originating with the legendary Gathelus, who married Scota, the daughter of Pharoah, and was the contemporary of Moses.

It was a sacred stone from Ireland, whence the Scots originally came. The Irish kings were crowned on it at Tara. Fergus, son of Eric, brought it to Dunstaffnage in Argyll for his coronation.

At Dunstaffnage (or, alternatively, Dunadd) the Stone was set beside a magic cauldron which always supplied exactly the right amount of food for the number of people present.

The Stone was St Columba's portable altar.

The Stone as an Object of Desire:

The Danes battled the Scots near Scone for possession of the Stone some time before 904. They were defeated.

Edward I wanted the Stone because it had magic powers, or at least that is what the Scots believed.

Edward I wanted the Stone simply because possessing your enemy's sacred relics saps their morale.

The Stone as a Fake:

There are many stories about fake Stones. The stone was hidden before Edward I arrived and he was palmed off with a hastily made facsimile or some random bit of church or castle architecture. The real Stone is therefore hidden. Suggestions for its location include DUNSINANE HILL, DULL or a 'Very Secret Hiding Place' known only to the initiated, the Freemasons, etc.

When it was stolen from Westminster Abbey in the 1950s by some eager Scottish Nationalists, it's said they copied the Stone before handing back a fake. It would therefore be the fake that now sits in Edinburgh Castle and the real stone is hidden Somewhere Secret.

The Stone as Destiny:

> *Unless the fates are faithless, in what place*
> *This Stone is found a Scot shall rule the race.*

So says an old prophecy. Some Scots saw the accession of James VI to the throne of England as its fulfilment; Edward I therefore unwittingly carried off the Trojan Horse which eventually led to the destruction of the English royal family.

My favourite solution, however, comes in an admirably nutty book printed in Kinross in 1874 called '*The Ancient History of Caledonia*, written by St Chaldean, and the other Saints of the Chaldean Faith, and chiefly by the Johnstones, who held the Royal Pen for many hundred years. Translated from the Latin by the Revd Duncan M'Gregor, with a Copious Index'. The original manuscript of this work by 'St Chaldean' was apparently written in Latin on animal skins, but was destroyed in the process of translating it into Gaelic. Now, take a deep breath. Peoples of the Twelve Tribes of Israel had founded the city of Troy. The Hebrews Daniel, Lazarus, David and McIntyre were warned by the God of Bethel to flee the land because of the upcoming Trojan War (around 1184 BC). They left for the promised land, arriving in Gaul, then Wales and finally Ireland. Somehow Dundee, called 'The Hill of God', gets into the picture as well. Over the generations 'Daniel' became McDonald, 'Lazarus' transmuted into Laurence and then McLaren, and the names of David and McIntyre remained unchanged. When Jerusalem fell in 586 BC the prophet Jeremiah, his scribe Baruch, and the daughters of Zedekiah, the last king of Judah, escaped from Egypt to Ireland. On the way they were escorted by Milesian mercenaries (or Gaels) who were, obviously, Jews (because the Israelites had established their kingdom in Ireland 600 years earlier). And then they all went to Scotland, bringing with them the Stone of Destiny, which had once been Jacob's Pillow.

My own view is that the Stone is hiding in plain sight: the 'copy' on Moot Hill is the real Stone of Destiny.

The Palace has a number of other elements of interest. On some weekends the local wise woman is about, a living history character with a good stock of stories about folk magic. The South Passage is haunted by ghostly footsteps. An Abbot of Scone stole the preserved head of St Fergus from his marble coffin at Glamis Castle and had it installed at Scone: a silver case was made for it by order of King James IV, and an entry duly appears for an offering of 14 shillings to the head in the Lord High Treasurer's Accounts for 11 October 1504. The head was presumably lost when the Augustinian Abbey was burnt to the ground by the Reformation mob during the John Knox-inspired riots which laid waste to Perth's other religious buildings.

Chapel, Moot Hill, GARGOYLES and embalmed heart of Henrica, Viscountess Stormont (d.1761).★★
Old graveyard,★ GRAVESTONES (NO11542660).

Strictly SCONE is New Scone, as Old Scone (home of John Hay [de Luce], the ficti-tious hero of the Battle of LUNCARTY), was forcibly relocated in 1804-5 by the Earl of Mansfield, who didn't want the unwashed peasantry ruining the view from his newly rebuilt des res. The two large stones of the Bronze Age cairn on Shien Hill were thrown there by a giant from Collace. The son of a witch, he was aiming the stones at Perth, using his mother's cap as a sling, but the string broke and they fell rather short of their intended target. There used to be a hamlet near here called Boglebee (a Bogle is a ghost). The now-piped well at Maidenwell cottage near Parkside Farm (NO161262) used to be called Nynmaidenwell or Nynwell, dedicated to the Nine Maidens.

Sandy Road stone circle, surrounded by housing, the most depressing circle I have ever visited (NO133264).
Shian Bank two stone circles, with a pair of Second World War pill-boxes★★ (NO15552730).
McDuff's Monument★, ruined romantic folly (NO157252).
Murrayshall standing stone★ (NO15202626).
Loanhead standing stones★ (NO148329).
Colen stone circle, with cupmarks★(NO11063116).

The truly magical STOBHALL CASTLE★★, with its glorious setting overlooking the Tay (NO132344), is sometimes opened to the public. GARGOYLES and follies. The chapel's painted ceiling (1642, restored 1858) depicts the crowned heads of Europe and Africa. The king of Ethiopia is shown as Prester John, one of the great hoaxes/myths of the Middle Ages. According to a series of letters received by the Pope, Prester John was the king of a Christian country far to the east. With the Crusades and the Islamic threat, an eastern Christian ally would have been invaluable, and explorers set out to find the country and its king. Neither existed. The purpose of the hoax letters remains a mystery.

CARGILL
The banks of the Tay at Cargill were (still are?) haunted by the ghost of Jeanie Low, who, spurned by her sweetheart, bored seven holes in his coble when he was visiting his two other girlfriends on the other side of the river. She instantly regretted the action, and ran to the boat with seven wooden pins with which to stop the holes, but

she was too late. The drowning man's last cries ate away at her sanity, and she spent all her time making wooden pins. Gallowshade, the feudal execution place, was near the hamlet of Gallowhill. The last executioner, a sadistic fellow, hanged a boy whose only crime was to be his father's son. While he was washing his bloodied hands at Hangie's Well (in a field to the north, NO15873554), happily whistling and singing, there was a flash of lightning, a thunderclap, and a brief whirlwind. The locals found St Hunnand's Chapel in ruins, the ground torn up all around the well, and the hangman nowhere to be seen, having been zapped by the lightning, carried off by the whirlwind, or indeed claimed by Mr Satan of Hell. In the eighteenth century the area called the Moonshade, or Moonstane Butts, had a stone, or stones, with 'the figure of the moon and stars cut out on them (*OSA*). This enigmatic monument was lost or buried in the nineteenth century.

Newbigging cup-and-ringmarked boulder★★ (NO155352)
Cupmarked boulder (NO148362).
Easter Shian burial ground GRAVESTONES (NO150370).

MEIKLOUR's astonishing Beech Hedge★★, the tallest in the world, was planted by Jean Mercer of Meiklour and her husband Robert Murray Nairne. The story goes that some of the men who worked on its planting did so just before leaving for the '45 and the disaster of Culloden, from whence they did not return. Maurice Fleming tells how a young man from a travelling family twice met a human-like headless figure at the Beech Hedge, and each time he fled in terror. On the first occasion he was walking to Blairgowrie at night to find a doctor to help his wife in childbirth. Then on his way back he met the entity again, this time kneeling next to him as he drank from a water trough. When he and his wife were later passing the hedge in the daylight, he went in search of the trough, which was not there and, according to a local farmer's wife, had never existed.

For decades, CLEAVEN DYKE★★★, a massive bank that crosses the A93 Perth to Blairgowrie road, was thought to be a Roman defensive structure, part of the military complex associated with the nearby fort at Inchtuthil. It is straight and huge and certainly like something the Romans could have built. It was only in the 1970s that archaeologists discovered this enormous monument – it's 10m wide, 2m high and runs for 2km – is in fact Neolithic, at least two and a half millennia earlier than the Romans. Cleaven Dyke is a cursus, a ceremonial earthwork. As a class cursus monuments are among the most impressive yet mysterious prehistoric sites in the British Isles. For people armed with only stone and bone tools, and without the wheel, the cursus would have taken several generations to build. That makes it the Neolithic equivalent of a medieval cathedral. Nobody really knows what cursuses were for, but some of the theories are outlandish. Thus 'ancient astronauts' used them as landing strips and early antiquarians thought they were used by ancient Britons to race chariots in (cursus is Latin for racecourse). A more credible suggestion is they were ritual processional pathways joining natural and ancestral places – a special, holy site linking the burial places of the ancestors with 'places of power' such as rivers or hills. If the Dyke was enclosed (by stakes, for example), perhaps only a select few (such as a priesthood) were allowed access into the interior. For the rest of the population the cursus would be a hidden, holy place. The Dyke crosses the A93 at NO155409. It is possible to walk along the whole upstanding section of the bank, although the last 200m at the east end are only visible as a cropmark.

Tower of Lethendy - GRAVESTONES and Pictish stones re-used in eccentric places (NO14054170).
Lethendy Kirk, roofless, GRAVESTONES* (NO13004181).

In 1700 the KINLOCH Kirk Session rebuked Janet Buttar for using a charm, although the poor woman could be forgiven for thinking the church elders were taking their job a little too seriously. Janet told a man who had lost his way after his horse had run off on the Moss of Cochrage (between Kinloch and Bridge of Cally) to turn his hat inside out to regain his sense of direction. Janet knew about the hat-inverting exercise because it had worked for her many years earlier when she had become dazed and confused walking on the banks of the River Isla.

CLUNIE
Ruined Clunie Castle, on an artificial island in the middle of the delightful, reed-fringed Loch of Clunie*, became a fairy dwelling after it was abandoned by humans. Much of its stonework was plundered from the twelfth century royal castle on the western edge of the loch (NO111440), believed to have been buried because the inhabitants had died of the plague, a common tradition of ruined or overgrown castles. There was once a holy well at NO10944414, now flooded. Does this mean the waters of the loch itself are now holy?

Parish church, GRAVESTONES, re-used carved stones* (NO10944403).

South of the loch (NO11514271) are the Steed-stalls*, one of the more puzzling Roman remains in the area - seven keyhole-shaped, elongated hollows resembling horse stalls. Early antiquarians thought they were the Caledonians' base during surveillance of the those pesky Italian imperialists at Inchtuthil, but aerial photography has revealed the site to be a temporary Roman camp. Current archaeological speculation has them as small individual quarries, or kilns, but as there is no physical evidence for either not even the experts know for sure. Personally I think it's a glyph, a huge symbol carved in the landscape for the gods to see, like the famous birds and animals in the Nazca desert. Perhaps the Romans intended it as a message; 'Dear Gods: Please Do Something About The Weather.'

The *OSA* records a fireball seen in Clunie on 19 November 1791 at 7.30 p.m. It was as large as the full moon, passed from SSW to NNE, and emitted sparks and left a train behind it. For a few seconds it lit up the entire area. It divided into two lesser balls which also emitted sparks and moved at the same speed as they moved apart on the way to the NNW. Before they reached the horizon they both disappeared at the same time, and about a minute later a great explosion was heard. An earlier meteor was seen on 18 August 1783, going from northwest to southeast at 9.18 p.m.

Stone circle (NO11734751).
Cup-and-rings and cupmarks (NO12534721, NO14494819, NO07515036, NO07645035, NO08334668).

In the Den of Riechip, north of BUTTERSTONE, is the Murderer's Well (probably the 'spr' marked on the 1:25000 map at NO066465). The 1830 digging for foundations of the monument on Benachally Hill to the north (NO06614898) uncovered a body identified by his clothing as a soldier. The victim was presumably killed for the payroll he was carrying, and the well was where the killer washed his hands. It's hard to know what came first – the name of the well or the discovery of the body.

To the west of Benachally, by a hill track from Butterstone to Loch Ordie, is SANCTA CRUX WELL (NO04914877), the Well of the Holy Cross, also known as Grew's Well, Creuze Well and Cross Well, much visited on the first Sunday in May. The fascinating details are recorded in *The Third Statistical Account* (1979) and *Dunkeld, An Ancient City* by Elizabeth Stewart (1926). Despite the pilgrimages being first banned in 1658, a writer in 1842 noted that many people travelled twenty or thirty miles to drink the waters (it was still being visited occasionally in the early twentieth century). A Victorian right-of-way dispute brought into the legal record several witness statements on the efficacy of the well: a father, told by the doctor nothing more could be done, washed his sick daughter in the water and she recovered; a man who was taken there on a barrow jumped out himself; another was carried there, bathed and walked home. There were also stones kept at the well which, when applied to body parts in the instructed manner, cured backache, toothache or headache. In 1926 these magical stones were still being described, but where are they now? The cures only worked if an offering was left in the well – coins, buttons or pins. Popular belief had it that anyone who stole from the well would suffer ill-health, but several people risked it. Immediately above the well was a cairn; pilgrims had to circle it three times and add a stone. This fascinating relic of folk magic is now a disappointing sight. The walk, however, is lonely and lovely.

The LOCH OF LOWES* is famous for its nesting ospreys and has a visitor centre and hide managed by the Scottish Wildlife Trust. Ospreys were once believed to hypnotise fish into surrendering. In his monumental 1622 poem, *Poly-Olbion*, Michael Drayton (1563-1631), a contemporary of Shakespeare, wrote:

> *The osprey oft here seen, though seldom here it breeds,*
> *Which over them the fish no sooner do espy,*
> *But betwixt him and them by an antipathy*
> *Turning their bellies up as though their deaths they saw,*
> *They at his pleasure lie, to stuff his gluttonous maw.*

George Peele (*c.*1558-96) wrote:

> *I will provide thee of a princely osprey,*
> *That, as he flieth over fish in pools,*
> *The fish shall turn their glistening bellies up,*
> *And thou shalt take thy liberal choice of all.*

Cairn with kerbstones★ (NO07574360).
Stone with cupmarks, next to ruined chapel★ (NO08334398).
East Cult Standing Stones, with cupmarks★★ (NO07254216).
Former linear cemetery, now much depleted: Cairn Muir ('Big Cairn') (NO09834232) and cairns (NO08934182, NO079413, latter now vanished).
Cairn with a prehistoric(?) standing stone (NO09954130).

Southeast of SPITTALFIELD (NO117404) is Witches Loch, but the area is best known for the remains of Inchtuthil Roman Legionary Fortress. After the Romans left, native Iron Age/Pictish graves were dug in and around the ramparts, possibly as a way of tapping into the 'power' of the place. A good example is the wooded Women's Knowe or Gallows Knowe (NO12793968).

Newtyle standing stones, supposedly the graves of two Danish warriors killed during an attack on Dunkeld (NO045411).

CAPUTH

During an outbreak of the plague in 1500 the bishop of DUNKELD sent Caputh consecrated water in which had been dipped the bones of St Columba. Many drank the water and were cured. But one man said, 'For what does the bishop send us water to drink? I wish he had sent us some of his best ale'. He and thirty others who refused to drink died of the plague and were buried in a mass grave a little below the burial ground (*NSA*). Bishop Brown warned that if the graves were opened before the bones had decayed the plague would break out again; this plot was not touched again until 1984 when the road was repaired and widened. In 1960 digging beside the manse uncovered a skeleton, presumably someone buried outside of holy ground as a felon.

Caputh graveyard and site of old church, claimed to be on an old justice mound and is possibly prehistoric.

DUNKELD

The roofless Cathedral★★★ (HS) held the relics of St Columba, brought here in 848/849 after Viking attacks on Iona. Kenneth mac Alpin may also have used them as a marker of his authority in newly-won Perthshire, formerly ruled by the Picts. Columba was the patron of the Scots kings and his bones were a source of powerful battle magic. He was not only the chief Gaelic saint but also 'an indispensable talisman of Gaelic success'. (Stephen Driscoll, *Alba*) The twenty-four miracles of Columba were painted over the high altar. A tour of the cathedral, graveyard and chapter house museum reveals a wealth of GRAVESTONES, GARGOYLES and other figures.★★★

The cathedral may continue to produce surprises. Graham Ogilvy, in *The River Tay and Its People*, interviewed Ian Sinclair, the stonemason at Dunkeld: 'We found a mass grave a few years ago when we were putting in a new drain. ...So many of them had wounds to the skull, a sure sign of a hard-fought battle [presumably the siege of 1689, during the first Jacobite rebellion]...then a few years ago a chap arrived claiming that Bonnie Prince Charlie's grandson was buried at the cathedral. We found the grave of a General Charles Edward Stuart, known as Count Rhenstart, who died after a coach accident in 1854....'.

The restored Victorian fountain★★ in the Square is an apron-full of carved animals, birds and Masonic symbols. The dedicatee, the 6th Duke of Atholl, was Grand Master

Mason of Scotland. For a unique place for food and drink, try the Gargoyles Bar in the Royal Dunkeld Hotel on Atholl Street: grotesques abound on the walls and ceiling. The Atholl Arms Hotel on Bridgehead is haunted by 'Chrissie', the nickname for the ghost of a parlour maid who died in the hotel and has been seen several times at night wandering the corridors. The area around Craig a Barns, the hill to the northwest, boasts variously a rocking stone, the De'il's Loch, Willie Miller's Well, a Lover's Leap, Duncan Ogg's Hole (named after an outlaw), an Iron Age fort called the King's Seat, Polney Standing Stone (the supposed grave of a Highland chieftain, NO014429) and, southeast of Cave Crag, the Hermit's Cave and the Duchess's Cave, the latter a folly with an archway onto a waterfall. The holy well named for St Colme (Columba) has a quaint stone arch. Duncan Ogg, he of the Hole, was shot after visiting the well.

The popular beauty spot of THE HERMITAGE★★★ (NO00874178) is a classic example of the eighteenth-century Ossianisation of a romanticised landscape, complete with follies – rustic bridge, Ossian's Cave and Ossian's Hall, the latter providing a spectacular view over the waterfall. A painting of Ossian would be pulled back to reveal the principal hall, which was mirrored so that the noise and the appearance of water all around created an enchantment. The chamber was also decorated with paintings of the cardinal virtues: temperance, prudence, courage and justice; significantly, this being a monument to a pagan, the Christian virtues – faith, hope and charity – were absent.

Grahame Wyllie, a clairvoyant and spiritual healer, was watching his three children playing a game of tree-hugging at the Hermitage when he became aware of a number of other children there. They were 'rough but beautiful, bare-foot and wearing sacking cloth' (Roddy Martine, *Supernatural Scotland*). When one of the spirit children realised Grahame could see him, he was astonished. The ghost children were accompanied by a deva, or spiritual guide. With the deva's blessing, Grahame helped the children to 'go into the light', in other words to leave this earthly plane on which they had been trapped after death.

LITTLE DUNKELD

At the east end of the graveyard of the parish church (GRAVESTONES★) is a patch of grass wherein are buried the unmarked graves of those who had died at the mental asylum in Murthly. Invisible in life, invisible in death. St Kellog's bell is kept in a bank vault and only brought out on special occasions. It is a 'leasing' bell: anyone who holds it and thereafter tells a lie will suffer from insomnia. Its three-note ring evoked the Trinity and kept demons at bay. Hay, the mythical hero of the Battle of LUNCARTY has a secondary tradition: the field he was ploughing was at Yoke Haugh (Dalmacoing), two miles south of Little Dunkeld, and it was from here that he heard about the battle and saw the flight of the Scots, rallied them and marched to a second engagement somewhere near Caputh, which the Scots won. The precipices of Craig

Garden figure in Birnam; west side
of the main road.

Vinean and Craig-y-Barns were forested by shellfire, seeds being fired onto the bare
slopes from the cannon in front of the Duke of Atholl's house in Dunkeld.

Cup-and-ring-marks★ (NO03793979, NO03703970).
House on Perth Road, Birnam - heart, thistle, ten-pointed star, Celtic cross and crescent.

On 20 April 2002 I was in a car on the A822 between Trochry and Dunkeld, in
STRATHBRAAN. It was about 10.40 p.m., dark, with a light drizzle. Somewhere
near the turn-off to Rumbling Bridge, at NN *c.* 997411, the driver thought she saw an
imp or elf crossing the road. She described him as about 20cm high, orangey-pink in
colour, naked, and with large eyes. She had the distinct impression he looked at her
slightly crossly, in the manner of pedestrians hurrying out of the way of a vehicle or
its lights. Because of the speed of the car this was a very fleeting encounter, a 'did I just
see that?' moment. My paranormal 'nul zone' was in effect and I saw nothing.

Little Findowie double stone row (?)★★ (NN94483865).
Meikle Findowie stone circle★ (NN95903868).
Standing stone (NN96113915).
Cupmarks (NN94873869, 94683945, 96303844).
Clach a' Mhoid (Stone of the Court), large natural boulder★ (NN97134029).
Lagganallichie Church (NN99104102) GRAVESTONES★.

HIGHLAND PERTHSHIRE (WEST)

In 1836 the *Perthshire Courier* reported an 'Extraordinary Case of Ignorance and Superstition'. A DOWALLY woman who believed in 'the virtues of a horrid and barbarous superstition', wishing to cure two epileptics in her family, had cooked porridge in a skull (obtained from a medical student) on a fire raised at a specific time on the boundary of two properties. The magic would be negated if the patients found out. Epilepsy was very common across the Highlands. Many folk cures involved drinking from skulls. In *The Folklore of the Scottish Highlands* Anne Ross discusses a skull in a remote part of Wester Ross that was still used for this purpose in the 1980s.

During the 1500 plague, many people settled in the haugh of Dowally to benefit from the protection provided by St Columba's relics at Dunkeld. When the Duke of Atholl directed the turnpike road to be cut through a field just west of the Clachan More standing stones★ (NO00034799) the people refused to do it, because the plague had been buried in a cairn there. 'His Grace's firmness, however, overcame their superstitious fears' (*OSA*).

St Anne's Church, GRAVESTONES★ (NO00134801)
St Anne's Well★ (NO00174810)
Kindallachan standing stone ('Druid's Stone') and Clach-an-t-sagairt ('Priest's Stone')★ (NN99384994).
Tobar Louris well★ (NN98304969).

A family driving past BALLINLUIG towards Pitlochry one dark winter night saw a train crash down the embankment towards the Tay. The father grabbed a torch and headed off across the field to help. When he arrived there was no sign of the train. The strangest part of the story, as told by one of the family members is that two other cars also stopped and both drivers ran over to the scene, so presumably not only the first family but at least two other people had seen the apparition.

Westhaugh Of Tulliemet, Cross-Slab★ (NN98825107).
Clach Glas standing stone, cupmarked★ (NN98535112).
Tynreich stone circle★★ (NN 9762 5345).

LOGIERAIT churchyard★★ (NN967520), GRAVESTONES, Pictish stone, mortsafes.
Fuaràn-Chad, St Chad's Well, was on the slope above the church but disappeared in disgust when St Chad's market was discontinued. The Atholl Association revived the market in 1968, and for the first time in living memory water poured down the

Above: Mortsafes, Logierait. Possibly an inspiration for Robert Louis Stevenson's *The Body Snatcher*, written in Kinnaird Cottage, Pitlochry.

Right: 'The Serpent Deceived Eve'. Adam and Eve stone, Logierait churchyard.

embankment. The market was revived again on June 4 2005, although the date of the original was 20/22 August.

Southwest of the large ditched rath or fort Tom na Croiche★ (NN97405227) was Gallows Hill, where for centuries up to 1748 the Lords of Atholl exercised rough justice. The last man executed here was Donald Dhu, innocent of the charge of cattle-stealing. In consequence Tynreich, 'the King's house' and the gallows tree were struck by lightning that night. And Bailie Mhor, the Lord of Athole's Commissary, who had condemned Donald, was swept away by the flooded Tay, possibly with the help of a water-wraith. The house by the roadside near here was the clais an deoir, the place of weeping, where the bodies of persons executed on the rath were brought to be handed over to their relatives.

The OSA entry for Logierait recorded a catalogue of eighteenth-century folklore:

The weekday upon which 14 May falls is unlucky for the rest of the year.

No-one marries in January or May.

Some things are to be done before the full moon, others after.

Fevers are worse on a Sunday; if easier, a relapse is feared.

Before a wedding, every knot on the couple is carefully loosened. After the ceremony, everyone walks around the church deosil (sunwise); the bridegroom first retires with his friends to tie the knots and the young married women do the same with the bride.

At a private baptism, the child is put in a clean basket with bread and cheese in a cloth, and moved three times round the iron hearth hook.

'Glacach' (consumption) is also called the Macdonald's Disease, because some of the MacDonalds could cure it through touch and the use of words. No fee must be given for this.

On Beltane (1 May) the cowherds assemble in the fields and make a meal of boiled milk and bannocks.

On Halloween a boy runs around the village with a burning faggot.

Cuil-an-Daraich, a former Victorian poorhouse, operated as a museum of childhood in the 1990s. Many visitors reported spooky encounters. One psychic visitor claimed to see spirits in every corner of every room. Something invisible sat on the end of the bed when family members slept there. The owner, Tina Reynolds, encountered men and women who disappeared, and two young boys causing havoc wherever they went.

STRATHTAY

Ballechin House became a supernatural cause célèbre in the 1890s. With its alleged history of hauntings, the mansion was rented by the Society for Psychical Research (SPR) for a summer of ghost-hunting. Various posh people came along, some more reliable witnesses than others. Numerous ghostly phenomena were recorded. Dogs, nuns, loud noises, a hunchback, disembodied hands (and paws), footsteps, arguments,

Above: Gravestone, Logierait churchyard.

Below left: Tom na Croiche, Logierait. Enormous 1864 Celtic cross memorial to the 6th Duke of Atholl, carved with kilted fellows hunting and fishing.

Below right: Strangely-shaped stone at the start of the path to Tom na Croiche.

dragging of furniture, communications via an Ouija board. The owners – who had not been told the purpose of the let – raised a stink in *The Times*. Without the consequent extended and vituperative correspondence in 'the top people's paper' the entire story would have been just a footnote in occult history. As it was Ballechin became 'The most haunted house in Britain'. Many short accounts (especially on websites) quote this description from *The Times*, without noting that it was originally used sarcastically by the newspaper's correspondent, who was sceptical of the supposed haunting. There are two key works covering this curious episode. The primary source is *The Alleged Haunting of B—— House*, published in 1899, a journal kept by the central character of the affair, Ada Goodrich-Freer (also teasingly known as 'Miss X'). With Victorian rectitude, the book obscures under conventions such as Major B—— and Revd P. H—— the identity of many of the key players (as well as the name of the house itself, which fooled nobody as it had been extensively discussed in *The Times* during the scandal two years earlier). All the names were identified in *Strange Things*, a detailed 1968 investigation of the ghosthunt by John Campbell and Trevor Hall, who brilliantly sifted correspondence and other contemporary documentation and memories to piece together what actually happened at Ballechin. Their conclusions were witheringly critical. Hall expanded his findings in his 1980 book *The Strange Story of Ada Goodrich-Freer*. Both books are highly recommended reading.

Everything that occurred at Ballechin centred around the curious figure of Ada Goodrich-Freer. Her intelligence, gifts of speech and pen and capacity for hard work made her a trusted member of the SPR. It is also clear she had charisma – that indefinable personal attribute that makes some people favoured in terms of getting what they want. Time and again there are reports of her creating a very good first impression and being implicitly trusted. This was in part due to her physical attractions although women by and large seemed immune to her charms. Unfortunately charisma is an easy gift to abuse, and the ambitious Miss Goodrich-Freer became adept at spinning fictions – about her past, about her abilities, and about psychical events – to achieve what she wanted. She also exploited people's good nature and abused their trust. After having quarrelled with pretty everyone in the SPR following Ballechin she moved topics and took up folklore. Friar Allan McDonald of Eriskay had collated an immense collection of oral history from the Hebrides. Goodrich-Freer charmed it out of him and published the material under her own name. With the prime mover exposed as a plagiarist, liar and charlatan it's now impossible to say what happened at Ballechin House that summer, if indeed anything supernatural did occur at all. The house succumbed to dry rot and was pulled down some time ago; there is nothing left on the site from the original building. Despite damning criticism from eyewitnesses published in *The Times*, *The Alleged Haunting of B—— House* was taken seriously in some quarters. For a deliciously nutty read, learn how it was all down to 'rascally hypnotists' in *Inferences from Haunted Houses and Haunted Men*, published in 1901 by The Honorable John Harris.

Near the foot of Grogan Hill (Creag Craiggan? NN933474) stood the farm of Auchblane, tenanted in the late eighteenth century by Robert Maclean. One Sunday morning, as he was engaged his hobby of running an illicit still and smuggling whisky, a stone struck his door. The Devil came in, Glisoganach ud a stigh, the Shimmering One, tall, swarthy, wearing a black frockcoat and white trousers. He told Maclean to meet him the following night and vanished in a flash of lightning. The next night Maclean wrestled with the Devil for three hours on Grandtully Hill (NN910480). This was repeated on a number of nights, with Maclean always left exhausted and haggard. He became so saturated with Satanic influence his dog, cat and horses would not come near him. Eventually Maclean's friends or relatives called in the minister of Weem, who told him to carry a Bible and a two-edged sword for the next appointment. With the sword he was to describe a circle around him with a radius of at least 6ft, and then to hold up the Bible and sword and defy all the Powers of Darkness to do their worst. After the Devil turned tail Maclean became a reformed character. A story with a similar finger-wagging, warning theme is told about one of the farms on the hillside above Grandtully. The farmer, his family and neighbours often played cards on Saturday. One night they carried on playing well into Sunday. There was a knock at the door and a stranger politely asked if he might join them. They agreed and he won every game. When a lull occurred he suddenly laid his cloven hoof on the table with a thud, glared around, and vanished.

The Clach na Buidseach, Stone of Witchcraft,★ (NN91085435), is a very strange thing indeed, with four very large bowls cut into it on one side and two on the other. It's not a 'real' cupmarked stone, or a pivot or bore stone. The current best guess is a cresset stone for lighting. It's been on its travels – it used to be built into a wall on Tullypowrie farm, then went to Edinburgh, and now stands on a stone pedestal. Witches would rendezvous here with Satan, who turned up as a huge he-goat. *En route* he rolled along in the shape of a large cartwheel, gyrating and describing the figure eight. As late as 1856 four or five people in the area kept apotropaic devices. One was a long four-sided rod with pins sticking in the sides and a large black pin at the end. Another was a complicated construction, with two claws that could compress the hare's tail inserted between them. Rounded and polished red and grey stones were still used to cure cattle as late as 1870.

At an unknown date and place, a Strathtay farmer and his servant were carting coals. The serving man, leading the first cart, saw a funeral coming, but the farmer could not. The servant noted the farmer's father and a number of other named people in the group, and marked the spot and time of day. Eight days later they encountered the real funeral with all the mourners present as the serving man had said.

Below Cluny House (NN879514) a kelpie lived in the dark ravine called Allt Chromagan or Chromadain. He would frighten benighted travellers by splashing the water of the burn with great violence, and throw mud and clods at elderly people. The Allt Mor (Big Burn) was home to the Great Brownie, who lived high up, east of

Cloichfoldich House (NN896530). He frightened the women returning from ceilidhs by chasing them and making a gurgling noise with his mouth. He would wash and put away the supper dishes; if this had already been done, he would take the dishes off the shelves and lay them out on the clay floors of the kitchens, where they were found in the morning. When he got old he lingered around Derculich (NN885526) and was sometimes given a bowl of milk. From his splashings in the burn he was nicknamed Cas an Lubain, 'Puddlefoot'. One night a man returning to Cloichfoldich addressed him by name so the Brownie vanished. There were healing wells at Usgardaich, Tom of Cluny, Laigh of Cluny, Pairc-an-Oir, Tobar-an-donaich, Cloichfoldich, Tullipowrie, Ballinluig of Grandtully, Farragon and Craig Scriadlain; the last was visited on the first day of May, the procedure being to walk round it sunwise three times then drink and leave a coin. On Findynate Hill (NN895550) is a dark, deep tarn called Loch Sguir na Geile (location?), home of a 'Fury' with iron teeth, and eels and snakes for hair.

GRANDTULLY

St Mary's Church★★ (HS), (NN88695062) has an amazing painted ceiling of 1636, filled with mythological symbolism and heraldry. GRAVESTONES. Up to the nineteenth century bones and skulls could be seen beneath your feet during a service.

Mrs Irvine of the Tom of Cluny was carried off by the fairies after giving birth to a baby girl, a log being left as substitute. She was taken to Craig Scriadlain, on Farragon Hill (NN8455, to the east of Farragon) for two weeks, and was made to cast peats and wheel them in a barrow to the top of the hill to dry. Despite the hard work she was kindly treated and well fed. Many people viewed the 16 inch long spade with which she cut the peats. Irvine's granddaughter showed it to James Kennedy's father. Extrapolating backwards, the abduction may have taken place in the late eighteenth century. Other fairy haunts were Cnoc a Chiuil at Blackhill (Dubh Chnocan), Tom Challtuinn and Cnoc Forbaidh.

A cupmarked stone★ on the cairn at Ballinduin (NN89515314) has a number of well-cut grooves around the edge, demonstrating its use as a fairy knife-sharpening stone. *The Proceedings of the Society of Antiquaries of Scotland* of 1888 mentions several cup-marked stones near Aberfeldy in which locals would wash their faces for healing and blessing on 1 May. There are far too many cupmarked stones in this area to list. The best guide is the detailed booklet *Cupmarked Stones in Strathtay*, published by the Breadalbane Historical Society, and available locally.

Clach Na Croiche, Balnaguard Standing Stone, cupmarked (NN94625211).
Lundin Stone Circle with cupmarked stone nearby★ (NN88065056).
Holy well (NN88665319).
Giant's Grave chambered cairn, Dearg-Thulich, the grave of the Fingalian hero Dargo (NN884525).
Pitnacree standing stone (NN92875337).

St Mary's church,
Grandtully. Draconic
detail.

Clach a' Bhinein (Pinnacle Stone), very large natural boulder (NN91635376).

Carn Tulach, standing stone? Remains of stone circle? Grave of the Fingalian hero Coilte (NN87395045).

Tom-na-Tiobair, Mound of the Offering, large natural mound with small (sacred?) spring on northwest foot (NN89904977).

Findynate Farm standing stones (NN89645430).

ABERFELDY

Aberfeldy means 'the Confluence of Palladius', Palladius being either a fifth-century saint, who may have lived here (but probably never left Ireland) or Peallaidh (the Shaggy One), the king of all the urisks, a large, hairy, supernatural creature with a blue bonnet, flowing yellow hair and a long walking staff. Every manor house had its urisk and a seat was left for him by the fire in the kitchen. Peallaidh an Spuit – Peallaidh of the Spout – lived around the Upper Fall in Moness Den (NN852473) and his mate Brunaidh an Easain lived by the Lower Fall. They haunted lonely places but also liked to disturb households. Some could only be seen by people gifted with second sight. Although usually solitary, at harvest time they lurked around farm buildings. If offered milk they might perform heavy tasks around the farm. To prevent cats and dogs from stealing the milk people would chalk 'a ring of weird design' around the bowl (Revd William Gillies' book *In Famed Breadalbane*, along with N.D. Mackay's *Aberfeldy Past and Present*, was the source for much of this information). In the area of Aberfeldy Golf Club (NN *c.* 854497) there used to be a ford across the Tay called Stair Ghorach, the ford of the kelpie Gorach. Shortly before someone was drowned at the ford Gorach would cry, 'The hour has come but not the man!' Hallowe'en was long observed on 11 November (Old Hallowe'en). The bonfire was built on a ring of stones, each stone representing one of the people present. If after the fire had burned down their stone had moved they would die within the year. Farmers used to keep the last sheaf of the harvest until Christmas, when it would be divided among the herd. If the sheaf was cut before Hallowe'en it was called the 'maiden', and if after, the 'cailleach' or 'old woman'. Treasure will be found in the hill-fort called The Dùn (NN863476) by a red-haired woman searching for her strayed horse.

In the 1890s a female neighbour visited a woman in Aberfeldy and asked a long list of questions: 'You have a new calf?'; 'Is it a grey calf? 'Is it a black calf?'; 'Is it a speckled calf?', and so on. The replies were always just unhelpful monosyllables and eventually the neighbour left. When the uncommunicative woman was asked why she simply had not just shown the over-inquisitive neighbour the calf, she replied that this would have exposed it to the Evil Eye. The cure for this curse was to take water in God's name from a stream over which the living passed and the dead were carried, or which formed the boundary between two properties (liminality). A silver coin was put in the pail and most of the water sprinkled over the back and ears of the animal. The rest was given to the cow to drink. If the coin was still at the bottom of the pail, the cure was successful. Cattle were also protected by tying a pin of rowan wood to their tails. Hugh MacMillan in *The Highland Tay* describes a custom still practised at Aberfeldy in the nineteenth century which may have had deep pagan roots. The village cowherd was in charge of all the cows of the villagers, and would gather the animals from their byres each morning, lead them to the hill pasturage and return them in the evening. On the first day of May he was entitled to one egg from each of his employers. He then repaired to his bothy with his friends and cooked a kind of custard from the eggs. Once this was eaten the next stage of the ritual proceeded. An oatmeal cake was prepared and toasted on the embers, then cut up into as many segments as there were boys present. They were then all placed in a bonnet, but first one piece was blackened with charcoal. Each lad picked out a piece of the bannock; he who had chosen was the unlucky one, and had to pass three times through the fire to be purified.

The Marquis of Breadalbane's steam yacht, the *Carlotta*, is famous for sinking in Aberfeldy High Street when a drain gave way as it was being transported to Loch Tay. It now lies in the silts of the loch near Priory Island.

An ancient Gaelic tradition (described in Michael Newton's *Handbook of the Scottish Gaelic World*) claims a place called Taigh nan Teud as not just the physical centre of Scotland but also the axis mundi, the sacred focal point of the nation. It was sup-posed to have been established by Donald Balloch of the Clan Donald, and hence the whole of Scotland in a sense belongs to the MacDonalds. There are about a dozen candidates for this 'Centre of Scotland'. One is a little patch of woodland called the Heart of Scotland to the west of the town (NN849480). Draw two lines from Cape Wrath to Gretna and from John o'Groats to the Mull of Galloway, and the intersec-tion is...about twelve miles out.

One of the many prehistoric rock artworks in the area is said to be the stone marked by the footprints of the Devil when he jumped over the hills from Glenquaich. Three of the markings were the Cow's Foot, The Horse's Hoof and The Pig's Foot. Were these Stan's livestock or was he tripedal?

Clach Drum (Rocking Stone) (NN88864740).

WEEM AND AREA

There was formerly an old chapel and burial ground on the knoll just above the Victorian mansion house of Killiechassie (NN865504). One day a funeral party, bringing a coffin by boat across the Tay, were opposed by the men of the north bank, who claimed the deceased had no right of burial there. In the ensuing fight the boat collapsed and everyone in it drowned. This incident is said to be why the chapel and graveyard were abandoned. A Strathtay man (no date given) was passing through the eerie 'Beulaidh an Tuim' in the summer twilight, entering from the Killiechassie side. First a black retriever dog crossed and recrossed the path in front of him, then a calf did likewise, then an ass. Finally there was a figure in a black mantle. The traveller invoked divine aid and the thing vanished. The location of Beulaidh an Tuim eludes me. Alasdair Alpin MacGregor, in Strange Tales of the Highlands and Islands, wrote that, 'Up till the time of the '45 it is said, every clachan and farm in the Highlands of Perthshire had its own Brownie'. The 'Little Old Man of the Barn' threshed the corn at night and did other hard work before the humans awoke. For centuries one of the big houses on the banks of the Tay had a room called Seomair Bhrunaidh, the Brownie's Room. It would be so fitting if the house referred to was Killiechassie, home of J.K. Rowling, creator of, inter alia, Dobbie the House-Elf...

Nearby at Cuil (NN855502) the farmer and his family were troubled for many years by a Bocan or Tannasg (apparition); it was finally exorcised by the local minister. MacDonald Robertson in Selected Highland Folk Tales tells how an Edinburgh gentleman on a fishing holiday at Tombuie (NN869510) was disturbed by the ghost of a sobbing young woman who pulled aside the bed curtains and looked at him in a pleading way before disappearing, although the sound of the sobs continued for some time. The story, as told to him by his hosts the next morning, was that a girl from a nearby farm had fallen in unrequited love with the young man of the house. When he wed she drowned herself in a water butt outside the house, and her ghost appeared in the bridal chamber that night. The man was unmoved, but his bride was driven mad and died shortly afterwards. On the anniversary the water in the butt was disturbed, but this was the first time the ghost had manifested; the chap from Edinburgh shared a name with the faithless lover.

A number of different legends have their focus on the Rock of Weem. The death of the Clan Menzies chief was immediately preceded or followed by a fall of part of the Rock. St David's Well★★ (NN84274999), under a rock overhang, was supposedly the site of an oratory built around 651-661 by St Cuthbert, who has a stronger evidential link with Melrose. He brought forth the well from the rock, erected a tall stone cross and out of a single stone carved himself a bath, in which he would spend the night in prayer. In imitation the Devil also built a stone-carved bath, but the saint expelled him with a huge cudgel. The local king accused Cuthbert of sleeping with his daughter. In answer to the saint's prayers the ground swallowed up the girl at a place called Corruen. Because of this he never permitted a female to enter his church. St Cuthbert's Bath later became the resort of health-seekers; I don't think there ever was a standalone vessel – the 'bath' was the well-basin that is still filled with water from a spring; it may have been cut or enlarged from the rock. Cuthbert was super-seded by Sir David Menzies (1377-1449), a laird who became a monk, gave away most of his land to his son John and, possibly suffering from a depressive illness, withdrew from the world to here about 1428. David became the patron saint, hence St David's Well. Spring-cleaning in the 1830s yielded numerous coins.

Somewhere below the Well there used to be a great cave which connected with another at Loch Glassie (NN850528, 2km distant and 230m higher). The main story, as recorded in ballad form by the Revd John McLean, Minister of Grandtully, tells how long ago on a Sunday, the daughter and step-daughter of the Lady of Weem heard the lowing of a lost calf from the cave. One sister had a Bible, the power of which prevented her from entering, but the other, who had no such supernatural protection, went in to explore. The song then has a question and response structure between the two sisters. The Bible-protected girl asks when her little sister will come home. The reply is that she cannot come home until the Day of Judgment, as there are seven iron gates between her and the entrance, and they are guarded by a man in a scarlet cloak. Again the other girl asks when her little sister will come home, but the hopeless response is 'when the time of seed-sowing and lint-pulling shall coincide', in other words, never. Her lifeless body was discovered in Loch Glassie with a long spiral of fiery light ascending from her breasts. Inevitably there are variants on this story: for example, both daughters enter the cave but only one is protected because she has some pages from the Bible, or, in another, the girls were actually sent to gather kail and were induced to enter the cave by the lowing of a calf.

A further version has it that the two girls loved each other but the mother of the younger girl hated her stepdaughter, who, being older, was of course heir to the estate. She entered into a plot with a villain who lived in the Cave of Weem; he wore a loose red hood or cloak and was thought to have been either the Devil or a brownie disguised as a fierce monk. The fiend stole a calf and placed it behind the first of the five (or seven, or nine) iron gates in the cave. The stepmother then sent the two girls to look for the calf, but before she did so she gave her own daughter a miniature of the Virgin Mary on a necklace (or a cross, or a Bible) so that the beast would know whom he was to abduct. But on the way to the cave the younger sister gave the charm to her older sister as a gift. So when they entered the cave it was the younger sister who was abducted and carried through the several self-opening and closing gates and the large chambers with gems studding the ceilings. The older child

St David's Well, Weem. To the right was a burial ground. The well (front left) could flood the area if the covering stone was removed.

Wood spirit, Rock of Weem. The woodland paths up to St David's Well teem with similar modern carvings.

In the wildwood, the mighty wildwood, the dragon sleeps tonight. Rock of Weem.

returned to the castle, and her stepmother, appalled at the mistake, sent the girl back to rescue her sister, without success.

Loch Glassie was home to a water horse. It abducted and drowned six Strathtay girls who had gone out to pet and mount him; a semi-bald scabby-headed boy survived (despite the Each Uisge screaming at him to stop) and told his parents. The bodies of the girls were found floating in the loch.

Weem Old Parish Kirk,★★ GRAVESTONES
Balhomais stone circle★ (NN82384926).
Boltachan Burn standing stone, cupmarked★ (NN84715160).

Two sanctuary crosses at DULL were taken in the early nineteenth century by Mr Campbell, the factor at Castle Menzies, for gateposts at his house Tom-na-Dashan, now Camserney Cottage. Campbell was warned this action would bring about his doom. The story was told that after attending a farmers' dinner at the Breadalbane Hotel in Aberfeldy, he rode home in the early hours – and his body was found at the gate to his house in the morning. Seeing this as divine vengeance, the locals restored the stones to their original places. But this is legend-mongering. The factor had actually inquired at the Coshieville Inn for a good horse to take him to Rannoch. The only one available was very high-spirited, but against advice he took it anyway. The horse bolted, took the old road to Fortingall and leapt a wall, falling on the rider and killing him. There is no suggestion his death was connected with the removal of the crosses, which were not restored to their original position, and are now in Weem Old Kirk.

Tobar Eonan, Adomnan's Well, is variously claimed for immediately outside the south wall of the manse garden (NN80304907), or the foot of a brae at NN80724927. To add to the confusion the *NSA* describes the latter as St Ninian's Well, a healing well whose 'imaginary virtues have long since ceased, and with them its deluded votaries'.

Dull Church★★, GRAVESTONES.
Carse Farm stone circles, with cupmarks ★ (NN80224873, NN80284846).
Nether Tullicro standing stone(?) (NN81324913).

KELTNEYBURN

The Keltnie Bridge was the site of a battle between the Picts and the Fingalians, leading to the extermination of the latter. Tom an t-sabhail, the hill or mound of protection or safety, a glacial mound, was their stronghold. In around 1570 it was called 'the old hall' (*NSA*). Garth Castle (NN764504), privately owned, was restored in very unusual fashion in 1963. On 16 August 1545 Mariota, the wife of the vicious laird

Above left: Weem Old Church. One of the sanctuary crosses from Dull, with funeral hatchment. The church also houses fragments of the vandalized cross from St David's Well.

Above right: Weem Old Church. Menzies tomb, lunar detail.

Below: Weem Old Church. Detail of the magnificent Menzies tomb, a riot of statues and carved symbolism.

Above left: Dull, village square. The single remaining sanctuary cross with a missing arm courtesy of a runaway horse and cart.

Above right: Balhomais cupmarked stone, on the north bank of Loch Tay.

Niall Stewart, was killed by a stone thrown from the castle parapet. Stewart got away with the murder and Mariota's ghost walks amid the trees. Two wells at Garth were still being used in the nineteenth century, Fuaran a' Gruarach ('spring of the measles') and Fuaran a' Druibh Chasad ('spring of the cough').

When introducing the fabulous mountain of SCHIEHALLION it is compulsory to say the name means 'the fairy hill of the Caledonians'. But this is just one inter-pretation. The *OSA* gives it as 'The Maiden's Breast'. Other versions include 'nest or brooding place of storms', 'the haunt of the monstrous fairy Cailin', 'the resort of the maiden or queen of the fairies' and 'the Caledonian Otherworld'. Scrapes on the side of the mountain are the claw- or broomstick-marks of the Cailleach Bheur, the great witch-hag of the Highlands. Supernatural black dogs are also said to pad around the mountain. The *NSA* described how young people from the entire area around would travel miles to visit a spring on the south side of the mountain on 1 May (Old Style, actually 12 May). The water cured kidney stones and urinary complaints; it was par-ticularly lucky to get the first draught, 'the cream of the spring'. I don't have a location for this spring – there is a Mineral Well (NN708501) but this seems too far away.

Above left: Cross-slab fragment, Dull Church.
The early Christian monastery here was possibly founded by St Adamnan/Eonan (679-704).
A mound to the east is traditionally known as Adomnan's grave.

Above right: Keltneyburn. The Iron Fairy smithy here does an excellent line in dragons.
Other metallic creatures can be seen all around the area.

Below: Gravestone, Dull Church. The kirk and area are filled with items of interest.

The limestone caves of Uamh Tom a' Mhor-fhir (NN707534), in Gleann Mor on the south foot of Schiehallion, give entry to the Otherworld. The name means the Cave on the Hill of the Big Men, the Giants Cave, or, according to the *NSA* in 1845, it is Tom-a-mhorair, 'the Earl's Eminence'. The giants may be the Fingalians, who sleep beneath the mountains awaiting the blast of Fingal's horn to rouse them into action. Their name turns up in Strath Fionan, a valley on the north of Schiehallion. Gobhar Bacach, the lame goat, limps around the area, ready to supply milk to the heroes when they return. Mystical goat-milk – breakfast of champions. The Tom a' Mhor-fhir cave is full of chambers, and a door which opens of its own accord; if you step through it closes behind you and cannot be opened. Yet another 'disappearing piper' vanished in the depths. The cave travels under Schiehallion to another entrance several miles east. None of these features have yet been noted by speleologists. In *Zenith* graphic novelist Grant Morrison sets a secret military underground base beneath Schiehallion. A hunchback from Braes of Foss passed Tom a' Mhor-fhir near midnight and on the Cnoc an Tiobart knoll saw the fairies dancing and singing 'Disathurna's Didomhnaich' (Saturday and Sunday). In a melodious voice he joined in, adding 'Diluain's Dimairt' (Monday and Tuesday). The fairies were delighted with this addition and sang it while dancing around him. Three approached him and granted him good health and wealth and the removal of his hump. When he reached his destination at Tempar his friend, another hunchback, did not recognise him. The friend set off to the cave, where he heard the fairies singing 'Disathurna's Didomhnaich. Diluain's Dimairt'. He joined in, in a tuneless voice, with 'Diciadain's Dirdaoin' (Wednesday and Thursday). The fairies were very angry. They jumped on him and pinched him, then three came forward and cursed him with a double hump, making him the ugliest man on earth, and he grew bigger and bigger. He made his way home disconsolate. Soon he was so big he could not get into the house. He slept outside and it took seventeen blankets to cover him. By the time he died twenty-four coffins were required to carry his remains. This tale is related in A.D. Cunningham's *Tales of Rannoch*; various versions are told widely across Scotland. A local variation has the first man being blessed because he was not just a tuneful singer but had a good heart. Two of his neighbours, neither tuneful nor good, also wanted to see the fairies. One was roughed up and given a hunchback and the second lost an eye. When Lizanne Henderson and Edward J. Cowan were writing their book, *Scottish Fairy Belief* (2001), someone told them that he had encountered a fairy near the top of Schiehallion.

LOCH TAY

Loch Tay is at the heart of Breadalbane, an area rich in folklore. Here the cattle knelt down on midnight on Christmas Eve, while fairy cows grazed on the slopes and even in the waters of the loch. The death of one of the Breadalbane family was presaged by a bull bellowing and climbing a hill; as it crested the rise, death occurred. The original story has Black Duncan of the Cowl, Donncha du a churraichd, bringing in a bull's head at a feast as a signal for the massacre of a number of MacGregors, whom he had invited in a friendly manner to the castle. A similar story is told elsewhere in Scotland. Another version has the MacGregors, on the way to the feast, meeting an old man on Drummond Hill who over and over again said to a large stone by the side of the road, 'It's to the grey stone I tell it'. When questioned, he intoned, 'When the head of the black bull comes upon the table the progenies of Gregor should take the alarm'. Duly forewarned, when the bull's head arrived the clan took their treacherous hosts hostage for safe passage (J.G. Campbell, *The Gaelic Otherworld*). Black Duncan (1552-1631), the seventh laird of Glenorchy, was said to be a black magician, the usual accusation against a thrusting, ambitious élite-figure who'd read a book or two. He forbade his tenants 'to cut any brier or thorn save in the waxing of the moon', an injunction possibly related to witchcraft or folk magic.

Other local death omens include unearthly sounds of shouting, distress, screaming or weeping where no human being could be. For the Maclachans, death was presaged by a little bird; for two septs of the McGregors, Clann Dhonncha dhui and Clann Dhonncha bhig, the omens were a little bird or a light like that of a candle, respectively. Before the death of a gentleman a light or meteor called Dreag or Driug was seen taking the route of the funeral party. It was only for 'big men' that these lights appeared and an irreverent tailor once expressed a wish that the whole sky was full of them. The Cruban Stone, Clach a Chrùbain, possibly gryphite, a fossil shell, cured diseases of the joints. It was lent only under the pledge of two cows, which were forfeit if it was not returned. The name is from crùban, a squatting posture caused by pain in the feet. When a woman gave birth a fire was carried around her to protect her against evil spirits such as the Gabble Ratchet and the Seven Whistlers, the latter being the spirits of dead babies who were guided by the call of ravens (Robin Hull, *Ravens Over The Hill*). Caution was advised against 'strong and undue' wishing. A woman wished for the return of her dead brother. Some time later his ghost appeared, greatly annoyed, and asked her what she wanted. She told him her husband beat her. The ghost went to the man as he was ploughing and struck him dead. In one of the townships overlooking the Tay a beggar was given shelter in a joiner's workshop. In the night he saw a ghost in a white shroud climb into a recently-completed coffin, but the coffin proved too short, and the spirit then vanished. The following day the vagrant told the joiner what he had witnessed, and, on checking the corpse, the coffin was indeed found to be undersized. And there is the tale told (in D.C. Cuthbertson's *Highlands, Highways and Heroes*) of Big John, a mighty man from this area. He was in the army, and strict orders were given that no man was to pass a certain milestone under severe penalty. But just beyond this boundary was the inn. So John carried the milestone with him to the pub, thus satisfying both his thirst and the letter – if not quite the spirit – of his orders.

On 12 September 1784 the loch experienced something resembling a mini-tsunami. As reported in the *OSA*, at nine in the morning, with the weather calm, the water in the bay at Kenmore retired about five yards and then flowed back again four or five minutes later. It repeated this three or four times in fifteen minutes, then suddenly all the water rushed from the east and the west in opposite currents – and when they met there was great foaming and a clashing noise. A wave five feet high drew up, leaving the bottom of the loch dry to the distance of about 90 to 100 yards. The wave rode westward, slowly diminishing as it went, until it disappeared after five minutes. Subsequently the loch waters sloshed about like tea in a saucer, flowing back into the bay and going four or five yards beyond its usual shore, ebbing about ten yards, and then repeating in ever decreasing cycles for two hours at seven minute intervals, until at last the water resumed its normal level. While this was going on the River Tay, which leaves the loch at Kenmore, ran backward, and the channel was left dry about 12 feet from either side. Under the bridge – which is about 60 or 70 yards from the loch - the current failed and the bed of the river appeared where there had been 18 inches of water. The after-shocks, or whatever they were, continued for the next five days, with ebbings and flowings seen about the same time of day, and for the same duration, but with less force, and the phenomenon continued in a reduced form for another month, until 15 October, sometimes in the morning and sometimes in the afternoon. Another episode occurred a decade later on 13 July 1794 but was shorter and less violent. It all sounds like earthquake-related activity, and attempts have been made to link the first episode with the concurrent Lisbon earthquake of 1784, but there have been other European earthquakes (and numerous tremors centred at COMRIE) since, and no further disturbances to the loch.

If there is tectonic activity in the area it may be that, in line with earth mysteries researcher Paul Devereaux's theory of 'Earth Lights', it also creates the strange lights which have been sighted in and on the loch over the centuries. Two examples from different eras will give the flavour of the phenomenon: the first has a 'geological mystery' air about it, while the second in very much in the 'ghost (or corpse) lights' tradition. On 21 August 1997 David Hardy and Susan Underhill were driving along the north side of the loch when they saw lights deep underneath the water surface. The lights merged to form a greenish globe which rose towards the surface. The reflection of the full moon could be seen elsewhere on the water, so that was not the source. The globe may have been 30-40 feet in diameter. As it rose towards the surface it changed from green to white; it moved westward in the direction of Killin for sev-eral minutes and then disappeared (www.leyman.demon.co.uk/nmistim.htm). In the nineteenth century, when the eldest son of the Cameron family of Morenish (towards the west end of the loch) returned home from military service overseas, he found his two brothers had died of fever and been buried at Kenmore (at the loch's east end). He decided to exhume the coffins and take them by boat to be reburied at Killin. On the night preceding the move, two bright balls of fire were seen moving across the surface of the water, taking the exact route later followed by the water-borne coffins (Alasdair Alpin MacGregor, *Strange Tales of the Highlands & Islands*).

KENMORE

The records of the Kirk Session (John Christie, *Witchcraft in Kenmore*) give us an extraordinary insight into the vituperative world of eighteenth-century rural folk magic, with all its petty hatreds and peasant preoccupations:

On 4 January 1730 Elspeth NcIgorrive complained that John Mcintyre and his wife Mary NcArthure had accused her of witchcraft.

On 30 August 1730 Margaret McGrigar, a widow from Tomb, denied accusing John Lumsden of killing her children through witchcraft.

In June and July 1747 Margaret Robertson of Rumuckie complained that she was unjustly charged with witchcraft and enchantments. This seems to have been a bitter dispute between neighbours, with a great deal of ill-wishing and (non-magical) cursing. After a wearisome number of interviews the Kirk Session rebuked both Janet Clerich (for making a baseless and slanderous accusation of witchcraft) and her neighbour Margaret Robertson (for basically being rude and difficult).

On 19 July 1747 Janet McIntaggart and her fifteen year old sister Margaret, both of Wester Acharn, were charged with using charms and enchantments against their neighbour Alexander Fisher of Wester Acharn. The McIntaggarts' animals were giving milk but the 'substance' or goodness was taken away. They suspected Fisher or his wife Ann Fletcher had something to do with it. So first they milked three drops from their neighbours' sheep to recover the 'substance'. This worked but they went further. Margaret went into all the houses locally with a concealed eggshell containing a small amount of milk; the charm would identify the household which had 'stolen' their milk and actually take it back. Lo and behold it was Alexander Fisher's house, but his wife spotted the 'egg shell in the Devil's name' and raised the alarm. After extensive consideration the Kirk Session effectively decided the two McIntaggart girls had been listening to too many gossipy old women from the area and had picked up bad ideas; both were rebuked.

On 1 July 1753 Donald Thomson and his wife Margaret Walker of Shian used 'unlawful charms' to increase the milk yield of their cattle, and their servant Janet McNicol was accused of practicing a charm early in the morning, crossing back and forth over a burn, and bowing to the ground as if taking something from the earth, or putting something into it. Both the couple and Janet were incensed at the accusation, which once again came from envious neighbours; it seemed everyone in the area 'knew' the household were using charms. Witnesses said Margaret cut four hairs from her own cow's tail and placed them in a knotted napkin around her neck; this was seen as a definitive charm. In the end, after once again an endless display of neighbourly enmity among the witnesses, the Session told Margaret to cease from doing anything which might look like a charm, and rebuked Janet. The servant, however, was having none of it, continued to deny the charges and hoped that God would bring down vengeance on those who had slandered her. Despite the Session's best efforts, she refused to submit to the judgement.

On 20 and 23 February 1757 Anne McInucatar of Croitantaoghan and Donald McNab of Lawers complained that Duncan McInucatar of Croitantaoghan had accused them of using charms and enchantments. This seems to have to have been a family dispute. Anne was Duncan's grandmother and had taken against him because of his choice of wife. Duncan's view was that Donald McNab had been Anne's agent during some dark business on Duncan's wedding day. Witnesses testified that Anne McInucatar had been seen secretly taking water from the loch and hiding the bottle in a cairn to be later picked up by her daughter. The inference here was that it was some kind of charm. Anne and her daughter were also said to have lurked around bothies at night on errands to no good (once again, the implication was of charms and enchantments). What clearly came over in the case was that several of the witnesses were, if not actually frightened, then at least in awe of the elderly Anne McInucatar; her temper, her strong personality and her reputation for folk magic were clearly quite intimidating to all the younger menfolk in the area. Unfortunately the records of this fascinating case just peter out and so we will never know what happened.

Here is folk magic and folk culture in stark reality. Neighbours are virtually at war over milk yields; everyone wants to police other people for any kind of imagined magical infraction; and enmity, envy and busybodiness eventually leads to public slanging matches at the Kirk Session. Ah, the good old days! Note that although the statute against witchcraft was repealed in 1736, people in Breadalbane were still accusing each other of magical crimes more than twenty years later and instead of the Session stitching people up for witchcraft, it is the accused who are complaining about being slandered. In earlier days, an accusation of witchcraft was a short route to great unpleasantness and possibly death; here, in contrast, it is a matter of seeking redress for a damaged reputation. And as for the members of the Session, you can almost sense them shaking their heads over the antics of their mean-spirited, refractory and bloody-minded flock.

INCHADNEY

Kenmore was originally called Inch-Aidan, Aidan's Island, named after the seventh-century saint whose soul St Cuthbert saw being carried up to heaven by angels. The former church (NN789468) was at the centre of a Christian landscape that catered for both body and soul – church, burial ground, holy wells, a standing cross and marketplace. Markets were held here until 1575 - the main one was on 18 July, the Nine Virgins' Day, supposedly linked to the community of nuns on the Isle of Loch Tay, but in reality commemorating the magico-mystical Nine Maidens. This once busy area is now just a field. When the church was abandoned in 1760 its holy power was not simply discarded, but conserved and transferred in multiple acts of Christian magic. The earth of the graveyard was transported to consecrate the small burial grounds of Ardtalnaig and Stronfearnan, and some of the tombstones were taken to the new church in Kenmore village - they can be identified because they are placed at the foot of the graves. According to local tradition, the very last burials at Inchadney were one person from Bolfracks and another from Fearnan. At this time there was a strong belief in the Faire-chlaoidh – the spirit of the last person buried who had to keep watch at the entrance to a graveyard until the next burial.

To avoid either becoming a Faire-chlaoidh without hope of relief, the relatives arranged that both burials should take place simultaneously. (On another occasion, when two funerals were scheduled to take place the same day, the mourners of one ran with the coffin to be sure to get there first.) The toothache well An Tobar★ still survives (NN788473), signposted 'holy well'. Visiting day was 1 May. Coins, pins and a stone cup found in the well are in the Museum of Scotland. Tobar Nan Dileag, the well of drips, NN805465, was still being used to cure children of whooping cough in the early twentieth century.

TAYMOUTH CASTLE★★★ is a glorious monument to aristocratic eccentricity, with Gothicised interior and a 'secret room' used by Queen Victoria and Prince Albert (hidden behind library bookshelves). In the nineteenth century the grounds were home to emus, American bison, buffalo, white Caledonian cattle and re-introduced capercailie. The castle's Mac an Sgialaiche pipers were said to have received their pipes from the fairies. In the sixteenth century when the laird Cailean Liath (Grey Colin) wanted to build the castle at the east end of Loch Tay he first chose Acharn, but an old woman told him it would be too cold there and he should build it where the first thrush could be heard. GARGOYLES, follies.

CROFTMORAIG STONE CIRCLE★★★ (NN79754726), is an easily-visited double ring which was rebuilt and ritually re-used for over a thousand years. The large cup-marked boulder was 'obviously' the sacrifice stone. Robert Burns 'said his prayers in it' on his famous visit to Breadalbane ('The Birks o' Aberfeldy' and a' that.)

Hugh MacMillan in *The Highland Tay* tells how the people of the neighbouring hamlet of Stix (NN802474) shared the grass of the surrounding parks. As late as 1901 they marked their allotments during the hay-making season with tree badges – branches of oak, birch, alder, fir, willow, lime and sycamore; each family had its own ancient tree symbol.

LOCH TAY NORTH SHORE

DRUMMOND HILL

A urisk called Caobarlan had his home in the Deep Burn (NN *c*.7646). His favourite pastime was throwing earth and stones at drunken pedestrians as they wandered home late at night from Kenmore to Fearnan. A Fearnan woman who was cursed with a feckless husband had to go out one night in search of her missing cow. Passing Caobarlan's den, she was so scared she said out loud, 'Blessing on thy name, Fellow that lives in the burn; early or late from thee I take no fear'. The words prompted the urisk to appear and thank her – all his life he had been waiting for 'one of the children of Adam' to bless him. In return he helped the woman find her cow, and when they returned to the house Caobarlan used his fists on the husband, cursing him for being a lazy good-for-nothing who even let his wife go out at night in search of their cow.

Taymouth Castle. The grounds are full of mock-military follies, including castellated bridges, forts, lookout towers and memorials.

Taymouth Castle. Gargoyles on the neo-Gothic chapel.

Having done his bit of marriage guidance counselling, and received his long-awaited blessing, the urisk left the area forever. Another urisk, Cas Luath (Fleet Foot) was frequently encountered in the old wood of Letterellan (NN c.731444).

And late one autumn night a farmer was passing Allt Coire Phadairlidh, 'the burn of Paderlan' (NN698424) when he felt something small and lithe jumping on his horse behind him. Guessing it was a young urisk, he wrapped his plaid tightly round himself and the creature, so that it could not escape, and rode as fast as he could to his home at Balnasuim. There he instructed his sons to bar the door, build up a fire, and place the end of the old coulter of the plough on the flames. Soon the fearsome Paderlan was duly banging at the door demanding the return of his son. The farmer made a bargain with the urisk – he would get his child back if he promised to leave Breadalbane

Taymouth Castle. Fantastically-shaped water-worn stones guard bridges on the south side.

One of the Newhall Bridge standing stones with Taymouth Castle north-east Gateway.

Croft Moraig. 'Two large hollows just outside the stone circle were interpreted as graves. During the 1965 excavation a student was persuaded to curl up in one to prove its adequacy'. (Aubrey Burl, *Carnac to Callanish*).

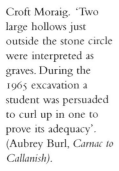

Above: Fair Stone Of Fearnan, Lagfern. The Latin cross on each side may be associated with St Ciaran's primitive church a little further north.

Right: Clach-na-Cruich, St Ciaran's Seat. Rainwater from the large natural cavity was used as a cure for measles. The enclosing tipi belongs to the nearby Culdees Bunkhouse, Fearnan.

forever. Eventually Paderlan reluctantly agreed, but insisted on sealing the deal with a handshake. The wily old farmer then pushed the hot end of the coulter through the window. Paderlan took hold of it and his hand twisted like a corkscrew. And he was never seen in the area again.

Clach an Tuirc (the Boar Stone), cupmarked★ (NN72184497).

A man from Killin was passing MACHUIM stone circle★ (NN68204015) one night when he heard music. The fairies welcomed him and gave him a white horse. It flew through the air at great speed, overshooting his destination. He shouted 'Woah' and the horse threw him off its back, right down a chimney of a house in Tyndrum. His sudden appearance in the hearth startled a wedding party, but he stayed there the night and made his way back to Killin, where he was still telling the story in the 1880s.

LAWERS

Although Thomas the Rhymer and The Brahan Seer take the lead nationally when it comes to prophecies, it's the Lady of Lawers who has the local market sewn up. Her numerous prophecies are said to have been written down in the Red Book of Balloch, shaped like a barrel with hoops of iron and kept at Taymouth Castle. This is one of those 'facts' that cannot be verified, as the book, if it ever existed (how do you read − or even write in - a barrel-shaped book?) is long lost and there is no reliable transcription of its contents. However, the prophecies were certainly in wide oral circulation by the nineteenth century. Unfortunately we cannot now tell what were 'genuinely' hers and which ones were later grafted on to her celebrity. My main references for the prophecies are Elizabeth Sutherland's *Ravens and Black Rain*, a magnificent study of Scottish seers; The Gaelic Otherworld, J.G. Campbell's folklore *magnum opus*; and Alastair Duncan Miller's *A Bit Of Breadalbane*. The prophecies follow:

'The ridging stones will never be put on the roof. If they are, then all my words are false.' This came true in her lifetime. In 1669 the sandstone blocks destined for the new Lawers church arrived by boat and were unloaded on the loch shore, but were then swept into the water by a storm. Some of the blocks can still be seen, buried in the shingle. The speedy result for the prediction meant the others were feared and respected.

'The tree will grow and when it reaches the gable the church will be split asunder, and this will also happen when the red cairn on Ben Lawers falls.' The ash tree, which she may have planted beside the north side of the church, reached the gable in 1833. A violent thunderstorm that year demolished the west loft of the church, causing it to be abandoned as a place of worship. The cairn, built by sappers and miners, collapsed ten years later, 1843, the year of the Disruption of the Church of Scotland.

'When the ash tree reaches the ridge, the House of Balloch will be without an heir.' In 1862 the second Marquis of Breadalbane died without a son (although of course the tree was at the ridge height for some time).

'Evil will come to him that harms it' [of the tree]. In 1895 John Campbell of Milton farm felled the tree with an axe. Shortly after he was gored by his own Highland bull, the neighbour who had assisted him went mad and the young horse used to drag away part of the tree unexpectedly fell down dead.

'There will be a mill on every stream and a plough in every field, and the two sides of Loch Tay will become a kail garden.' Agricultural improvements.

'The jaw of the sheep will drive the plough from the ground' and 'The land will first be sifted and then riddled of its people.' Also 'The homesteads on Loch Tay will be so far apart that a cock will not hear its neighbour crow.' Clearances and modern farming. From 1835-1838 the Marquis of Breadalbane evicted over 500 families and the loch side population fell from over 3,500 to around 100.

'The feather of the goose will drive memory from man.' Passing of the oral tradition.

'The earldom will not descend beyond a grandson in one line. Great and perplexing doubts will arise as to an heir.' The first Earl's grandson died without an heir. In 1782 the title went to a relative whose son became the second Marquis, but he too died without an heir in 1862. It took five years to decide which claimant should inherit, eventually settling on John Campbell of Glenfalloch, but his son, the third Marquis, died heirless in 1922.

'In time the estate of Balloch will yield only one rent and then none at all' and 'In time the estates of Balloch which were put together in hides will fall asunder in lace.' In the mid-nineteenth century the second Marquis had 500,000 acres put together in hides, or large lumps, acquired by marriage or more dubious means. The evicted tenants considered him a tyrant. One, John Kennedy, wrote a bitter attack in Gaelic soon after 1834. It appeared in English in *Punch* in 1903. The last lines read 'Breadalbane's land – the fair, the grand – Will no' be aye the Marquis's', which clearly refers to the prophecy. In 1922 many acres had to be sold off to pay death duties. By 1933 about half the land had gone in small pieces, or 'lace'. In 1946 they had only Kinnell House at Killin and one farm paying rent.

'The last laird will pass over Glenogle with a grey pony leaving nothing behind.' In 1946 a retired gardener saw the Countess of Breadalbane on her way from Killin Station in a trap drawn by a grey pony. By 1948 even Kinnell House had gone to the Chief of Macnab.

'A strange heir will come to Balloch when the Boar's Stone at Fearnan topples over, and the house will be at its height of honour when the face of a certain rock is concealed by wood.' Not fulfilled. The chunky Boar's Stone, Clach an Tuirc (NN72184497) is very happy where it is.

'A ship driven by smoke will sink in Loch Tay with great loss of life'. Up till 1939 pleasure steamers plied the loch, but the last Marquis, among many others, refused to travel on them. Note the remarkable prediction of a steamship.

'Ben Lawers will become so cold that it will chill and waste the land for seven miles.' Not fulfilled. In the 1980s this was seen as forecasting a nuclear winter.

'The lands of Macnab will be joined to those of Breadalbane when two trees join together on Inchbuile and grow as one.' In 1820 a branch from a pine tree growing on the Macnabs' burial island, Inchbuile at Killin, fell and grafted onto another tree. 'Growing as one'. The Macnab chief fled bankrupt to Canada and his chief creditor, the first Marquis of Breadlabane, bought the lands. In 1948 the 22nd chief of Macnab bought back the ancestral lands and the grafted branch began to die. Another prophecy, not part of the official canon, talks about fire coaches crossing Drumochter Pass, possibly a prediction of the railway. Rennie McOwan says there used to be a stone near the summit of Ben Lawers carved with words somehow attributed to the Lady: 'Spend as you get, and get as you spend. Save, and for whom? Remember death!' The stone was stolen sometime in the nineteenth century.

So who was the Lady of Lawers? Tradition has her as either a Stewart or a MacCombaich (Colquhoun) from Appin in Argyll who around 1645 married a younger son (or brother) of the impoverished Sir James Campbell, sixth Laird of Lawers. Her house was said to be Milton Farm, opposite the church. But despite extensive genealogical research, we don't know her name, or even if she actually existed. The church★ that features in the prophecies still stands, just about (NN683394), on the lochside east of the current village. Inevitably the Lady is said to haunt the ruins.

In one of Alasdair Alpin MacGregor's *Strange Tales*, a shrill whistle from the south side of the loch summoned the Lawers ferryman one evening, but when the man arrived at the ferry-place there was no-one around. Then something like a large sack of wool came rolling down the slope and into his boat. Now terrified, the ferryman rowed back, and as soon as the boat touched the north shore, the peculiar cargo transformed into a large white bird which noisily flew to the burial ground at Lawers. A day or two later, the ferryman repeated the journey, this time transporting the corpse of a young woman who had died suddenly.

According to the Revd Gillies around 1760 or thereabouts a witch called Cailleach Dhomhnuill Bhric, Donald Breac's Old Wife, was active in Lawers. Her powers included the ability to cause cattle to abort, or prevent them giving milk; 'freezing' horses, so they would not eat, drink or work and making children sick, even to cause their death. On Beltane, the first day of May, a blacksmith called Martin saw a hare acting strangely and speaking, saying: 'Transfer the summer's growth and the harvest's crop from the smith's croft to the adjoining one'. The next door croft belonged to Donald Breac and his wife. There was a gun being repaired at the smithy, and Martin immediately called his apprentice to fire it at the hare. The first shot had no effect and the hare changed into a woman and then back again; although thoroughly spooked, the smith reloaded with a silver sixpence and fired it the name of God. The wounded hare made straight for Donald's house, entering through a cat flap. The Breacs were not seen for the next twenty-four hours, so Martin and his apprentice called upon them. Being refused admittance, they threatened to set fire to the roof. This did the trick, and inside they found a scene of disorder. Breac's wife was limping, the sixpence having penetrated her thigh to the bone; and all around her were the implements of her craft: 'charms, urns, hair tethers, stone balls, wooden cups, dried kail stocks, and a bladder full of cow's hair and raven's feathers', the last two of which, when dried and powdered, were used to blind people. The witch confessed her crimes, repented of the evil she had done and destroyed her magical items. The blacksmith extracted the silver bullet. A cripple for the rest of her life, the old woman made peace with her neighbours and died a good Christian, being buried in the gateway of Lawers graveyard.

Easter Croft-an-tygan standing stone★ (NN67063942). Nearby a house on the north side of the road has a modern stone circle in its garden.
Strange carving of a trefoil within a circle, probably from the hippy era as it was first reported in 1975 (NN64673819).

BEN LAWERS

As reported in Rennie McOwan's excellent *Magic Mountains*, two experienced mountaineers were forced by bad weather to come down from the ridge on Ben Lawers to Lochan nan Cat (NN645425). They walked the long trek to the road separately. When they met up, one wanted to know the name of the Victorian lodge they had passed about a mile back. The other man, Alan Boath, said no such lodge existed, and brought out the map to prove it, but his friend was absolutely insistent it had been there, and gave a full description, right down to the blue and white curtains. Despite testimony from other climbers, Boath's friend continues to believe he saw the building near the lochan. Loch Tay was created by a careless dairymaid watering a herd of dun cows on the slopes of Ben Lawers. So powerful was a spring in the Corrie of Carie, on the southwest side of the mountain that it had to be kept secure by a strong door, but one evening the girl was late in finishing her work and forgot to lock the door. The fountain flowed all night and the next morning Loch Tay was in existence.

A woman at BLARMORE (NN642370) was constantly harassed by the young son of the fearsome urisk Sligeachan, who lived in the pool called Linne na slige. The urisk pestered the woman to tell him her name, but she cannily replied, 'My name is Myself, and nobody but Myself'. Eventually she got so fed up with his pranks and stealing that she poured scalding water over his legs. When his father asked him who had done this, the answer (inevitably) was 'Myself, and nobody but Myself'. This tale is told not only in other parts of Scotland but across Europe.

CLADH DABHI

Until at least 1901 two of St Fillan's Healing Stones were kept on a tombstone dated 1817 at the now overgrown Cladh Dabhi graveyard (NN598347). Women travelled for miles to apply the stones to their breasts to cure pectoral inflammation. These mill socket stones were from the original five at Killin, now restored to the Breadalbane Folklore Centre there and available for consultation.

MORENISH

As reported by the Revd Gillies, on 20 February 1622 Donald Taillour McGillechrist accused his neighbour, a woman called McVane, of using a pock of earth from Tom nan Aingeil, the Knoll of the Angels, in Killin, to curse his farmwork and corn. The court in Killin dismissed the case and instructed no one else to use the pock of earth or carry on similar activities, as 'it inclined to no good but an evil custom'. A man came across two women 'gathering the dew' on a croft at Morenish (NN *c.*6135). The ritual involved drawing a rope of hair over the dewy grass, repeating a spell that would bring them the milk of their neighbours' cattle. The man cut the rope and gave the women a scolding. There is no date for this incident, but another one took place as late as 1888 somewhere on the south side of the loch, where a woman was seen using a rope to take the milk from the cattle of one John Crerar. A hair rope used in this kind of folk magic can be seen at the Museum of Scotland in Edinburgh.

LOCH TAY – SOUTH SHORE

The loch is the Scottish centre for the study of crannogs, artificial islands used for centuries from the Iron Age on (a wonderful medieval example features in Terry Gilliam's film *Jabberwocky*, the companion to *Monty Python and the Holy Grail*). A survey in 1979 identified eighteen crannogs; the early tradition spoke of twenty-four. Many are now permanently submerged; others appear in dry summers. The most obvious, Priory Island (NN 766454), also known as the Isle of Loch Tay and Eilean nam Ban (Island of the Women), was the home of the urisk Brunaidh an Eilean, ('the Island Brownie').

ACHARN
'Our guide opened a door, and we entered a dungeon-like passage, and, after walking some yards in total darkness, found ourselves in a quaint apartment stuck over with moss, hung about with stuffed foxes and other wild animals, and ornamented with a library of wooden books covered with old leather backs, and mock furniture of a hermit's cell. At the end of the room, through a large bow window, we saw the waterfall...a very beautiful prospect.' So wrote Dorothy Wordsworth in 1803. The Hermitage, or Hermit's Cave, was built around 1760 for the Third Earl of Breadalbane, who advertised unsuccessfully for a real, permanent eremite. The guide in 1869, Donald Anderson, would dress up with a long beard of lichens and clothes of animal skins. Guided visits probably stopped during the First World War. After lying derelict and vandalised for decades the Hermitage (NN75674318) was repaired in 1990 and the balcony again gives a sudden view of the high waterfall, so you too can know the Sublime as experienced by Enlightenment thrill-seekers.

Acharn Falls stone circle★★ (NN76784249).

In an old sheep house at CALLELOCHAN FARM (NN719423) all the urisks of the area would hold regular meetings, with Peallaidh (see ABERFELDY) as the 'tyler' (the

The Crannog Centre, Loch Tay. Next door, at Portbane, An Tiobairt healing well was used to treat consumption.

doorkeeper of a masonic lodge). Other urisks included Cleitean, Cludarlan, Uisdean, Martain and Slochdail a chuirt. A local shepherd wanted to find out what the urisks talked about, but could not understand their language. Trying to get a better view from his hiding place, he knocked over a shearing stool. The startled urisks ran pell-mell through the door and were never seen in the area again.

An elderly man called John, on his way to Ardtalnaig was accosted by a huge grey dog at An Carn Mor, the big cairn, at CLAGGAN (NN717385). The dog acted as his shadow, copying everything the man did, whether stopping, walking, or speeding up. He ran into the farmhouse, terrified. Despite his pleading the Mackays, tenants of the farm, refused to leave the house as his escort and insisted he stayed the night.

FORTINGALL & GLEN LYON

Glen Lyon is catnip to mystical types. It is the Glen of the Goddess, the Valley of the Sun God, a focus for anything with the word 'Celtic' in the title. Even Jesus allegedly came here to learn from the Druids. An official tourist leaflet even describes it as a 'centre of ley lines'. All this said, it is a wonderful place.

FORTINGALL★★★
In *The Folklore of the Scottish Highlands* Anne Ross relates an account of a Hallowe'en she herself obtained from a man who took part in the festival as a boy. A huge communal bonfire was built on the tumulus known as Càrn nam Marbh, 'The Mound of the Dead'★★ (NN74064693). For months in advance, the young people gathered materials from the hills, but on the day it was the older men who actually built the bonfire on the mound. Then the whole community would join hands and dance in a ring around the

Fortingall. The Plague
Stone, Clach Phlàigh, on
the Mound of the Dead.
Note the supernatural/
folkloric details of the
story on the plaque.

great blaze, moving first in one direction, then the other. The younger boys would take
burning sticks from the fire and run with them, finally throwing them into the air and
dancing over them where they fell. Boys held leaping competitions over the embers,
and when the fire finally died out, the children would head for home for games of
ducking apples and fireside divination. Meanwhile the adults repaired to the Fortingall
Hotel for drinking and dancing. The local keeper eventually banned the gathering of
cover from the hillside (it was interfering with the game). With one key element missing, the tradition withered, and the last Hallowe'en bonfire, with its archaic traces of
folk magic, was lit on the Mound of the Dead in 1924. A man gifted with second sight
told D.C. Cuthbertson he saw twelve nuns wearing rough cloth beside the stone. He
thought they were modern nuns staying at the village. He looked away and looked back
and they had disappeared. His impression was that they had lost their lives while nursing
the villagers during the plague, and were buried at the stone. Another of Anne Ross's
elderly informants told her he had witnessed a Glen Lyon man carrying out a curse
using a circle of blackened stones, the right state of the moon, and ritual chants. Despite
being in normal health at the time, the victim of the curse sickened and died. The locals
found out and the evil-doer was evicted from his holdings by the landlord. The magical
murder took place in the 1890s and the location of the circle is still known.

Next to the church★★ (GRAVESTONES, cupmarked stone) is the Fortingall Yew★★, one
of the oldest trees in the world. The church was originally dedicated to St Cedd. In
the area we have Dal-mo-cheode (St Cedd's Field) and Feille-mo-cheode (St Cedd's
Fair). Part of his relics were said to have been returned to the area and buried under
Leac-mo-cheode, the Flag-stone of St Cedd. Also there is Tigh-n-naomh, the Saint's
House, at Duneaves (NN74874687). Duneaves is derived from the ancient Celtic term
nemeton, a sacred place, often with a sacred grove or a single tree.

Bizarrely, Fortingall is claimed to be the birthplace of Pontius Pilate, surely the last
person you'd want on your 'famous sons of' list. The origins of this story are lost but
they are relatively modern, probably eighteenth century. This area has therefore been

Fortingall. Water-worn stones from the River Lyon act as apotropaic guardians on the gateposts of the church, the village hall, and, here, Glenlyon House. Note the horseshoe.

'Pilatised'. King Metallanus, who ruled the Scots from Fortingall between 10BC and AD29 (500 years before the Scots actually arrived from Ireland), received an ambassador from the Emperor Augustus at his palace at Creag a' Chasteil/An Dun Geal, 'medieval homestead' (NN74754759). Either the diplomat himself or one of his staff fell in love with a young girl called Menzies, a close relation of the king, who gave birth to Pontius at the Roman camp. For the record, the Romans were never actually here at any time and the Pilate story ranks as one of the least credible tales in this book.

Duncan Campbell, in *The Lairds of Glenlyon*, relates how John Campbell of Glenlyon House, An Coirneal Dubh, the Black Colonel, spent his life in the belief that he was cursed because his ancestor had been responsible for the massacre at Glencoe. In the aftermath of Culloden he found it his duty as a soldier for the Crown to persecute friends and neighbours who had fought for Prince Charlie, even though his own father and brother were Jacobite fugitives. He fought the battles of the British Empire for twenty-two years around the world, never being wounded. Campbell was a brave, inspiring leader but he never laughed (except on approaching battle) and seemed to carry a gloom around with him. In 1769 the great soldier finally retired and returned to Glenlyon House. On a shooting party his brother Archie Roy fired at a hare while Campbell was in the line of fire. Although the colonel's cloak was riddled with shot, he himself was unharmed. 'Don't be afraid', he said, 'I am not touched. The curse of Glencoe is a spell upon me. I have been in mortal strife many a time, and remained untouched by ball or steel while friends and foes were falling round me. I must drie my weird.' In 1771, back in action against the rebellious American colonies, he arranged a fake firing squad for a court-martialled marine who had been

Fortingall. Clach-math-Luag, the Stone of St Moluag, a massive boulder to which scolds were once chained. Note the water-worn stone.

Fortingall. Strange structure found on the south bank of the River Lyon, near Duneaves. Pagan fire/water ritual site? Or something more mundane?

The 'Roman camp' or 'Praetorium' – a moated medieval homestead.

secretly reprieved; the soldier was to be psychologically punished with the build-up to the execution, but not actually killed. In pulling out the reprieve the Colonel accidentally dropped a white handkerchief, the signal to fire, and the man was shot dead. Campbell clapped his hand to his forehead and exclaimed, 'The curse of God and of Glencoe is here; I am a ruined man'. The incident left a permanent impression on him, and shortly afterwards he left military service forever.

Glenlyon House was once home to Clach Bhuaidh (the Stone of Virtue), which kept soldiers immune from serious wounds. You will not be surprised to learn that, of all the men who went off to the Jacobite army at Culloden, the only fatality was the one who did not drink the water in which had been dipped the Clach Bhuaidh – a tailor who said the charm was not merely superstitious but actually sinful. Academic Brendan Murphy was restoring a house called Achloe at Fortingall in the 1980s. While work was ongoing he received a visit from an old friend, David. They had a lot of catching up to do and so, by the light of oil lamps they got stuck in to a bottle of rum. As described by Roddy Martine in *Supernatural Scotland*, an ordinary, long-haired young woman in casual dress walked in during the conversation. She said very little, just smiled and nodded, and then after a while just walked out. David asked Brendan who she was. Brendan, however, had assumed she was with his friend. 'It really was a very strange shared experience which neither of us is likely to forget', said Brendan.

Fortingall stone circles★★ (NN74514695, NN74534697, NN74544692).
Prehistoric ritual landscape★★ southwest of village: Dalraoich Standing Stones★, NN73144641, cupmarked stone, long cairn and the Lyon Bridge round cairn topped with a cupmarked stone★ (NN73174657), the latter being Uaigh an t-Seanalair, the General's Grave ('Pilate's father').

GLEN LYON★★★ from east to west.
Just to the west of Macgregor's Leap (NN72234761) on the south side of the road is 'The Soldier's Grave Mound'. Opposite is a mineral wishing well. At Halloween 1838 a man disturbed a circle of cats round the Clach Taghairm nan Chat, the Stone of the Devil Cat, (NN711478, but now lost) in the BLACK WOOD OF CHESTHILL, Coille Dhubh. A huge black cat sitting on top of the stone led an attack on the man. Fighting for his life, he reached the safety of a nearby house, but with a dead wildcat fastened to his back. Water-worn stones at the entrance to CHESTHILL (NN699473).

On a bank a little east of INVERINIAN is Cathair Innian, the stone seat of St Ninian (NN654476). It repaired itself whenever it was chipped, and anyone who damaged it would rue the day. A lifting stone, the 'Testing Stone of the Fianna', supposedly stands at NN620478, although I clearly did not pass the test as I couldn't even find it. Before the time of St Columba three 'goblin saints' (uruigean) came to Glen Lyon. One was Peallaidh (see ABERFELDY) who lived on the mountainside in a shieling still called Ruighe Pheallaidh (NN63254827) close to the Easa-Pheallaidh waterfall. Peallaidh

Cladh Chunna disused graveyard, Inverar, Glen Lyon. Note the apotopraic water-worn stones. St Cunna's well nearby is lost, as is St Wynnin's well at Inverar.

Roromore Farm, Glen Lyon. The ghost of a Roman centurion was seen here one morning.

The footprint on the Rock of Craigianie, marked by a modern cairn. The 'footprint' is a natural cavity shown here with a modern size 12 boot for comparison.

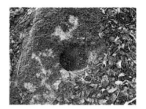

Above: The 'plague rock', 100m west of St Adomnan's Stone, in a line of hazel trees on the north side of the road. The low, flat stone is in front of the fourth tree from the east.

Left: St Adomnan's Stone, with a crude cross on each face, on a natural mound opposite the Rock of Craigianie.

the supernatural urisk and Palladius the early Christian saint are often confused and may be the same individual, a kind of *genius loci* for the area. Another urisk, Triubhas Dubh (Black Breeks) also lived somewhere near here. Palladius/Pheallaidh left his footprint on the Rock of Craigianie★ on the north side of the road.

St Adomnan's Stone★ marks the place where Adomnan, by the power of prayer, diverted a devastating plague into a nearby rock.

In June 2000 I went on The Path, an art-landscape project produced by Angus Farquhar's nva organization, a night-long walk around a route up and down Gleann-Da-Eig. Lights, weird sounds, Tibetan singing bowls and recordings of locals' encounters with strange lights enhanced the already numinous qualities of the landscape here. The centrepiece was the astonishing Clach air a sgoltadh,★★ the SPLIT STONE, which stands west of Gleann-Da-Eig, (*c.* N608465). Although natural, it has inevitably attracted attention because of its shape, hence its other names, Fionn's Rock (Fingal split the stone with a fiery arrow) or the Praying Hands of Mary. Another story says it split at the moment of the defeat at Culloden. Another split stone, Clach an t-Sioslaich, Chisholm's Stone (NN59234695) traditionally marks the place where a chief was killed on a raid. The damage actually occurred in the nineteenth century.

The present farmer tells how his father lifted the 'plague rock' many years ago; it was simply used to anchor a fence pole like these.

Across the road from the plague stone is what looks suspiciously like a stone circle but is just the remains of a denuded wall.

Up until about 1830 unbaptised infants were buried in this natural mound, Sithean a Bhaile-mheadhonaich, near Roroyere.

Aviform simulacrum near Sithean a Bhaile-mheadhonaich.

INNERWICK church★, GRAVESTONES, the only remaining kirk in the Glen, houses a 1950s stained glass window of St Andrews in a kilt, as well as the Benrudh Bell, possibly Adomnan's, from the seventh century. It moved around several consecutive churches on different sites and for centuries was locked up in a niche in CLADH BHRANNO graveyard (GRAVESTONES★, NN58184676). The War Memorial (NN588477) is capped by another water-worn boulder. The art gallery in BRIDGE OF BALGIE has a wonderful collection of naturally-shaped rocks and wood, including a water-worn stone. Roddy Martine describes how at a Hogmanay party in the area in the 1980s a large jolly man in an old-fashioned tweed coat happily drank steadily for several hours, enjoying his own company and attending to the fire. Nobody remembers actually speaking with him, and he disappeared when the owners returned. Glen Lyon in winter has a population of less than a hundred; nobody in the area knows who he was and no-one has seen him since.

MEGGERNIE CASTLE (NN555461) famously has a bisected ghost, encountered by two guests in 1862, E.J. Simons of Ullesthorpe, Leicestershire, and Beaumont Fetherstone, known as Beau, who wrote about his experience. Simons was woken in the early hours by a burning sensation on his cheek, like a scalding kiss; he saw the upper half of a woman drift into the closet. Beau, in the adjoining room, woke at 2am with a pink light in the room to see the floating head and shoulders move back towards the closet, the location of a sealed-off door that joined the two rooms. Simons was certain the hot kiss must have scalded his cheek but there was no mark on his face when he looked in the mirror. He did not mention the pink light. So as not to influence each other's story the two men related their respective experiences separately to their host Herbert Wood. Their stories matched. At the breakfast table Simons was about to describe the event when he was hushed by Mrs Wood, who feared the impact on the servants. It was already proving difficult to hold on to them – only a day or two before a kitchen-maid had told her she had seen the lower part of a female figure in the corridors; the same ghost had been seen several times in the corridors, the adjacent avenue of limes and in the graveyard. A week after the first encounter Simons was in a room writing letters when the heavy studded door swung open, the temperature dropped to below freezing and the top half of the ghost went gliding by. He made for his bedroom with the aid of the lamp and in walking along one of the ground floor passages he saw the ghost peering through its sole window. She was sad and beautiful and stayed long enough for Simons to bring the lamp close to the window to study her face. It then faded away. A year later, Beau met a woman at a hotel, who repeated her own encounter with the ghost, which was the mirror-image of Beau's and Simon's. In October 1928 Dr Mackay, staying in the room below the haunted chamber, saw the figure float past him at ceiling level – by now the floor level of the haunted room had been raised, but the ghost remained on the same level. The back-story is that Captain Menzies, the owner, suspicious of his wife's fidelity, murdered her and cut the body in two, and concealed the halves in the old

Meggernie Castle, home of the bisected ghost. Secret Tunnels allegedly run from the castle to the river and west to a small burial ground.

chest-of-drawers which stood in the closet between the two rooms. Then he went on a European jaunt, coming back with the story that his wife had drowned overseas. Under cover of darkness, he recovered the lower half and buried it in the graveyard. He was found dead the following morning, clearly murdered. His death was variously attributed to the ghost of his wife, or, more prosaically, the vengeance of her lover. The murder seems to have gone uninvestigated. But whatever happened, the upper part of the corpse remained hidden under the floorboards, in the closet between the two rooms, to be found during the early twentieth century renovations and buried. The most extensive version of this much-told story is in Alasdair Alpin MacGregor's *Phantom Footsteps*.

The famous eighteenth century freebooter Sergeant Mhor Cameron was rumoured to have concealed his loot in a cave on the mountain of CAM CHREAG (NN535491). A.D. Cunningham tells how a Rannoch farmer, Finlay Robertson, and two companions, were all hit as if by a massive electric shock while digging for the treasure. Finlay suffered from a speech impediment thereafter and none of the men ever returned to Cam Chreag.

Twelve structures scattered throughout the glen have always been called 'castles', and Fingalian ones at that, although they are actually all post-medieval homesteads. Three around CASHLIE are Caisteal an Deirg ('Castle of Dargo'), Caisteal an Duibhe ('Castle of the black hero') and Caisteal coin-a-bhacain ('Castle of the dog's kennel'). The latter is close to the Bhacain★★, a two foot high standing stone to which the Fian's hunting dogs were tied (NN485415). There was the Grey Hound, who once terrorised Glen Mhor, pouncing on stray humans and ripping them apart; and Fingal's own dog, Bran – yellow-pawed, green-backed, black-flanked and tethered with a chain of pure gold, the finest, fastest fiercest hunting hound ever. A ford over the Allt Cashlie burn (NN *c.* 489423) was in the early part of the nineteenth century occupied by something that threw clods and stones at people. One night a rumbustious traveller shouted, 'In the name of God I defy all from the pit' and a mysterious sound passed up the ravine. The throwing stopped, never to return. Archie McKerracher reports a flat mound called Sithean Tom na Cloin near Cashlie, where, until the middle of the nineteenth century, unbaptised children were buried. Sidhean Camaslaidh (NN46574202), a natural glacial moraine, has a fairy mound name but I have no further details.

In his book *Scottish Hills* (1946), Kersley Holmes related how he was walking in the area of Creach Mhor, south of Loch Lyon (NN391361) on a warm and sunny afternoon when he heard two loud stamps behind him, as if from a great foot. There were no sheep around and he felt a strange sense of dread. A friend told Holmes of a similar feeling of unease and dread in the area nearby. He had set out to spend the day fishing in one of the hill burns that run into the River Lyon. He started off full of enthusiasm and energy but when he arrived at his destination he found himself uneasy, and many things started to go wrong – more than would normally occur simply through accident. Then he came to a hollow filled with white stones and experienced such a strong sense that he was not wanted that he immediately left the area.

Beyond Loch Lyon, in GLEN CAILLICHE, lies one of the most astonishing sites in Europe, the Tigh-nam-Bodach★★★ (NN38054271). The small stone 'house', also known as the Tigh na Cailleach, houses three anthropomorphic water worn stones – the Old Woman (Cailleach), the Old Man (Bodach) and their Daughter (Nighean). Quite simply, this is a shrine to a nature deity, still in use. The creation story tells how a pregnant goddess, accompanied by her husband, arrived in the glen during a terrible snowstorm during Beltane (1 May). The local people built a house for the homeless and weather-battered couple and the Cailleach gave birth to a daughter there. A pact was made: as long as the people carried out the correct rehousing rituals at the start and end of summer, the glen would be blessed by the permanent presence of the divine beings. There were summer shielings here until at least 1782. Each May Day the figures were brought out, washed in the burn a little below the shrine, the Allt na Cailleach, and placed outside their newly cleaned and thatched home. Only then

The Bhacain. Women from the glen going on a long journey would lie underneath to avoid pregnancy - possibly a unique use for a standing stone.

could the cattle be moved up the hills. When the herds moved down in October, the family were replaced in their house, cosy in waterproof moss. These days the thatch has been replaced with stones and although the practice of summer transhumance has long passed and the high, remote glen is empty of people, buildings or roads, the bi-annual transfer and caring of the Cailleach and her Family continues to be carried out by successive generations of local people. For many years the custodian was Bob Bissett, head stalker on the Invermeran estate. Anne Ross met Bob (and through him, the Cailleach and her Family) when she lived in Glen Lyon in the 1950s. On her first meeting with the Cailleach the figure moved of its own accord right before her eyes, and she described the atmosphere around the area as unnervingly powerful, with a strong sense of being watched. Bob Bissett died not long ago; another custodian has taken his place and continues to ensure the Cailleach is well cared for. Ross thought the shrine might be Bronze Age. The stones are very heavy, and vary from 18 inches high (the Cailleach) to 3 inches (Nighean). Some people swear the Daughter is growing, and once every 100 years another child joins the family. A report from 1888 says there used to be 12 stones. Further members of the family can possibly be identified in roof and walls.

HIGHLAND PERTHSHIRE (NORTH)

'Athol…is infamous for witches and wicked women; the country, otherwise fertile enough, hath valleies bespred with forests: namely where that WOOD CALEDONIA dreadful to see to for the sundry turnings and windings in and our [out] therein, for the hideous horror of dark shades, for the Burrowes and dennes of wilde bulles with thicke manes…extended it selfe in old time farre and wide every way in these parts.' (*Scotland, an historical geography of Scotland*, printed 1610).

Atholl was a byword for witchcraft. In 1566 Margaret Fleming, the Countess of Atholl, used witchcraft to cast Mary Queen of Scots' labour pains onto the wet-nurse. Four years later a gift 'we suppose from the witches of Athole' was intercepted on its way to Mary: 'a pretty hart horn, not exceeding in quantity the palm of a man's hand, covered with gold'. The arms of Scotland were displayed above a crowned, enthroned queen. Under her feet a thistle covered a rose and a smaller lion submitted to a larger one. Beneath it all was written: 'Fall what may fall, the lion shall be lord of all'. This threatening heraldic symbolism was clearly meant to prophesise that Mary would eventually possess England as well. The chronicler Patrick Anderson, commenting on a witchcraft panic in 1597, said 'speciallie in Atholl both of men and women ther was in May at one convention upon a hill in Atholl to the number of 2300 and the Devill amongst them'. One imagines that the number was an exaggeration.

PITLOCHRY

As he related in his *Casebook of Ghosts* the 'gentleman supernaturalist' Elliott O'Donnell, pausing his bicycle at a junction a mile or two from Pitlochry, encountered a tall misty column with spidery arms that bounded after a horse-drawn haywagon. His landlady, Miss Flora Macdonald, told him when she was a teenager the 'death bogle' had pursued her own carriage and touched her father lightly on the hand, a touch which brought about his death within a year. Near the enbogle'd crossroads once stood the Old White House, where Flora Macdonald's mother, in a terrifying experience during her teenage years, encountered a candle that would not blow out and moved through the air, as if held by an unseen entity.

In the eighteenth century Stewart of Shierglass stabbed his brother-in-law, John Stewart of Bonskied, at the market in Pitlochry. William Marshall, in *Historic Scenes in Perthshire*, describes the then-current belief that if a murderer could see daylight under the body of his victim, he would escape punishment. So the killer hid himself by the wayside of the route he knew the victim's retainers must take when bearing the body back to Bonskied. With his ear to the ground he could just make out daylight beneath the dead man's plaid. Thus satisfied that fate had smiled upon him, he fled to the Continent for some time, but eventually returned home and was not troubled by the law. Sunnybrae Cottage (HS) is thought to be the location of the murder. In the fourteenth century Adam Fergusson killed his neighbour Baron Stewart with an arrow at the Bloody Stone of Dunfallandy, which used to stand above Wyandotte Cottage. Stewart had forbidden his daughter to marry Fergusson's son. The stone was fire-blackened, with a deep cup. It was probably a tallow-filled 'cresset' stone, lit to guide travellers on what was the line of an old road between Logierait and Dunfallandy. About 1979 it was buried under a roadmakers' quarry.

Tobar Traigh wishing well is in the wood to the south of Wyandotte Cottage, near the river bank. St Bride's Wishing Well, which cured lung disease, stood on the north bank of the Tummel near the suspension bridge to the Festival Theatre. It was filled in at the end of the nineteenth century when sewage from the treatment works polluted it.

The fragmentary Black Castle in Moulin (NN94705892) has a plague tradition with a number of variants: one has it that the victims were shut up in it and buried there, hence the local people would not remove any stones in case the infection escaped; another, that the owners of the castle were infected and the locals barred the door from the outside and burned them alive or alternatively that the castle was destroyed with artillery to ensure the plague did not spread. The usual date given is 1500.

Moulin Kirkyard, GRAVESTONES★ including one inscribed 'TIS MY LOT THIS DAY IT IS YOUR LOT TOMOROU' (NN94415923).
Balnakeilly standing stone★ (NN94635943).
Dane's Stone Standing Stone★. Deals at Moulin Market were struck by clasping hands at the stone (NN94255942).
Faire na Paitig stone circle (NO07456609).
Cupmarked rock (NO07656612).
Clachan an Diridh stone circle★. On May Day the stones were walked around deiseal, from east to west (NN92515574).
Faskally Cottages stone circle (NN93015877).
Tober Argan/St Feargain's Well, restored in the 1970s (NN94145822).
The Priest's Stone (or Chapel Stone), cross slab (NN915592).
Mains Of Killiechangie Pictish cross-slabs (NN96195482).
Dunfallandy Pictish Stone★★ (HS) (NN946565).

LOCH TUMMEL

The loch was home to the buarach bhaoi, the wild or wizard shackle, a kind of large leech-like eel that twisted itself like a shackle round horses' feet until they fell and drowned. It then sucked their blood, and had nine holes or eyes in the head and back out of which the blood re-emerged. J.G. Campbell reported how Bonskeid House

(NN89346108) was subject to either a poltergeist or a telekinetic attack in the 1820s or 1830s. Turnips appeared in mid-air or as if thrown through walls, knocking candles out of hands. Bedclothes were pulled off, lights blown out and furniture moved. A friend visiting from Rannoch saw the spinning wheel come down the stairs and fall apart on the floor of the room where the family were sitting; as it was not broken, he re-assembled it and carried it back upstairs, but within a few minutes the wheel came back down the stairs and once more fell apart. For more than a year the phenomena continued, seriously affecting the health of the proprietor. Then one day, as he was warming his feet on the hearth-stone, the stone began to move – and he saw the smile of pleasure on one of the servants. He realised she was the cause of the disturbances and sacked all the servants from Badenoch (his wife's home). Immediately all the disturbances ceased. Badenoch at the time had a reputation for witchcraft. When a new farmhouse was built nearby, gravestones were borrowed from the ancient burial ground at Cladh Chille (NN89046076). Mrs Stewart Sandeman of Bonskeid recorded in her memoirs that, 'While the farm-servants were at supper, stones came rattling down the chimney and when the inmates went to bed, low moaning sounds were heard which would not let them sleep'.

Craig Kynachan (NN761579) at the west end of the loch, holds a gold hoard, supposedly deposited by a former Bishop of Dunkeld. This is according to a dubious prophecy of Thomas the Rhymer which specified the treasure would be found by 'Niall of the Seven Nialls'. A young man with this very name, and a second sight-gifted seventh son of a seventh son to boot, spent years searching for the treasure without success. The Rhymer also apparently predicted the drowning of eighteen people on an overcrowded ferryboat crossing the Garry to Strathtummel in February 1767.

Foss Kirk, GRAVESTONES (NN790581).
Upper Gaskan stone circle and cupmarked stone★★ (NN74666113).
Tombreck cupmarked stone (NN79655812).
Cross-incised stone (NN7745698).
Na Clachan Aoraidh, the 'Stones of Worship', stone circle★ (NN838662008).

LOCH RANNOCH

The information boards of the Clans of Rannoch trail around the loch give details of sites and stories associated with seven clans - the MacDonalds, Menzies, MacGregors, MacDougalls, Camerons, Robertsons and Stewarts. Each site has an information board and parking, and a leaflet is available locally. The trail was conceived by Alec (A.D.) Cunningham, former deputy head of Rannoch School.

The Revd John Sinclair wrote extensively about a seer he called 'old Sarah'. Her actual name was Rachel Cameron, a crofter's wife who lived near Killichonan. She had been born a MacGregor of Ardlaroch in 1815. Her second sight had descended from one generation to another by way of red-haired daughters. Mrs Cameron's daughter Rachel, also red-headed, inherited the gift. If Rachel the elder was around eighty in 1895, her daughter was presumably around sixty. Most of the material seems to relate to the older Rachel, but there appears to have been some confusion between the two elderly women (both with the same name, gift and general location) and so some visions attributed to Rachel senior may have actually been Rachel junior.

Among the things Rachel 'saw' were phantom funerals and the taibhses ('future ghosts') of people involved in them. The identity of the taibhses told her who was missing – that is, who was dead. She also heard the sounds of the gravedigger at work, and the carpenter making coffins. Once, she saw good and evil angels fighting in the graveyard over the soul of a man who was to die shortly. And on a lighter note, she would do her best to see into the future for well-born ladies of a certain age who desired a husband before it was too late.

Not surprisingly, the ability to foretell death made her neighbours a little wary, but whenever someone went missing, Rachel was called in. She correctly identified the location of several victims of drowning. A farmer disappeared on his way home from market in Aberfeldy during bad weather. Rachel had never been to Aberfeldy or the district, but after being asked for help she prayed and had a waking dream. 'A sort of mist rose up, then cleared, and like a picture I saw a dead man lying in a reclining position, kept down by some tree roots at the bottom of a pool at the side of a river, below a queer bridge. I did not know the place'. She sent for one of the farmer's relatives who drew a sketch of the famous Wade Bridge. Rachel identified it, and insisted that was where the body was. The site had already been searched, but a second attempt found the body in the hole by the bridge, as described.

When the party searching for the miller of Camserney Mill arrived at her cottage, she knew in advance why they were coming, and showed them a drawing of a bridge and the arch where the body was lodged. In another case, she was consulted by post about a man drowned in Loch Awe, Argyll and obliged with a sketch map showing his location. And, more cryptically, she told the searchers for the drowned body of a Grandtully man that they would find what they were looking for in front of a many-windowed building. The men first looked in the river by a church, but found nothing, much to the satisfaction of the local parson, who deplored second sight as witchcraft. Then they tried again at St Coombs, another 'many-windowed dwelling', and the body was found.

The visions of funerals and graveyard scenes came involuntarily, without warning. But for specific purposes – such as searching out missing bodies – Rachel appears to have used some sort of divining cup. Unfortunately we are given no description, and nothing about how she used it. Quite probably this cup vanished after her death, its special and supernatural role unrecognised.

Rachel's fame spread, and in 1895 Lord Bute, a patron of the Society for Psychical Research, sent a commissioner to interview her as part of a survey into psychic phenomena. Lord Bute had originally asked Revd Sinclair to perform the interview, but the minister declined – although he was able to reluctantly tolerate Rachel's psychic ability, he didn't want to actually endorse this heathen superstition. The commissioner found that Rachel was deeply Christian – she quoted several episodes in the Old Testament which proved to her satisfaction that second sight was alive and well (and God-approved) in Biblical times.

Rachel's last recorded vision was in 1900, when she was asked to find a Rannoch-born groom who had disappeared in England while in service. She 'saw' that he had been murdered and first buried in a quarry near the stables, but then thrown into a lake by the murderers. The police found the crime scene in the quarry and then dragged the lake and found the body.

Around the 1850s a wright in KINLOCH RANNOCH saw or heard people coming for coffins in advance of the actual death. He also heard the planes and hammers at work, making the coffins. The visions disturbed him so much he emigrated to Australia. If you look south from Kinloch Rannoch you can see the profile of the Sleeping Giant of Bunrannoch, one of the Fingalian heroes awaiting the call to action.

LOCH RANNOCH NORTH SIDE
Clach a' Mharsainte (Stone of the Packman). A wandering pedlar sat down by the stone to rest with his pack on the stone. The pack slipped down the other side and the loop at the front throttled him (NN65405887).
Clans of Rannoch Board 1: the 'Grove of Hanging Trees'. One tree has a modern notice – 'Gallows Tree 1764'.

By CRAIGANOUR (NN61715896) is the P-shaped Chieftain standing stone, 'Clach na h-Iobairte'*. On the side facing the loch there is a tiny incised inverted 'T', which you may see as an axehead. A healing well lurks somewhere nearby. There are several Clach na h-Iobairte ('Stone of the Sacrifice' or 'the Offering') in Highland Perthshire. The spirits could be entreated with offerings such as milk or grain; forget all thoughts of 'sacrifice' involving knives, blood and the like.

At AULICH in the eighteenth century the miller encountered something that called itself The Black Walker of the Ford. For more than a year after the first meeting the miller left home at dusk and headed to a copse about half a mile away, from which cries and yells were heard throughout the night. The miller returned before dawn with blood on his dirk, but in the daylight it always proved to be nothing but earth. On the last occasion of the nightly Miller and Black Walker contests, the noises were even louder than before and in the morning the snow revealed a foot, or knee-print, in the snow next to the miller's tracks. In a curious coda to this episode some years later a man from the area who had emigrated to America returned and entered the mill, which caused the miller to rant and rave and throw a pick at the man, telling him never to return. Was this man the Black Walker?

Board 2 describes the self-inflicted torment of Sir Alexander Menzies, who having finally beheaded his arch enemy the Chief of Clan MacGregor, learnt from a prophecy of Thomas the Rhymer that 'with the last of the MacGregors will go the last of the Menzies'. In his later life Sir Alexander believed he had brought disaster on his clan.

In the 1820s or '30s the tramping of horses and the rattling of a conveyance were heard after dark coming to the farmhouse of Liaran (now LEARAN), but the source was invisible. Four or five days later a hearse (until then unknown in the area) came from Appin of Menzies with the body of a cousin of the family, killed by a horse kick.

Out in the loch is EILEAN NAM FAOILEAG, Island of the Gulls, or Tower Island, an artificial crannog. Board 3 describes how for many years it sheltered the fierce and much-feared fugitive MacGregors. A Robertson of Struan used the island as a prison for his legitimate wife in order that he might swear to the father of another woman that he had no wife living on Scottish ground. (Exactly the same story is told about Loch Con in GLEN ERROCHTY). In the early nineteenth century Baron Grantly built a two-storey crenellated folly as a supposed reconstruction of this island prison. Now ruined, the tower is said to have an uneasy atmosphere – at least one person who spent the night there had a bad experience.

The householder's herd-boy son at ARDLARACH was found in the morning sitting by the fire, having been transported there by the fairies through the night from his post at the Spital, near Dalnarcardoch on the A9 west of Calvine – a distance of 12 miles. The door was barred from the inside, so the only access was via the chimney. The lad was always known afterwards as Dòmhnall Ruadh nan Sìthchean (Red Donald of the Fairies).

The area between Rannoch Station and Kinloch Rannoch is covered with hundreds of large glacial erratics deposited during a throwing contest between two giants who lived on Rannoch Moor. These Fomorians were tricked into the competition by a clever young man who, like all his neighbours, was sick of the giants' wicked behaviour. After two days and nights of continuous stone-chucking, the two final boulders, larger than anything that had been thrown before, came to rest at Bridge of Gaur. The winner of the contest was promptly crushed to death by the loser, who then himself died of exhaustion. The Fomorians are one of the monstrous non-human tribes who invaded Ireland in the ancient mythological cycle, The Book of Invasions. Another two giants, Anier and Anear, completely deforested Rannoch Moor during a battle lasting thirty days and nights, leaving it a treeless, difficult area, the largest wilderness left in Britain.

Just 3km northwest of RANNOCH STATION (NN410602) on the West Highland railway the boundary between Perthshire and Highland passes through the dark, remote LOCHAN A' CHLAIDHEIMH, the Loch of the Sword. In the seventeenth century, in an attempt to finally settle a long-running territorial dispute between the Camerons and the Atholl clansmen of Rannoch, Ewan Cameron of Lochiel and the Earl of Atholl agreed to meet at this then unnamed loch, each accompanied by just one man. As he set off Cameron was warned by a well known witch called Gormsuil (the Blue-eyed One) that the one agreed companion was not sufficient: 'If you go to meet a wolf you will need more hounds'. So Cameron took sixty-five of his best men and hid them in the heather by the loch. Cameron and Atholl met but both were too hot-headed to compromise and soon both drew their swords. Atholl gave a shrill whistle and fifty of his warriors appeared behind their chief. The next section of the event has the hallmarks of having been improved over the years. Atholl is supposed to have said, 'These are my Atholl wedders come to graze on the Lochaber grass'. (A wedder, or whether, is a castrated ram.) Lochiel gave his own signal, his men appeared, and said, 'These are my Lochaber dogs and they are gey hungry for the flesh of the Atholl wedders'. Atholl realised he was outnumbered and so gave way, renouncing his claim to the disputed land. To ratify the agreement a sword was thrown into the loch. In the summer of 1812 the level of the loch was very low and the sword was found by a herd boy. It was taken to Dr Thomas Ross in Fort William, but when the great and the good realised what it was, the sword was carried, with due solemnity, by twelve men back to the Loch of the Sword, where, Excalibur-like, it was thrown back into the water.

In a hollow on Loch Rannoch-side which had a name for being haunted, a man met a terrifying spirit in the hours of darkness, and fought with it until dawn, at which time he was found exhausted, scratched and bleeding, having spent the night battling with a bush.

LOCH RANNOCH SOUTH SIDE

A young man going home at night along the loch was joined by a funeral procession. One of the poles of the bier was thrust into his hands, and he had to march in the procession for more than a mile. He was on the lochside of the coffin, and had great difficulty in keeping on the road. The other bearers of the ghostly coffin were laying the weight on him to try and push him off the road into the loch. A boy in Rannoch saw and accurately described his grandmother's funeral several days before it happened. Board 5 of the Clan Trail describes the Solas Raineach, or the Rannoch Light. This anomalous light phenomenon has often been seen on Meall Dubh (the Black Hill) on the opposite (north) side of the loch. It appears to be a ball of fire that skims the surface of the loch and hovers over the hillside. Alasdair Alpin MacGregor in *Strange Tales of the Highlands & Islands* says most of the time it rises and disappears at regular spots a short distance apart on the loch surface, but sometimes rises above the water and rolls up the hill. The loch was also inhabited by the water-bull, whose existence was still being vouched for in 1834. (For other anomalous loch-light phenomena, see LOCH TAY and LOCH EARN.)

An old man in DRUIM-A-CHAOIN was sceptical of dreag (death lights). One night he was called to the door because a light was approaching. He stepped into the public road in front of his house right into the path of the light. When it reached him it stood in front of him. The old man gazed steadily at it and an indistinct and shadowy form became visible in the middle of it. It slowly placed its palms together and extended them towards him. Then it suddenly said 'Whish' and passed over his head. In the same district a young man confronted the death light, by sticking his dirk in the middle of the road and standing behind it. When the light came to the dirk it stopped and after a time the young man saw a child's face in the light. He bent down to draw the dirk from the road and as he did so the light passed over his head.

Board 6 tells a grim tale of love rivalry and multiple infanticide. A group of Camerons from Glen Nevis settled at CAMGHOURAN, and engaged in inter-necine tribal warfare with their traditional enemies the Mackintoshes. Ewan Cameron of Camghouran and a MacIntosh of Moy both wanted the same woman. Cameron was successful and the couple lived happily and raised a family of boys. But at a market in Perth Cameron unpleasantly gazumped MacIntosh over a bunch of arrows. MacIntosh swore revenge on his dirk and he and his men went hot-foot to Camghouran, where he tried to force the woman to go with him. She refused, so he took her sons and dashed their brains out one by one on a stone. In some versions he killed three, in another six, before she broke down and agreed to go with him. But then her husband and his clansmen arrived, and killed all but one of the MacIntoshes. The survivor swam across the loch, only to be killed by a MacGregor.

The fairies were busily engaged in building a bridge from Camghouran to Innis Droighinn when someone wished them God-speed. All work instantly stopped and never resumed.

The BLACK WOOD OF RANNOCH is an eerie place that cries out for stories of the supernatural. Distillers of illicit whisky in the wood would always put out the first portion in a saucer for the fairies. A hunter who lived at Tigh na Coile on the edge of the Black Wood was about to shoot a hind and her calf when the creatures changed into a woman and child he knew locally. Terrified he bolted for home, pursued by the pair in deer form. Each time he aimed his gun at them they shapeshifted back to humans. Exhausted and frightened, he finally stumbled beyond the tree line, which they did not cross.

What sounds very much like a folktale is told about a wolf which was chased into the Black Wood in the early eighteenth century. The hunters set fire to the wood but the wolf swam the entire length of the loch and ran for Ben a'Chuailaich. It followed the smell of food into the kitchen of the local mill. Ignoring the cooking food, it tried to drag an infant from its cradle…then the mother came in and attacked and killed the wolf with the potato masher. From then the mill was known as 'Millinwadie' – Mill of the Wolf.

Board 7 near CARIE is about the Robertsons, the chief clan in Rannoch in the old days. One of their most warlike chiefs was Alexander Struan Robertson, who famously took part in all three Jacobite rebellions of 1689, 1715 and 1745. His mother was apparently a terrifying individual. She was said to have starved her brother to death so that she could ensure the succession and when she went walking the crows would follow her in great numbers.

Clach na Boile, 'Stone of Fury', standing stone (NN66995798).

Clach Sgoilte, the Split Stone (NN681576), is said to have split in half vertically on the day of Culloden. A Stewart woman, whose husband was with the Prince, was living in a house near the stone. When the stone split she said, with second sight, 'The cause of the Prince is lost and I myself am a widow'.

Lassintullich burial ground, Pictish stone, GRAVESTONES (NN69545773).
St Peter's healing well, now supplying a horse trough (healthy horses!) (NN69585769).

When nighttime travellers forded a small stream crossing the road on its way into LOCHAN AN DAIM, also known as Lochan Doimeig (NN718573), they were escorted for about 20m by a Something which variously showed itself as a dog, billy goat or a dark moving mass. In 1824 a gardener who had been working further south set out to walk back home to Killichonan, but, having been last seen at Coshieville, did not arrive at his destination. Several days' searching proved fruitless, until a woman told the search party she had had a dream about cutting rushes at the lochan. Shortly afterwards a local man told them he had dreamt exactly the same scene. Lochan an Daim was investigated, and the dead gardener was found, lying on a green mound, stretched out on his front as if in the act of taking a drink from the stream.

DRUMCHASTLE was supposed to have been built by a man who discovered treasure through a coincidence of dreams. He had dreamed of a great treasure on the North Inch of Perth, but had failed to find it. Despondent, he was leaving when he fell into conversation with a man who told him he should not take dreams seriously. As an example of this, he himself had frequently dreamt of a great treasure hidden in a certain spot in Rannoch, but he knew it was not there. The Rannoch man, recognising his home turf in the description, hurried back, found a hoard of gold coins, and built Drumchastle castle.

SRÒN AN TÀCHAIR, the Ghost-haunted Nose, is a rock between Kinloch Rannoch and Drumchastle, 'where faint mysterious noises were heard, and on passing which the wayfarer was left by the mysterious sprite which joined him in the hollow below'.

KILLIECRANKIE

War is the crucible of folklore. Wherever there is danger, slaughter, courage, victory and defeat, there you'll find a collection of associated legends and tales. On 27 July 1689 at the Battle of Killiecrankie★★★ a Highland Jacobite army supporting the deposed James VII defeated 3,000 Government troops loyal to William III. The Jacobites were led by John Grahame of Claverhouse, Viscount Dundee - popularly known as Bonnie Dundee. Dundee was a charismatic man and successful general. His men thought there was something special about him – as if a higher source was protecting him in battle. His enemies said he had protection from the Devil, the proof being his black charger called Satan (but actually he rode a sorrel mare).

The night before the battle, Dundee was woken in his tent by a vision of a man with blood dripping from a head wound. The spectre told him to get up, but then vanished. The second time it pointed to its head and ordered Dundee to 'Remember Brown of Priesthill!', a reference to Dundee's killing of the Covenanter John Brown. Dundee shouted for the guards - but no-one had entered the tent. He returned to sleep, to be awoken by the third visitation, when the ghost pointed to the plain of Killiecrankie below and said, 'I'll meet thee yonder'. Dundee abandoned sleep and called in a Highland chief and told him what had happened, but made him swear not to say anything if the battle was successful. At the height of the battle, Dundee was shot and killed. The Highlanders may have won the fight, but they had lost their leader. Almost immediately the folklore machine started; Killiecrankie 1689 became a sort of 'Highland Dealey Plaza'. There were dozens of claimants for who fired the fateful bullet, from where, and with what anti-supernatural weapons system. The favoured theory had Claverhouse killed by a silver bullet. In one version as he stooped to water his horse his plumed helm dragged up his steel jacket, and he was shot in the spine. John Howie of Lochgoin, a virulent anti-Jacobite, wildly claimed that 'his own waiting-servant, taking a resolution to rid the world of this truculent bloody monster, and knowing that he had proof of lead, shot him with a silver button he had taken off his own coat for that purpose' (quoted in Andrew Murray Scott's *Bonnie Dundee*). Dundee was buried at St Bride's Kirk, next to BLAIR CASTLE. Some time later it was dug up and his armour was stolen from the grave by tinkers. The body was re-buried (it's now under metal covers in the ruined church) and the armour eventually turned up at Blair Castle, where it can still be seen, but with a bullet hole in the centre of the chest when it is thought he was shot in the armpit when raising his arm.

The Pass of Killiecrankie. An excellent visitor centre tells the story of the battle, including the famous Soldier's Leap.

The Duke of Atholl thought this was too ignominious an end for a great hero, so he 'improved' the story by having his ghillie fire through the centre of the breastplate. We know this because the bullet has clearly been fired from the inside.

'Claverhouse's Stone'(NN90826319) is actually a prehistoric standing stone. A plaque on a small mound called Tomb Clavers or Mount Clavers (NN90506365) states that the mound marks the graves of the officers of both sides. In 2003 excavations showed this was just a memorial, with no burials.

Lord Balcarras of Colinsburgh was imprisoned in Edinburgh Castle on suspicion of Jacobitism. About daybreak his close friend Claverhouse appeared to him, drawing aside the curtain of the bed and looking straight at the Earl. Claverhouse then moved towards the mantelpiece, leaned against it for a while, and walked out of the chamber.

The earl called out repeatedly to his friend, but received no answer. The following day he learned about Dundee's death.

Some aspects of these stories can be traced, at least in its popular form, to Walter Scott. He coined the term Bonnie Dundee, a hero in *Old Mortality* (1816). In 'Wandering Willie's Tale' in *Redgauntlet* Dundee is a murdered ghoul, one hand clasped over the wound made by the silver bullet. In *Guy Mannering*, Bertram Donohoe, Laird of Ellengowan, joins Dundee at Killiecrankie – but it's Donohoe killed by a silver bullet.

Many people have had, and continue to have, strange experiences at Killiekrankie. The main focus is usually the anniversary of the battle, 27 July. Peter Underwood, in *This Haunted Isle*, mentions two people he talked to at the site, a local man from Pitlochry and a visitor. On separate occasions each had seen and heard Highlanders charging down the valley to the gorge and then disappearing. They also saw a red glow and heard the sounds of distant battle. One summer a cyclist touring the area stopped overnight on a rock at the foot of one of the cliffs. Her amazing encounter was told to Elliott O'Donnell who repeated it in her words in *Casebook of Ghosts*. At almost 2 a.m. she was woken by the sound of firearms. Then over the next few minutes she experienced a series of scenes from the battle: a Highlander running with huge bounds; the sounds of drums, fifes and flutes; and 'what appeared to be a whole army of scarlet-clad soldiers away at the far end of the pass with a mounted officer at the head'. She particularly noticed how tall the marching men seemed and, as they grew nearer, she clearly saw the white, set faces in the red glow that hung over the whole scene. She watched as they passed and disappeared round the bend of the Pass and listened as the marching sounds slowly died away. After the army passed an ash tree on the opposite side of the road swayed violently (there was no wind) and moaned and groaned. She tried to flee but could not. At this point she actually kicked against a body of an English soldier with a terrible wound in his chest. Then she saw dozens of bodies, men and horses, Highlanders and Englishmen, gory and silent. A Highland girl dropped from the ash tree and robbed the corpses of the English, cutting off fingers to get the rings and murdering ten wounded men in the process. In the most astonishing part of this account the corpse-robber actually saw the witness at this point, and rushed at her with a scream of rage. The witness conveniently fainted and when she came to it was morning and all the ghosts had gone. The whole encounter is vividly written, with precise description, such as a fleeing Highlander having a shoe buckle missing and a seam burst on his coat near the shoulder. This contrasts with mundane details as she tried to focus on the everyday in between the encounters – taking the fat off her beef sandwiches, and repairing a skirt button.

'Many years ago' a group of riders approaching the Pass met a tall figure in a cowl or hood. As it approached their horses panicked and subsequently refused to enter the Pass. This figure had been seen before, always at the same spot. At 12.40 a.m. on the night of 27/28 July 1955 (the anniversary of the battle) a man from Dundee and a companion were terrified to see five or six people in cloaks and three-pointed hats carrying an old-fashioned lantern. They were talking – one thing they said was 'Where do we go now?' The staff at the NTS centre have numerous stories told to them by visitors, such as a woman and her sons, entirely ignorant of the anniversary, experiencing a sense of terror and cold on a hot sunny on 27 July. Another man had heard the marching of an army near Pitlochry the night before.

I have one slight problem with hauntings taking place on the anniversary. The battle took place on 27 July 1689. Just sixty-three years later Britain adopted the Gregorian calendar; an eleven-day adjustment was needed to correct the former Julian calendar to match the reality of the seasons. Thus 2 September 1752 was followed by 14 September. So, unless the dead made the same calendrical adjustment as the living, this means the actual anniversary of the battle is 7 August.

BLAIR ATHOLL. Old Blair (formerly the Atholl estate factor's house, and before that a coaching inn, NN86766658) has a history of hauntings. Sometime just before 1920 the householder, Mrs Forbes, was recovering from influenza and had woken from a broken sleep to see a woman dressed in grey at the end of the bed. As Mrs Forbes looked, the grey lady disappeared. Much later, when another family moved in to the house, the daughter dreamt of a lady dressed in grey sitting in a walk-in cupboard. In the dream, the lady shovelled coal on her pillow – and indeed the bed was against a blocked fireplace. Then an aunt and her fiancé came for a visit. The aunt woke up in the middle of the night to see a figure of a woman, who was giving off a sense of evil. She was dressed in a black gown and moved from the bed to behind a curtain. Simultaneously, the fiancé was thrashing about in a nightmare. When he was awoken by his partner switching on the light, he explained he had been fighting off a woman in black who had been trying to harm him. And shortly later, a Church of England canon was visiting and slept in the same room. On preparing to sleep he sensed something sinister, so sprinkled some holy water (from St Alkmund's well in Derbyshire) on the bedclothes in the sign of the cross. This was something he had never done before. After this apotropaic ritual, he slept soundly.

St Brides Church★, Old Blair (NN86746649). Leaning against the church wall is a slab with twelve deep hollows which looks like a cupmarked stone but was probably a cresset stone, the hollows containing oil for torches.
Blair Castle★★, mythological statues around grounds; The Whim, Gothick folly.
Fairy Knoll, cairn – 'the Sighichin, or fairies, witnessed the legal transactions contracted on the hill' (OSA) (NN89876497).
Clach na h'Iobairt, Stone of the Offering, standing stone (NN87626526).
The Wade Stone, erected 1729 by General Wade when the road was first constructed, moved for the new A9 (formerly at NN69227166, now NN69327169).

Left: Pass of Killiecrankie. High up on the Victorian railway viaduct is a strange carved face. No-one knows what it is, who did it or why it is there.

Below: Modern painted cross at the south end of the Pass. Is it here to commemorate the victims of the battle or to lay the ghosts?

The local kirk recorded accusations of witchcraft and wishing evil:

29 May 1720, Blair Atholl – Elspet Robertson accused of imprecations against James McLaren, making his right hand swell and be so sick he was like to die.

14 October 1744, Strowan - Margaret Robertson accused of imprecating and wishing ill to Robert Robertson in Milntoun of Invervack.

21 May 1749, Blair Atholl – John Robertson in Wester Balhuain used charms on John Tossich's cow in Wester Monzie. He was accused of saying Elspeth McLauchlan had used witchcraft to sicken the cow, but in the kirk session denied it. Note that witchcraft ceased to be a capital crime in 1735, but clearly the belief in witchcraft persisted.

GLENTILT

John (JW) Dunne, author of mystical works such as *An Experiment with Time, The Serial Universe, The New Immortality and Nothing Dies*, had been experimenting with flying machines since 1900. In 1904, just one year after Kittyhawk, he built his first plane. Secret tests were conducted by the War Office, with the plane being driven by road and assembled in secret in a field up Glen Tilt in 1907. It was tested then and flown (by Dunne) the following year. It was tail-less, had backward-sloping wings and incorporated aerodynamic ideas from the zannonia leaf (of the cucumber family). It was very stable but lacked speed and manoeuvrability and was not taken up. This was probably the first powered flight in Britain.

One day the ground opened up at the confluence of the rivers Tilt and Fender and the men of the area disappeared down a hole at Tildune (Toil Daoine, 'hole of the men') and re-appeared across the river as oxen in Toldamh (Toll Daimh: 'hole of the oxen').

BEINN A' GHLO is a massive mountain east of Glen Tilt (NN9773). The Witch of Beinn a' Ghlo was infamous in the area, featuring in many shieling tales. William Scrope, in *Days of Deer Stalking* (1883) described her as 'of a very mischievous and malevolent disposition, driving cattle into morasses, where they perish, and riding the forest horses by night, till covered with mire and sweat they drop down from fatigue and exhaustion. She has the power of taking the shape of an eagle, raven, hind or any other animal that may suit her purpose. She destroys bridges and allures people to the margin of the flood by exhibiting a semblance of floating treasures, which they lose their lives grasping at'. Two Braemar poachers, Big John MacHardy and Donald Gruer, out in bad weather, came across a bothy in a small glen unknown to them near Glen Tilt. An old woman opened the door and told them they were expected. She fitted the stereotype of a witch – gaunt, sunken-eyed, long black hair and a tendency to chant weird songs and cackle. She indicated a rope with three knots: 'If I loose the first a soft wind will blow to gladden the hunter's heart; if I loose the second a strong blast will sweep over the hills; if I loose the third a terrific storm will arise that neither man nor beast will endure. The blast will stream down the corries, and this bare arm

Blair Castle. 'When the white cows come to Blair, the wheel of Blair Mill will turn round seven times with people's blood' (Thomas the Rhymer). White cattle arrived in the 1850s without sanguinary consequences.

will guide the course of the storm as I sit on my throne of Craig Gower on the top of Ben a' Ghlo'. It was clear she had brought the poachers to her door in the hope they would be carrying a recently-killed deer, for even as she served fresh salmon to the terrified men, she criticised them for bringing no venison. Their forfeit was to promise to deliver a fat hind for her at Fraser's Cairn at midnight on the first Monday of every month during the hind season. Failure to deliver would mean death on the mountains. The poachers promised to do as they were bid, and fell asleep. In the morning the hag had gone. There are many versions of this story; one of the best is in Affleck Grey's *Legends of the Cairngorms*. The *OSA* mentions Po-nam-ban, a pool into which bad women were thrown, near here, and describes a cave on the south side of the mountain. From a narrow mouth it opened out, narrowed again, then descended 'deeper than ever any person had the courage to venture'. A burn could be diverted into it; the people of the village far below would then hear the noise of water.

An unusual vampire story took place in about 1923 at an old bothy near FEALAR, a very remote shooting lodge (NO009799) northwest of Glen Tilt; it is not clear whether the bothy was at this lodge or was just in the vicinity. Two poachers wanted to stay the night but the door was locked, so they broke a window to gain entry. They lit a fire and one started to climb back out through the window to fetch water, when something tore at his leg and started sucking his blood. The pain was great – and so was his terror – but he managed to free himself. Both the men then bravely climbed out through the window and searched the area. All they could see were some white-winged objects and faint blue lights moving to and fro in the distance. They burst the door open, cooked a meal, and did not sleep a wink all night. The next day another search revealed nothing but their own footsteps. The bitten man carried the scars for the rest of his life and neither poacher ever returned to the area. The bothy seemed to have an evil reputation among the older inhabitants, although it is hard to tell if this existed before the vampire incident.

BRUAR

The antiques shop keeps the holdings of the mothballed Clan Donnachahidh (Robertson) Museum, including the Clach na Brataich, or Stone of the Standard, a magic piece of rock crystal used to cure diseases by dipping it in water three times. The afflicted person or animal then drank the charmed water. This was still taking place in the 1820s, when the Chief, Captain Alexander Robertson, would dip the crystal in a great china bowl filled with spring water (from a fairy spring or holy well) which he then distributed to a number of people who had come great distances to obtain it. A story of the origin of the Stone has it being found stuck to the bottom of the clan standard the night before the Battle of Bannockburn in 1314. Ever since, the Stone was carried by the Chief during times of war, and its varying colour foretold the outcome of the battle. These days, there is a very obvious flaw in the 5cm diameter sphere. This appeared on the eve of the Battle of Sherrifmuir in the Jacobite Rebellion of 1715. The battle marked the beginning of the decline of the Clan, ending with the loss of their lands.

Clach Na h-Iobairt, Stone of the Offering, standing stone★ (NN82146590).

STRUAN Church; GRAVESTONES★, Pictish Stone★, cross-marked possible preaching stone★ (NN80896534), was formerly dedicated to St Fillan. In times of drought (rare in Scotland!) the saint's statue was used as a rain charm, being dipped in the nearby St Fillan's Well, 'Tobar Faolen', at the foot of Tom an Tigh Mhor, a motte (NN807365360). Somehow the practice survived the Reformation, until the minister, John Hamilton, smashed the statue and flung the broken pieces into the Garry around 1717-1720. Soon afterwards his son died insane. The water from the well was reputed to cure insanity. For the story of St Fillan's Bell see PERTH MUSEUM.

Mystical Medicine: Clach an Druchasd, the whooping cough stone (NN818653) has a water-filled hollow. The cure was only effective if the water was drunk from a spoon made from the 'quick' horn of a living cow. People were bringing their children here as late as 1860. A rheumatism well, Tigh an tobar (NN82316542), was still visited on the first Sunday in May until the 1850s. A woman, crippled with rheumatism for many years, had been carried over the hill in a wheelbarrow. Having bathed in the spring, she walked the four miles home. The trees around the well were covered with various offerings, and coins and buttons were thrown into the water.

On the summit of Struan Point is An Teampan, Temple of Struan (NN787653), a conspicuous knoll with commanding views of Glen Garry. It is ringed by an ancient stone dyke and was planted with a circle of larch trees. Local historian John Kerr calls this 'a mysterious place' for it was clearly something important in earlier times and the name is suggestive.

At the head of GLEN ERROCHTY is Càrn na Sleabhach ('the Rock-Pile of the Gullies'), a fairy haunt. J.G. Campbell reports how a widow asked Alastair Chaluim, a peripatetic diviner, for her husband's whereabouts. Using a dòduman, a small four-sided spinning top, he replied: 'he is a baggage horse to the Fairies in Slevach Cairn, with a twisted willow within his mouth'. (I haven't been able to find the mound; was it submerged under the Loch Errochty reservoir?) An excise officer fled the ruined building northwest of Errochty Dam (NN6996630) after being pestered by 'supernatural beings' which were actually locals dressed as ghosts. A Robertson chief, Duncan the Fat, Donnachaidh Reamhair, married a wealthy woman from Lennox, but when he grew tired of her he tied her to a stake in an underground cave on the Isle of Dogs, in Loch Chon, (NN668679). He could thus swear that he had no wife living above ground and went off to woo the daughter of the chieftain of Glen Tilt. A duplicate story is told of another Robertson chief (or the same one?) in LOCH RANNOCH. Duncan was haunted by his former wife, a thin, white-faced spectre with eyes blood-red from weeping. At his death the chief was carried away by twelve ravens.

Achanruidh cupmarked rock, probably a 'bore-stone' for a flag (NN79416397).

A herdsboy called Iain spent the summers at the sheilings by the waterfall at NN623686. During one exceptionally dry season his cattle, starved and weak, went missing in the mist. When he found them they were eating rich green grass in a high corrie. He heard the grass singing a sweet song and realised he was in fairy territory. When he took the cattle down to the lochside to be milked, the previously dry beasts filled every pail available and then some.

LOCH ERICHT (NN5066), hides a drowned village, Eadail (or Feadaill), destroyed in some great flood. As with similar stories worldwide, buildings are said to be visible at the bottom of the loch in clear weather, and on calm evenings the church bell can still be heard tolling in the submarine currents. A man fishing from a boat at the west end of the loch pulled up with his anchor a gravestone marked 'Elspet Robertson died 1545'. This date is several hundred years later than the supposed inundation – for which there is absolutely no evidence. Ewen Òg, the shepherd at Coire Bhachdaidh (or Bhacaidh), (NN550720), first became aware of fairy visitors when he noticed small pits in his porridge – subsequent observations confirmed it was the little people pecking at the food when he put it out to cool in the evening. Ewen carved wooden dishes and spoons at a fairy scale, and encouraged his guests to use these rather than snack on his own larger dish. Over time the fairies started socialising with the shepherd in his remote bothy. One evening a female fairy came along, but there was no spoon or dish for her. She sat on the other side of the hut, not speaking but constantly grinning and making faces. Presumably this was fairy facial communication for 'can I have some food please?' but Ewen did not take the hint and asked her, 'Are you always like that, my lively maid?' The Gaelic word he used for 'maiden' can also be translated as 'twiglet'. Either his inept questioning or his lack of hospitality caused some offence and the fairies never again visited Ewen.

The northern border of Perthshire at the Drumochter Pass is marked by two distinctive adjacent mountains west of the A9: the Sow of Atholl, which is completely in Perthshire, and the Boar of Badenoch, across whose top the county border runs. The Boar had a reputation for some kind of mysterious phenomenon called the Spectre of the Boar, and also for being haunted by the ghosts of Duncan Macpherson, clan chief of the Macphersons of Crubenmor, and his ghillie. Affleck Grey recounts how sometime before the Second World War a gentleman named Henry Tegner was hunting deer in the area (NN *c*.621763) with his stalker Kennedy and a ghillie. It was a decent October day, dry, with low cloud. They spotted a herd on the Boar and, leaving the ghillie hidden near the foot, Tegner and Kennedy approached. Then the sun broke through the clouds and on the summit of the mountain they saw two huge figures. At first they appeared to travel at great speed across a streak of mist that now covered the peak, but then the giants stopped and looked down at the two frightened men from a distance of a hundred metres or so. After a moment, the figures faded into the mist, leaving an indelible 'supernatural' impression on the two men The deer were now gone, and when questioned the ghillie said he not seen anything of the mysterious figures. The stalker was convinced they had witnessed the Spectre, but on reflection Tegner noted the two figures seemed to mimic, in an exaggerated way, the movements of himself and Kennedy. They probably experienced a 'Glory' – a combination of sunlight and cloud or mist in which the viewer's shadow is magnified and projected onto the clouds. It can sometimes be seen from an aircraft when flying above the clouds (and may have given rise to associated UFO reports) and is not uncommon in the changing weather conditions in mountain areas. I've experienced something like it myself, and the effect is startling and eerie.

WEST OF PERTH

HUNTINGTOWER

A stormbound traveller took emergency lodging on the first floor of Huntingtower Castle★ (HS). The man woke in the night to find a distressed woman with green sleeves standing behind an empty chair. She vanished, leaving behind what appeared to be old bloodspots on the chair. The traveller spent a sleepless night and left the next morning.

Three days later he fell out of the ferryboat while crossing the Tay and drowned.

Several masked men burst into a lonely house on the estate and were about to murder an old man for his (non-existent) money when 'Lady Greensleeves' appeared at the window, scaring the robbers off and saving the old man's life. In another cottage nearby a young boy lay seriously ill. His widowed mother left the house briefly to search for a neighbour who was supposed to be fetching medicine from Perth. When she returned the boy was in full health, having been visited by the ghost, who had stroked his head three times and took the sickness away. The boy described her as having blue eyes, long blonde hair, and wearing a green dress with pearls on her sleeves. The lad lived long enough to tell the story to his grandchildren.

There was a chapel and holy well dedicated to St Convall here, near the mill-lade (NO c. 077255). In 1618, sixteen women were censured by the Kirk Session of Perth for superstitiously drinking from the well and depositing pins and headlaces.

Dog graves (NO07302568).
Cists (NO054260).
Neolithic burial mound NO069249).
Pit-circle/possible stone circle (NO39079251).

METHVEN
Violet Mar of 'Kildies' (either Culdeesland just south of Methven or Culdees near Muthill) was executed in Edinburgh on 24 October 1577 for using 'incantations, invocation of spirits and sorcery' in an attempt to kill the Regent Morton. Violet was probably from the higher levels of society; assizes were made up from the accused's peers, and Violet was judged by an assize of lairds. The political nature of the crime – an act of treason – also suggests she was a world away from the peasant brand of magical healing and petty cursing. There are three known attempts against the Regent's life: 1561, 1572 and June 1577. They did not involve magic. Violet's attempt is not recorded officially, and neither is her sentence. The historian of witchcraft P.G. Maxwell-Stuart (*Satan's Conspiracy*) suggests it was deliberately omitted and the case buried: a government cover-up! In 1643 John McIlvorie was implicated by another witch and put on trial in Crieff. The details of the case are scant and the sentence is unknown. Then the months of May and July 1662 saw a major outbreak of witch-hunting in the parish – many were accused and several executed. A clue as to what might have been going on is the Privy Council's notes about one of the cases – they urged caution about the use of torture, and the accused was to confess voluntarily and be of legal and mental competency to stand trial. 'Witches Wood' is at NO022262 on the west edge of the village.

The 23m high and very old Pepperwell Oak at the private and restored Methven Castle is supposed to have a stone in its heart, but it must be cut up to ascertain this. A house on the east side of the street leading from the Square to the Den still has inside it a water-filled well, covered with a grille. A sexton who was known to enjoy a drink fell asleep in a grave he had just dug. Some of the local scallywags placed the boards over the grave. When the gravedigger woke up he struggled through the boards and, seeing the burial yard empty on the Day of Judgement, said, 'Aye, it's a poor turnout for Methven'. (Thanks to Ross Young for this.) GRAVESTONES.

South of Methven is Tippermallo (NO022245), the home of Sir John Moncrieff, author of a hugely popular book called *Tippermalloch's Receipts, or The Poor Man's Physician*, first published in 1712 when the author was eighty-four years old. The 'receipts', or recipes, provided bizarre cures for every ill that flesh is heir to. Here are some of the cures:

Epilepsy – Take a skull from a grave and burn and powder the bone. Men can only be cured by a male cranium, and women by a female (see DOWALLY for an example).
Lethargy – Take the whole skin of a hare, including the ears and nails and drink hot as a powder.
Paralysis – anoint the parts with ointment made from earthworms.
Deafness – mix ants' eggs with the juice of an onion and drop it into the ear.
Measles – keep a sheep in the bedroom for the animal to draw the illness into itself.
Sleeplessness – apply living creatures to the head.
Pleurisy – take a mixture of ten parts carduus water (thistle water) to one part wild goat's blood.
Colic – apply a live duck, frog or suckling puppy to the part. NB this will kill the animal.
Over-eating – tie a piece of the iron-rich stone called eagle stone to the arm.
Headache – apply snails bruised in their shells to the forehead. Snails applied to the soles of the feet cures pestilential fever.
Whitlow in the finger (a painful inflammation) – put the finger into a cat's ear and it will be whole in half an hour.
Mania – wear amulets around the neck.

And some beauty tips:

To make hair golden – wash the hair in a solution of ivy ash.
To achieve clear skin – wash the face in the distilled water of snails.
To achieve a healthy 'outdoor' complexion – take the liver of a freshly-killed sheep and apply it to the face.
To counter baldness – burn doves' dung or small frogs; make a paste of the ash, and apply it to the scalp.

FOWLIS WESTER parish church★★ (NN928241) houses two superb Pictish stones. The spectacular taller stone has inevitably attracted folklore and fantasy. Two nine-teenth-century accounts (Mackinlay and Korner, see bibliography) claim it once stood at Bal-na-Croisk, near the entrance to the SMA' GLEN. In one version it was a memorial to a Roman soldier killed at the supposed battle of Fendoch in AD84, and was moved to Fowlis Wester when the church was built in the thirteenth century and the images then carved on it. In this story its original position was on the east side of the churchyard, and a Sunday shoe fair was held around it to entice people to attend church. The *NSA* says the stone records an actual event: during a wolfchase (the dog and riders) the beast ran through the village and bit the head of a boy (the man in the monster's jaws). There is nothing to support any of these stories. In September 1996, after their experiences of using dowsing rods on the Pictish stones in the museum at MEIGLE, Hilary Wilding and Nick Brazil's divining rods moved when brought close to this stone. The other cross-slab was found during restoration of the church in the early 1930s and is in superb condition. The rest of the site is also full of interest. The church, which has been built and rebuilt for centuries, has a lepers' squint and an inscribed aumbry. The churchyard archway is carved with the words 'Tak heid to thy foot when tho entrest the House of God, 1644' with the Hebrew word for Jehovah above (this is the Tetragrammaton, a word of great magical power). On the top of this gateway there used to be an ash tree that featured in a prophecy attributed (inevitably) to Thomas the Rhymer: 'When the tree is strong enough to bear a swallow's nest, the kirk will be surrounded by troopers; and when the tree can bear a crow's nest the kirk will be surrounded by cannon'. The first part of the prophecy is held to have come true when Sir Patrick Murray of Ochtertyre surrounded the church with troops one Sunday in an attempt to obtain the parochial registers – Murray wanted the names of all the men in the parish so he could help them 'volunteer' for the militia he was raising to fight Napoleon. The local women, however, had other thoughts on the subject and hid the registers under their clothes and made off with them. Unfortunately for the second part of the prophecy the tree was removed in the late nineteenth century before it could grow too large to damage the arch (William Marshall, *Historic Scenes in Perthshire*). A broken recumbent slab behind the church bears a carved sword and axe and a large cross-carved stone lies hidden beneath the new path. GRAVESTONES.

Tumulus and standing stone (NN92712329).
Stone pair** (NN92032404).
Cupmarked stone** (NN92092397).
Two stone circles and standing stones (NN924249).

ABERCAIRNEY

In 1589 John Millar of Middle Cairnie and Marjory Blaikie of Cairnie were accused of the bewitching and murder of Williame Robertsoun, but there are no further details in the judicial records. Fairy Knowe (NN91222348): 'a Si'un, a mount of peace, where the Druids held assizes and kindled large bonfires called Samhin or the fire of peace' (*NSA*). Hallowe'en fires were still being lit here in Victorian times.

Chambered cairn* (NN89242347).
Fort, home to Comhal, Fingal's father, defeated by the Romans at Fendoch (NN89052351).

MONZIE Castle (private) claims to have the world's three longest-lasting lightbulbs, installed in 1911. Their age was confirmed by an expert (it appears there are experts on historic light bulbs!).

Until, perhaps, the 1950s local boys and girls competed for the Wasp Cup, a silver cup presented to the child who handed in the most queen wasps stuck on a card for annual inspection. They got 1d or ½d per wasp, so there was keen rivalry and some cards had thirty or forty queens (each queen can produce 10,000 wasps).

Boys from forty-two nations attended the 1939 Rover Scout Moot at the castle; a photograph in Colin Mayall's *Around Crieff and Strathearn* shows Peter McGregor, piper to the Laird of Monzie, posing with the be-kilted dummy which was thrown from the battlements of the castle each morning as 'an old Scottish tradition'.

The stately pile itself has carved stone gables, initials and mottos in three ancient languages. The Witch's Stone★, by the castle drive (NN87982431) is associated with Kate McNiven (see CRIEFF) and is one of the sites given for her death. In 1936 the stone stood in the middle of a Roman road-like causeway 120m long, but there is no visible evidence of this now, and a burial mound which may have been associated with the stone has also disappeared. There was a healing spring in the area but in the 1770s two trees which grew over it fell, and 'the virtue of the well fell with them' (*OSA*).

Stone circle, cupmarked stone★★ and vanished subterranean feature (NN88162417).
Two stones from possible destroyed stone circle (NN87982517).
Cupmarked rocks (NN88972700, 88102756, 88102731, 88382706, 91112598, 91122597 and 88772633). One has 'figures of people's feet, with those of the hooves of horses, cows and sheep' (*OSA*).

In 1593 John Campbell of Ardkinglass on the west coast consulted a Margaret Cambell about a murder he had committed and how she could help by getting various Lorn witches to assist him. Ardkinglass asked Margaret if her witches named God or Christ in their incantations and she replied they did. He then said he knew a man whose magic was much more powerful because he did not use the holy names, and he had seven demons or spirit-guides attending him. This was Patrick MacQueen, the minister of Monzie (he was appointed to the parish in 1595 and is recorded as minister in Rothesay in 1589). One might assume it was unusual for a Protestant minister to be a practising witch (P.G. Maxwell-Stuart, *Satan's Conspiracy*).

The SMA' GLEN is a feast of archaeological curiosities and folklore. A Bronze Age bronze hoard was found at Corrymuckloch (NN89533507) in 1995. The high status objects were deposited in a peat bog. A half-metre long cross★ is carved onto a boulder at the mouth of Glen Fender (NN90773757); there are two possible cupmarks at the base of the shaft. Could the cross be designed to counteract the terrible pagan powers of all the prehistoric rock art nearby? Fingal lived near the Roman fort at Fendoch, and later, when Gara had burned his house, in the Iron Age hillfort on

Dùn Mór (NN90773032). His father Comhal is buried under a cairn in the area. About 1730 soldiers under General Wade were building the highway and needed to move a huge stone: doing so took vast labour using levers and jacks, until it tumbled over and over out of the way. A Captain Burt, Wade's English officer of engineers, left a first hand account in *Letters from a Gentleman in the North of Scotland*: 'Digging a little into that part of the ground where the centre of the base has stood, there was found a small cavity, about 2ft square, stone-lined, containing ashes, scraps of bones and half-burnt ends of stalks of heath…soon after the discovery was known to the Highlanders, they assembled from distant parts…carefully gathered up the relics, and marched with them, in solemn procession, to a new place of burial, and there discharged their firearms over the grave, as supposing the deceased had been a military officer' [my informant, himself a native of the hills, said] 'they believe that if a dead body should be known to lie above ground or be disinterred by malice, or the accident of torrents of water &c., and care was not immediately taken to perform to it the proper rites, then there would arise such storms and tempests as would destroy their corn, blow away their huts, and all sorts of other misfortunes would follow till that duty was performed'.

Today Ossian's Stone★★ (NN89533060) remains as a huge upright boulder by the road but can Burt's account be taken at face value? Toppling this behemoth just once would be a major undertaking; making it tumble over and over seems unlikely in the extreme. And what about the cist? The stone is massive – and there is no example in the British Isles of a prehistoric burial covered by a single titanic rock. All in all, Burt's story may have been as embroidered as James Macpherson's fake 'The Poems of Ossian' (1796) which belatedly gave the stone its name. The entire site within the fences is a scheduled monument filled with intriguing lumps and bumps. There are the remains of a wall (a report of 1791 mentions a circular dyke 200ft in circumference and 3ft high) and two small (prehistoric?) stones. The hillock nearest the road is traditionally the Soldier's Mound. During General Wade's road-making one of the soldiers died and was interred here. Over a century later two veteran troopers decided to drink to the memory of the comrade buried in the mound. The toast was given, 'Honour to the brave fellow who sleeps beneath!' and then a loud voice was heard as if from the mound: 'Ay, ay, lads, wait 'til I get a sneeshan!' The prankster was Neil Gow, famous fiddler and Perthshire's eighteenth-century version of Jimi Hendrix.

Giant's Grave standing stone and cairn (NN90452962).
Cupmarks (NN89733543, 89323529, 89173508, 89043469, 89293532 and 89273521).

UPPER GLEN ALMOND. The narrow glen following the Allt Coire Chultrain southwest from the ford over the River Almond southeast of Conichan gives access to a series of remote sites which demonstrate the way names, legends and places can be confused, especially by writers who have never been to the area. The *OSA* described a cave on Eagle's Rock (NN833318) which could hide sixty warriors and

Ossian's Stone. 'Does then the Bard sleep here indeed? / Or is it but a groundless creed? / What matters it? – I blame them not / Whose Fancy in this lonely Spot / Was moved; and in such way expressed / Their notion of its perfect rest.... therefore, was it rightly said / That Ossian, last of all his race! / Lies buried in this lonely place.' (William Wordsworth, *Memorials Of A Tour In Scotland*)

was where Gara fled after burning Fingal's house. If there is a cave here then it has remained invisible even to the shepherd who has worked twenty years in the area. Near this cave was the only tree in the vicinity, a tall pine; death came to anyone cutting a branch from it. Continuing southwest 1.5km from here (NN828305) is the Thief's Cave, with the same 'tree of fate' story. Here it was an oak and the cave was home to the notorious sheepstealer Alastair Bane. One night, wanting to roast a fat fowl but having no spit, he tore a branch from the tree and the fire led his pursuers to Alastair and eventually Alastair to the gallows. Again, there is no cave here, just a rock face with scattered boulders. Midway on the moorland between these two non-caves (NN83393120), and marked on the 1:25000 map as 'Shelter', is the real deal: a pile of six huge, natural boulders standing out impressively in the largely featureless landscape and creating a space big enough to park a car in. This is the cave supposedly on Eagle's Rock. It's completely natural but, again, several writers have misidentified it as the Kirk of The Wood (or Kirk of the Grove or Church on the Green), an evocative name in Scottish history because the last time it was used was supposed to be when sixty men (or twice this, depending on who is telling the story) took the sacrament on the way to fight (and die) at Culloden. But there's no chapel here. One hundred and forty metres east of here are the low drystone walls of some kind of building; the NW-SE orientation is wrong for a religious building so this has probably been mistaken for the chapel. Twentieth-century writers with a certain mindset have taken to calling the rock shelter, for no good reason, the Druid's Cave or Druid's Stone. It is, however, in the Middle of Nowhere, the kind of 'Nowhere' which allows your imagination room to roam, especially if you've just taken shelter in it from the predatory weather. What may be the lone pine tree of the legend is still there, to the north on the view down to Glen Almond, standing stark and weatherbeaten in an otherwise treeless landscape.

Somewhere in Upper Glenalmond there may be a large stone called Clach-a Buachaille, the herdsman's stone. A shepherd dreamt a treasure was hidden under it, and as he passed it each morning and evening he thought he could hear the clink of gold. Early on a summer morning he started digging, but when his spade struck the earth he heard a shrill voice cry: 'Black John! Black John! Beware of that stone!' He looked around and saw no-one, so went back to work. Again the warning came, but again he ignored it. But his labours had undermined the stone, and it collapsed on him and killed him. If he was alone and he died on the spot, one wonders how any-one else knew what happened?

Tomenbowie burial ground (NN83633248), GRAVESTONES★.
Clach na Tiompan chambered tomb and standing stone★★ (NN83013284).
Stone circle (NN82593299).

GLEN QUAICH

A dragon lived on the crannog close to the southwest shore of Loch Freuchie, guard-ing a rowan tree whose red berries could heal wounds and prolong life. The hero Froach (Freuchie) dared the dragon and stole the berries to heal his beloved, but the lass's wicked mother sent him back for more and on the second attempt the reptile nabbed him. His sweetheart bravely swam out to Froach with a dagger, but both hero and dragon died in the fight. The story's origins are in 'The Lay of Froach', an ancient fragment of the Fingalian cycle of stories. Exactly the same story is found in Ireland, Loch Awe and the Ross of Mull, which shows the way itinerant storytellers – just like stand-up comedians – adapt their material to the local audience.

A urisk called Adaidh lived in Glen Lochan, the short pass between Glens Quaich and Almond (NN8435). His cave is at the foot of a rock near Lochan a' Mhuilinn. Unlike most urisks, he seems to have been a benevolent spirit, tending flocks and looking after sick sheep (indeed, he is credited with introducing sheep farming to the area, which would make him a mighty age indeed). One night a Glen Almond woman was about to give birth. Adaidh took a horse from the stable and rode to Glen Quaich, bringing the midwife back with him. As they were passing Adaidh's lochan home, both on the same horse, the unsuspecting midwife became afraid that the urisk would come and abduct them. 'You need not fear for Adaidh', the urisk replied, 'he will not be nearer to you tonight than he is at the present moment'.

St Cottaig's well still exists as a stone-lined 'wishing-well' (NN83943951) near Auchnacloich. Tom an t-Sithean, The Fairy Knoll (NN84153985) is a wooded glacial moraine. North of Shian (NN84594135) is a very unusual stone circle★★ of thirty-two small white quartz stones, none more than half a metre high, although most only just protrude from the ground. It can be quite hard to find – look along the east side of the Shian Burn. This is a very strange place, with a look and feel very different to most circles. It is possibly in this general area that Canon Anthony Duncan encountered supernatural entities in the 1970s. The Canon, who had a reputation for being a gifted psychic, was driving with his wife and a friend around Glen Quaich. At the top of a steep climb which their car just about made, they stopped at small plateau with a very distinctive rock close to the right hand side of the road (this may be Ossian's Stone in SMA' GLEN but the account, in Alan Richardson's *Spirits of the Stones*, definitely mentions Glen Quaich). It was raining heavily and there was no other vehicle or person in sight. They got out of the car and immediately found themselves in what the Canon could only describe as fairyland. 'We were quite overcome by the sheer, breathtaking beauty of little things. It was as if we were being taken by the hand and shown beauty that we could not otherwise have noticed....And then I suddenly became aware that the profound silence was alive and that it was made up of a wonderful harmony. I looked up at the tops of the mountains all round us and realised, with a shock, but somehow without too much surprise, that they were all singing! And I heard them, and I heard the harmony of them....And then I became aware of a very powerful presence, quite close to hand...the awareness of presence by the rock by the side of the road was almost overpowering. But there was nothing alarming about it and so I did what I always do when confronted by something 'other'. I said 'Peace be with you!' The immediate sense of welcome was tremendous. We were 'friends' at once. I have a mental image of a very large Pan-like figure, an Elemental, but that is an essentially subjective construct, I did not 'see' – except that I almost did! We were wet through and it was time to get into the car and drive on. We all turned and said 'thank-you' to all the natural beauty and wonder we had experienced, and I gave a priestly blessing to my new acquaintance and his little kingdom'. The Canon stopped at the same spot a few years later but knew he could not recapture what had been experienced the first time and so did not even try. As he said, 'These things are "given", they are not to be sought after'. Note that all three of the group experienced the 'otherness' of the place.

Surrounded by desolate moorland south of Loch Hoil is a large heap of grey stones, Carn na mna uilc, 'Witches Cairn', (NN86074236). Even in the early twentieth century it was common for passers-by to cast a stone on the heap. Inevitably it is said to mark the spot where pursuers caught the last witch in the district and executed her, but 'Canmore' (www.rcahms.gov.uk) quotes the gamekeepers at Gatehouse and Lochans saying it was built by burial parties traveling from Glen Quaich to Aberfeldy.

STAREDAM, WATERLOO is famously given a bad press in Sir Walter Scott's *The Fair Maid of Perth*. The book's endnotes describe the place's eeriness: 'The whole aspect of the place fitted it for being the scene of trial and punishment...at the east end of Roch-an-roy wood, [there are] some oaks on which the Highlanders were hung, and which long went under the name of the "Hanged-men's-trees"'. Neither Scott nor the *NSA* mention the obvious Christian cross carved on the northeast stone of the stone pair at Staredam★ (NO04993828). Could this mean the cross was carved to neutralise pagan power sometime after 1845? Of course, absence of evidence is not evidence of absence, and simple crosses are impossible to date, so this is just speculation.

A minister, William Eason, was deprived of his living in Auchtergiven because on behalf of his sick wife he had consulted 'a woman who is suspected by every on[e] that knows her to have ane familiar spirit', in other words she was a witch (Roy Pugh, *The De'il's Ain*). Possibly coincidentally an impressive 2.2m tall menhir by the side of the minor road to Meikle Obney is known as the Witch's Stone★ (NO04243752).

BANKFOOT
Pitsundry stone circle (one stone remains)★ (NO05593445).
St Bride's Well (NO05313452).
Former St Bride's church, now graveyard (NO04923418), GRAVESTONES.
Loak Standing Stone (NO07573305).
Loak Court Hill, prehistoric burial mound (NO07733301).
Sack Stone (NN99753597).

MURTHLY Castle (private) is home to the quasi-medieval Chapel of St Anthony the Eremite, 1846, the first Catholic place of worship to be opened after the Reformation, with a huge mural of the Vision of Constantine.

The builder was Sir William Drummond Stewart, a classic Victorian eccentric. Having travelled in the Wild West, he returned with two Indians, who lived in the castle's Garden House for several years, and a herd of buffalo, which grazed on Duncan's Hill. Elsewhere on the estate is a fantasy bridge in the style of a Roman aqueduct, a dilapidated Classical temple and a large, genuine standing stone★ (O7053956). But all of this great stuff pales when compared with the Dead Walk★, an avenue of yew trees leading from the castle to the chapel. The laird must never walk along to the avenue to the chapel; that route is only for his funeral procession. The extent to which the 'curse' is believed in is variable; the present laird told me it is more of a family custom, and at the age of twenty-eight his grandfather, obviously not one for Superstitious Stuff And Nonsense, removed the barriers at each end of the walk and went for a saunter. But there were Dark Mutterings among the staff.

Witches Stone, Cloven Stone and Saddle Stone, Muir of Ord – not antique and of little interest.
Murthly stone circle★; the adjacent new housing development, Druid's Park(!) has robbed the site of some of its atmosphere (NO10273851).
Kinclaven Castle★★, great atmosphere, resembles a Mayan temple overtaken by the jungle (NO15813773).
Kinclaven church (NO151385) GRAVESTONES★★.

Chapel of St Anthony the Eremite. Sir William was removed from the vault as post-mortem
punishment for desecrating the original mortuary chapel. After nineteen years in an artificial
cave he was re-interred by the current laird's grandfather.

Over Benchill standing stone, topped with a large red sandstone sundial in place since
at least 1911★ (NO09513224).

The Battle of LUNCARTY is a conflict central to both the nation and a local aristocratic family. It's also one of the most blatant examples of propaganda masquerading
as history. Here's the usual story as repeated in dozens of popular books and hundreds
of websites. It's AD 980. The Danes invade and camp on the east bank of the Tay, with
the Scottish army on the other side of the river. The Vikings cross the trap-dyke at
Stanley by night to attempt a surprise attack, but a bare-footed Norse soldier steps on
a thistle and cries out. Despite this early warning, the Scots take a beating and retreat.
A doughty farmer, who just happens to be ploughing nearby with his sons, stops
the rout by blocking the path with his plough above his head. The Scots army rallies
and thrashes the Danes. The king (Kenneth III) ennobles the horny-handed son of
toil and gives him the name Hay and the choice of as much land as a greyhound can
cover or a falcon can fly. He chooses the falcon and consequently gets a tidy amount
of territory to the east of Perth. The Hay family rule wisely and the Viking-punctur-
ing thistle becomes the emblem of Scotland.

   It's all down to the historian Hector Boece. For years there were so few appar-
ently-authoritative early narratives of Scottish history that his *Scottish History* (1526)
was regarded as gospel. But as the 2006 *Encyclopædia Britannica* says, 'Boece's history is

Left: The Dead Walk, Murthly Castle. The section by the castle was felled by a laird's widow until she was prevailed upon not to Mess with Tradition; the yews were subsequently replanted.

Opposite: The King's Stone, Luncarty, with Denmarkfield Farm and the site of the supposed battle behind. The stone originally was named for the Danish general, but monarchs have better name-power.

a glorification of the Scottish nation, based on legendary sources, and is more inter-esting as romance than as history'. No earlier writer mentions the battle; there is no other source.

Boece provides a creation myth for the Hays. The falcon flight legitimises their great land possessions and shows them with their feet under the table from the tenth century, except the Hays don't actually turn up in records until 200 years later. The first charter of the Errol lands was granted towards the end of the twelfth century. A knight called Le Sieur de la Haye accompanied William the Conqueror into England and before this the La Hayes were lords in Normandy. So the Hays are in fact Anglo-Norman Johnny-come-latelies. Hector gives them a false legitimacy and the propaganda certainly worked: the Burial Table of the Hays of Errol at Coupar Angus Abbey, dated 1346, refers to the first of their line as the conqueror of the Danes. Hector's words have also colonised both landscape and mythology. The farm on the supposed battlefield is called Denmarkfield (NO097286). Sir John Sinclair, the insti-gator of *The Statistical Account of Scotland*, visited the site to verify that the landscape provided incontrovertible proof that the battle had taken place exactly as described by Boece. He was duly shown the encampments of the two armies, Hay's original home ('Gullan', opposite Luncarty), the spot where Hay rallied his fleeing country-men ('Turn Again Hill') and the field being ploughed at the time, left untouched with a border of grass around it. The standing stone★ (NO09712828) became the King's Stone.

There's not one, but two Falcon Stones where the bird finally landed. The falcon took off from an oak in an orchard on the south side of Barnhill Brae, near Perth; under the terms of his lease, the gardener had to preserve the tree.

James Hay (1771-1838), fourth Hay of Seggieden in the Carse, collected family documents and traditions on the battle. The man who rallied the Scots was called De Luce, an unlikely name in tenth-century Scotland. When Kenneth asked for him he was found sitting on his plough, tired out, and said 'Ooh Hey' or 'Hay'. So the king said, that's your name now. (It all makes perfect sense when you see it like that.) De Luce's wife objected to the name change and so was drowned in the river, where she called out 'D'Luce' and then 'Luce' until she could no longer keep her head above water, so she "put the nails of her thumbs together and imitated the way commonly used in those days of killing the animal whose name resembled that of her husband'. I confess I'm baffled by this account!

What is obscured by this is what might actually have been going on archaeologically at Denmarkfield. As well as the King's Stone there was a second standing stone (now buried) near the farm (NO09402844). All the old accounts mention numerous tumuli. Cists, skeletons and weapons were found when the mounds were flattened. There was also a long oval earth rampart. Naturally earlier writers assumed all this was from the wake of the battle, but I think it all tells us of a large-scale ritual landscape from the Bronze Age (the tumuli, cists and grave goods) and possibly the Neolithic (could the rampart be a long cairn?).

In 1656 four witches were reported in Redgorton, but we do not know their names or alleged crimes. Hidden in Luncarty Woods to the south of Marshall Way (NO099298) is an old beech used as a toothache tree, in use at least up to the 1960s. A nail would be first inserted into the gum until it drew blood; hammering it into the trunk transferred the pain to the tree (sympathetic magic).

Cramflat standing stone★ (NO08853032).
Gellybank standing stones (NO08213134).
Kirkhill Burial Ground (NO09413006), GRAVESTONES★.
Redgorton Church (NO08362839), GRAVESTONES★.

MONEYDIE. '[Here] there is a quick thorn, of very antique appearance…the people have a mortal dread to lop off, or cut any part of it, and affirm…that some persons, who had the temerity to hurt it, were afterwards severely punished for their sacrilege' (OSA). Workmen in 1825 came upon a possible plague pit in the foundations of the new church. Warlock Ireland lived at what is now Millhole (NO044305). Many stories are told about his powers. He was insulted in Perth High Street and instantly gave the man a pair of horns on his head, which he only removed when his business in the town was done. He enchanted all the rats of the mill to march over the Shochie Burn into a wood, where they fought each other until none were left alive. He made a pact with the Devil, the price of which was a blood sacrifice. He called for Fanny, his dog, but it was Fanny his wife who came, and so by the rules of the pact, she was the sacrifice (this is a story told elsewhere of dragon-killers, and dates back to Greek mythology). When he died the Warlock hinted at some treasure he had hidden, but the secret seems to have been buried with him (Forrester, *Logiealmond*).

PITCAIRNGREEN

Three faux standing stones constructed by Lord Thomas Graham, near Lynedoch Cottage (NO03792870, 03582902 and 02962898).
Grave of Bessie Bell and Mary Gray, who retired here to escape the plague but died of it in 1645, a story told in a famous ballad and repeated many times since (NO02832881).

A headless minister haunted Craggans Wood and the moorland around Shannoch, north of CHAPELHILL (NO000310). He carried a knapsack with a large Bible and preached although we are not told how he managed to speak in the absence of a head. The ghost was eventually laid by a Kindrum elder, Gilbert Pullar, the confrontation taking place on a very misty day at the east end of Burmieston Farm (NO008327).

Opposite the minor road that leads toward Keillour from East Tulchan on the road to BUCHANTY is an overgrown former formal avenue that leads, after about 300 vegetation-choked metres, to the former Mercer burial ground★ (NN958285). Eleven cruciform gravestones mark the graves of some of the more prominent Victorian

Vulval simulacrum,
Luncarty Woods.

members of the very prominent Mercer family, who, according to one of the stones, 'are aulder than auld Perthe'. The gate pillars are each surmounted by a metre-high metal stork with a serpent in its beak. The sculptural motif is repeated on a marble slab on the inner side of one of the pillars and on the sculptured decorations on the former General Accident building on PERTH's High Street.

STRATHEARN

ABERNETHY★★
Medieval round tower★★, Pictish symbol stone★★, burial ground, GRAVESTONES★ (NO189163).
The early Christian monastery here has several competing legendary, Pictish and saintly founding stories. The Nine Maidens, a popular mystical grouping, were buried at the foot of a great oak tree - as late as the seventeenth century the Kirk Session of Glamis had to forbid maidens going on pilgrimage to the oak on 15 June.

The Celtic scholar Ronald Black found a cluster of similar wells, chapels, fairs and altars across east Scotland dedicated to the Nine Maidens; he concluded that the cult was somehow connected with river worship, located around the main tributaries of the Tay. Stuart McHardy, in *The Quest for The Nine Maidens*, goes further, taking in Greek, Roman, Celtic and Norse mythology, King Arthur, magical nines, and mystical groups and islands of women. There are unusual carved skewputts on Mornington Stables, School Wynd (now the local museum), and at the west end of Main Street★. Ralph Merrifield, in *The Archaeology of Ritual and Magic* mentions some 'acoustic pots' found near Abernethy. These devices were placed high in the walls of the chancel or nave of late medieval churches, or under the choir seats, to amplify the singing. But over time the real meaning of the pots was lost, and they were built into domestic walls. The Abernethy examples were on the outside, where they obviously had no acoustic function. Merrifield suggests they were thought to trap evil before it entered the house.

The area's witchcraft lore has imprinted itself on the landscape:

Witches Road, 'named in memory of the twenty-two members of the local coven who were burned on Abernethy Hill', according to the Abernethy Glen Circular Walks leaflet. The number is dubious: the only accused witches recorded here were Elspeth Young, Jonet Crystie and Margaret Mathie, who were tried on 23 January 1662. No details of their confessions have survived.

Witches' Graves, or 'Long Man's Grave', (NO189153) a long, shallow depression, probably a former blackhouse.

Bogles Quarry (Bogles are spirits), disused, where the witches resolved their disputes.

Witches Hole (NO183154), a small cave.

Wizard's Stone, unknown location of a warlock's execution.

Castle Law hill-fort; when the Picts were attacked by the Romans they threw a silver cradle into the small loch on the summit (NO183153).

Katie Thirsty Well, possibly dedicated to St Catherine and/or St Drostan (NO194129).

GLENFARG

The Sunday Post (15 August 1976) reported a big cat, 'the size of a fully grown Labrador' with long pointed and tufted ears and eyes that glowed orange in the dark, frightened a Glenfarg woman and her dog on 10 August. There were other sightings of the lynx, including one in Glenfarg main street.

Arngask old parish church, GRAVESTONES, cupmarked stone★ (NO140108).
Clochridgestone stone with slot for cross(?) (NO146134).

DRON★

Former Druidic oracular rocking stone (NO137141).
Edmund's Grave, named for a Roman (?) general (NO147145).
Cupmarked stone (NO118151).
Graveyard (NO141158), GRAVESTONES★

Above left: Dron Church. A 'melted', honeycombed boulder – eroded gravestone or monument?

Above right: The Bore Stone, Moncrieffe House. May I suggest these two holes resemble the elliptical eyes of the Greys, the ubiquitous aliens of UFO-lore?

BRIDGE OF EARN. Moncrieffe Arms coaching inn, on the main road, (now a nursing home): 1970s reports of sobs coming from empty areas and footsteps on floorboards from carpeted rooms. Mr Young, the then owner, came across a locked bathroom in use; seconds later the door was open and the bathroom empty of occupant or bathwater and the towels cold and dry.

Moncrieffe House (private). Bore (or Boar) Stone★★ (NO136193), large Pictish cross-slab moved from NN973181, several km west, in 1885. 'There are many traditions and legends connected with this relic, but they are too absurd to be committed to writing' (*NSA*). Here are some of them: the tenant at Gask once tried to remove the stone to bridge his mill-race. It took many horses to drag it down the hill. The man was subsequently plagued with catastrophes. When he returned the stone just one pair of horses easily took it up the hill. The arms of the cross are hollow, so obviously it was a pillory. Some of the weathered carved animals look vaguely like boars, so it was the gathering place for wild boar hunts. About 50m west are the nine stones of a reconstructed stone circle★ which once stood where the M90 now drones. Miss Moncrieffe stipulated that the site be excavated and the stones re-erected next to her house. Moncrieffe House and the ruined chapel to the east have numerous GARGOYLES.

Graveyard, GRAVESTONES★ (NO113190).
Balmanno Castle, GARGOYLES (NO144155).
Ecclesiamagirdle House and graveyard, GARGOYLES, GRAVESTONES★ (NO107163).

KINTILLO

In 1658 Issobell McKendley of Dunning diagnosed Janet Imrie with 'a glisk of the ill wind'. (Glisk - a glance, evil eye.) On Issobell's instructions Janet's mother Margaret Imrie and mother-in-law Margaret Dick thrust Janet three times through a circle of blankets, followed by a stone or clod. The illness was transferred to Margaret Dick's son, Hugh Scot, who duly fell ill. Issobel also told them to wash Janet's feet in the millstream and take her to church after the blanket session. Margaret Imrie later divulged more about Issobel's cures to the kirk session at Dunbarney. Three small stones were put in the hair (or bed) of Margaret Dick's daughter Christian Scot. Both Margaret Imrie's husband Ninian Balman and Agnes Dron's husband John Wright transferred their illnesses to a chicken passed through their newly washed shirts. The investigation lasted from June 1658 to July 1660 before everyone involved had con-fessed their 'guilt'. Penances were imposed on the Dunbarney parishioners, while Mrs McKendley, being from Dunning, was reported to the Auchterarder Presbytery. Two years later she was executed for witchcraft. In the same year on 5 January at Dunbarney the Kirk Session sent a letter to 'the man that tries the witches'. Who this was, or why he was needed, is not clear. On 21 September 1662 Alison Simpson's trial for witchcraft cost £8. There are no records of her anywhere else.

RHYND

On 9 January 1662 the Privy Council, the major politico-judicial power in the land, issued a commission to try Margaret Dron from Rhynd for witchcraft. This was nor-mal practice. Margaret had already confessed to the local kirk session (i.e. the religious authorities) to making a pact with the Devil and the commission entitled the local great and good to prosecute her in a civil court. If guilty, she could be legally executed, not by the church but by the duly authorised civil authorities. Then on 1 April the Council discovered the minister, James Gillespie, and fifteen other members of the local gentry had used the commission to not only execute Margaret Dron, but also, illegally, Eupham Hougan, Issobell Marshall and Issobell McKessock. The women had been tortured by sleep deprivation and pricking (and, not surprisingly, had confessed) and then summarily executed. Confident of their own invulnerability (after all, they were gentry, men of standing and influence, and their leader was a man of God), the death squad had also illegally imprisoned and tortured Kathrin Bowar, Jonet Scrogges, Elspeth Tod, Cristian Vallandge and a woman named Gray. The torture was designed to make the women hang themselves. The Privy Council transported the still-living five to Edinburgh for safe-keeping; it is possible they were released. Gillespie and his cronies just received a reprimand. (P.G. Maxwell-Stuart, *An Abundance of Witches.*)

Parish church, ruined, GRAVESTONES (NO18261854).

FORGANDENNY parish church, GRAVESTONES★★ (NO088184). Steve McIntyre had experienced negative energy years ago in a Perth flat, so before building a house on a plot next to the church in Forgandenny in 1998 he decided to 'look into the leylines' and did a bit of dowsing, even camping out to get a feel of the place before building. (*Perthshire Advertiser*, 4 November 2005)

Two witchcraft commissions were appointed locally in 1660 and 1663. The first executed two Forgandenny women, Elizabeth Clow and Jonnet Armand, and the second condemned eleven witches to the stake or drowning in the River Earn.

In the grounds of Strathallan School (NO090183) is Lady's Well (i.e. the Virgin Mary's Well) a vaulted well-house in poor condition, possibly a plague-proof water supply for the former seventeenth-century mansion. The actual holy well is the stream issuing from a small stone-lined culvert hidden in the vegetation just to the northwest.

> *In the Dryburn Well, beneath a stane,*
> *Ye'll find the key of Cairnavain,*
> *That'll mak a' Scotland rich, ane by ane.*

Cairnavain is at NO069083. Nearby are Chapel Burn and Chapelburn Well. A Christian site, two wells, a prehistoric cairn and a treasure legend. Intriguing.

FORTEVIOT

Cropmarks of megalithic monuments and huge vanished henges show Forteviot was a major Neolithic centre. If some of these structures were still standing in the Dark Ages their aura of power may have persuaded the Picts to establish a royal palace here. Kenneth mac Alpin may have fought the Pictish king Bruidi at Forteviot. Prior to the battle, as was common in medieval times, there were signs and portents. Two comets were seen. The air resounded with the sounds of battle by day, and at night armies fought in the sky and warriors with fiery swords clashed overhead. And finally the Pictish bishop's crozier was burned to ashes by a strange fire which fell from heaven during a service. All these were seen to prefigure the military defeat of the Picts, which may or may not have happened. A plaque in the village reads: 'This village was rebuilt by J Alexander first Baron of Forteviot in year 1925-26 and occupies part of the site of the Pictish capital FOTHUIR TABAICHT a royal residence from the VII to the XII centuries. Here died Kenneth MacAlpin in AD 860'.

Kenneth was succeeded by his brother Donald, whose short reign at Forteviot was characterised by ill omens. A six-week-old child warned its mother to flee the country to escape the coming warfare. Cattle and sheep roared in a strange manner before falling down dead. And in Galloway poisonous snakes fell from the sky in huge numbers.

Church, GRAVESTONES* and Celtic bronze hand-bell (NO050174).

DUNNING**

A dragon was killed here by St Serf. It may have been the one from the Dragon's hole on Kinnoull Hill, but we are given no further details about its size or habits, never mind its role as a metaphor for paganism overcome by Christianity. St Serf's church* (HS) now houses the magnificent ninth century Dupplin Cross**, brought here from another site (NO05051897) to preserve it from weathering. It is superbly displayed and there is an excellent interpretation panel and booklet. During my visit my friend Dave Walker, who is notoriously sensitive to electromagnetic and other radiations, felt distinctly uncomfortable at the east end of the church (the end opposite the Cross) and had to leave. Graveyard, GRAVESTONES*.

Standing stones* (NO018146 and NO022118), the supposed 'graves' respectively of Doncha, Abbot of Dunkeld, and Dubdon, Mormaer of Atholl, both killed at the Battle of Duncrub in 965.
Keltie Castle, with ghostly associations possibly connected with the female skeleton found walled-up in one of the rooms during renovations (NO008133).
Alleged site of burning of a wizard and two witches (NO023153).

At NN988131, and visible from the B8062 west of Dunning, is The Ship or Tarnavie (supposedly a corruption of the Latin *Terra Navis*, 'ship of earth'). This large natural mound resembles an upturned boat, hence the legend of a Viking boat burial. The *OSA* of 1779 relates an incident which took place 'some time ago'. A man attempted to dig for turf on the side of the mound but as soon as he opened the ground with the spade, an old man 'supposed to have been the spirit of the mountain' appeared through the opening and 'with an angry countenance and tone of voice, asked the countryman why he was tirring (uncovering) his house over his head?' He then vanished. The man was terribly frightened, and 'none has since ventured to disturb the repose of the imaginary spirit'.

It's not often you get a monument to a 'road-to-Damascus-type' religious experience reported in Scotland, which is why the Ebenezer Stone* is so interesting. On one side of this small headstone-like monument is a quote from Isaiah 50 v.10:

Who is among you that feareth the Lord,

that obeyeth the voice of his servant
that walketh in darkness
and hath no light?
Let him trust in the name of the Lord
and stay upon his God.

Plus the word Ebenezer ('Stone of Help') and, in Latin:

HIC	*HERE*
EX TENEBRIS	*OUT OF DARKNESS*
LUX LUXIT	*LIGHT SHONE*
ERGO	*THEREFORE*
PATER, FILIUS ET	*THE FATHER SON AND*
SPIRITUS SANCTUS	*HOLY GHOST*
MEUS DEUS,	*(SHALL BE) MY GOD*
ET NOMEN	*AND THE NAME OF*
HUJUS LOCI	*OF THIS PLACE*
LUX	*LIGHT*

It was erected by Auchterarder resident James Lawson (1747-88). Either he had an epiphany that showed him his future direction, or it may mean he experienced an actual vision of light. Despite his poverty Lawson studied for the church, only to suffer a lifetime's rejection from the establishment. Eventually he was ordained as a minister by the secessionist Relief Church just a few years before he died aged forty-one. In the twentieth century a group of worshippers would regularly sing hymns accompanied by a pedal organ transported on a farm cart, in later years replaced by an accordion. The stone is not in its original location – it was moved downhill in the 1950s when the farmer piped the watercourse, and now stands between the farms of Wester and Easter Gatherleys (NO0411). (Source: *Dunning Parish Historical Magazine*)

The witch monument to Maggie Wall★★★ is a mystery wrapped in a riddle encased in an enigma, one of the most bizarre and fascinating monuments not just in Perthshire but the whole of the UK. Located west of Dunning on the roadside of the B8062 (NO006140), it consists of a tall cross atop a rough cairn of boulders with the painted words 'Maggie Wall burnt here 1657 as a witch'.

Who was this witch, so well known that she, alone among the thousands of executed witches, gets her own named memorial? No-one knows. There is no trace of her in the ecclesiastical records or the surviving witch-trial documents – or of anyone called Walls or Wallace. Of course, the records could have been lost, but it's not that simple. Other witches do appear in the contemporary records. In 1657, the year Maggie was supposed to have died, the Synod visited Dunning to excommunicate and censure Johnnie Guthrie for charming (a 'cunning man'). There are no further

Maggie Wall's Monument. In 1998 the cross was broken and a sandstone replacement installed. Every so often the paint is renewed and flowers left, but by whom?

details of what charms he used and how he used them, and no mention is made of his fate. But the major outbreak of witch hunting in Dunning and the area around took place five years later. On 7 May 1662 a commission composed of the great and the good (including members of the prominent local families Drummond, Hay, Moncrieff, Oliphant and Rollo) accused a large number of women of witchcraft. On 28 May eight of them were executed. Possibly the others were released, as there is no further record of them. The cases were:

Name	Residence	Result
Issobell McKendley	Dunning	Executed (See KINTILLO)
Elspeth Reid	Dunning	Executed
Jonet Toyes	Dunning	Executed
Jonet Airth	Pothill of Aberuthven	Executed
Helen Ilson	Forteviot	Executed
Margret Crose	Forteviot	Executed
Jonet Martin	Nethergask, Findo Gask	Executed?
Jonet Young	Clathimore, Findo Gask	Executed
Jonet Bining	Clathimore, Findo Gask	Released?
Agnes Ramsey	Clathimore, Findo Gask	Released?
Jonet Allan	Overgask, Findo Gask	Released?
Jonet Robe	Woodend of Findo Gask	Released?
Issobell Goold	Dunning	Released?
Agnes Hutsone	Dunning	Released?
Anna Law	Dunning	Released?

So, if all these cases are in the records (as well as Johnnie Guthrie's in 1657) why isn't Maggie's?

Inspection of the monument itself just creates further mysteries. The earliest reliable record is in 1859. The cross-shaft is an eighteenth-century lintel and other stones in the monument have drill-holes with a style characteristic of the same century. At a guess, then, Maggie Wall's supposedly seventeenth-century monument is probably early nineteenth century in date - although of course it might have replaced an earlier one.

So who built the monument? No-one knows. Why does a woman burned as a witch have a cross on her grave? No-one knows. Could the name be apocryphal, used to represent all the witch-dead rather than one specific individual? Is there even a body there? Then there is the writing. Over the years a notion has been mooted that its refurbishment is carried out under cover of darkness by a feminist cabal dedicated to preserving the memory of a past victim of injustice. Occasionally folk are suggested as the perpetuators of this tradition. Perhaps some of the re-painters are even reading this book!

In 1966 the *News of the World* printed a photograph of a young couple posing in front of the monument. They were on holiday and they were fascinated by witchcraft. Their names were Ian Brady and Myra Hindley, the 'Moors Murderers'.

ABERDALGIE AND DUPPLIN
Parish church, GRAVESTONES* (NO079202).
Kirkton of Mailer burial ground, GRAVESTONES (NO109200).
Hilton of Moncrieffe Standing Stone, fallen and graffitied (NO110206).
Old Dupplin church ruins, GRAVESTONES* (NO064194).

In 1682 the minister of KINKELL, Richard Duncan, was executed at Crieff for murder. The corpse of a child fathered on his servant Catherine Stalker was found under his own hearth-stone, but suspicion of 'dirty tricks' surrounds the conviction, as Duncan was involved in a longstanding row with many influential locals. He was reprieved but the messenger arrived twenty minutes too late. Duncan protested his innocence to the end and predicted that after his hanging a white dove would alight on the gallows as proof and it duly did so.

Trinity Gask church, GRAVESTONES* and anti-plague Trinity Well (NN963183).
St Bean's church, Kinkell, GRAVESTONES* (NN93801621).
'Witch Knowe', actually a Roman Signal Station (NN997195).
Madderty parish church, GRAVESTONES* (NN953225).

MUTHILL
The 'Princess of Morocco from Muthill' is one of those tales that is so far-fetched that it could perhaps be true. Helen Gloag was born on 14 February 1750 (perhaps) in a cottage at the Mill of Steps, just outside Muthill. When her blacksmith father married for the second time the teenage Helen left home in a huff of spirited red-headedness and took ship to America. The ship was captured by North African pirates who enslaved Helen. She captivated and married the Emperor of Morocco and had two sons by him. Whether this meant she was actually the Empress or a member of

the harem is not clear. The story was first published in 1780, with lightweight circumstantial evidence. A later publication, *The Antiquities of Strathearn*, took the story further. Here, Helen's two sons get involved in a dynastic struggle with pretenders to the Moroccan throne after the death of the Emperor. Using their mother's nationality as a fulcrum, they inveigle military aid from the British. Unfortunately the princes were killed in the infighting and the whole episode comes to nothing. Even if this whole fabulous tale is not true, one feels it should be. But be warned: with a few minor details changed, much the same story is told about a young woman in GLENSHEE.

TULLIBARDINE

Around 1548 an eighteen-year-old shepherdess, Isobel Watson, fell asleep in the open air near Tullibardine and was transported by the fairies through a rock to a big house underground. In 1590, when she was sixty, and on trial for witchcraft in Stirling, she gave very considerable details (recorded in P.G. Maxwell-Stuart, *Satan's Conspiracy*) about this and her other stays with the sìthean, whom she visited at each new moon, apparently over many years. She did not consume anything there because she knew eating fairy food put you in their power. The house was filled with many people, both tall and short. She gave her own child to the fairies as a quid pro quo for them healing her husband, who had suffered a long-term illness brought about by falling asleep on a fairy hill. (The fairies swapped the two-year-old for a lookalike changeling; she refused to feed it and her husband threw the creature on the fire, an action which almost burned down their house.) She then agreed to serve the fairies if they would give the infant back to her. To mark this, Thomas McRory, a former lover who was now dead, cut her deeply on her forehead with a knife. She visited the fairies along with James Hog, Isobel Leith, James Brown, Margaret Bill, and James Tod, a fiddler who played while they danced. She sometimes danced with the fairies themselves. William Finton and his wife helped the fairies to lift large stones. James Watson had been taken by the fairies. A lady with the generic witch name NicNiven (see CRIEFF) was the Fairy Queen's midwife, and later Isobel herself took that role. The Fairy King anointed her with some egg yolk-like oil on her head, arm, throat and breast; as long as some of the oil remained on her, no man could harm her. The King also removed some or all of her hair. The King's daughter gave her some wheat, a piece of woollen cloth, and a fingerbone, which were designed to protect Isobel from the violence she frequently suffered at the hands of the fairies each new moon. Isobel also claimed to have received the bone from either her aunt or John Row, the minister of Perth (c.1526-1560). The bone may therefore have been a saint's relic or a magical item. Isobel later gave the three gifts to James Kynard when he asked her to cure his toothache. She was scarred on the middle finger of her left hand from a fairy's bite. She had seen fairies in the market place, but they were invisible to other humans in the crowd. People who stayed with the sìthean for seven years were given to Hell as a tithe – a common belief found elsewhere, in for example Tam Lin, the famous ballad of fairy abduction and true love.

It's hard to know what to make of Isobel's confession. Many parts are contradictory and incoherent, no doubt partly because she was questioned on several different occasions about events forty years earlier. She was also either mentally befuddled, or the clerk was very bad at recording the evidence. The record shows clearly that Isobel's inquisitors had a pre-defined set of beliefs and they shaped her testimony to fit. For example, she said she was visited on one occasion by an angel and at another time by Jesus Christ; the former offered her a deal (protection in return for service) and the latter told the details of a minor theft. To the churchmen these visitations were clearly impossible and they spent much time convincing Isobel that her visitors could only have been the Devil in disguise. Similarly, the sìthean could not just be minor spirit entities (with whom interaction was not strictly a crime) but actually Satanic. Isobel Watson was executed for witchcraft on 23 June 1590.

There is a holy well just west of Tullibardine collegiate church (HS) (NN906134). On May Day morning you walked around it nine times before drinking the water, then nine times around the adjacent set of stones to bring good luck.

ABERUTHVEN
St Kattan's chapel, GRAVESTONES★ (NN973151)
Standing stone★ (NN977164).

AUCHTERARDER★★
The Perthshire Courier of 29 October 1840 described how a 'respectable mansion in the neighbourhood' came under a poltergeist attack: 'Money rumbled in the drawers, and leaped from places, where it was not under lock and key, to the floor. Tables shook– the plate rack, or its contents, danced and rattled with startling fury – the house bells would ring for many minutes on end'. The article coyly suggests that the spirit was officially exorcised.

At 11 p.m. on Friday 6 August 1993 David Hardy and Susan Underhill were driving along the A823 northwest of Auchterarder. On the straight section of the road just before the junction with the A822 road to Crieff (NN *c.* 8814), they came across a circle of cats occupying the entire road. There were something like thirty to fifty cats and they were focused on the centre of the circle, although there was nothing visible. They blithely ignored the car and its astonished occupants for about four to five minutes and then, their mysterious business concluded, wandered off in different directions. (www.leyman.demon.co.uk/nmistim.htm)

Alexander Drummond, a healer professionally active for fifty years, cured hundreds of people and animals of madness, epilepsy, hallucinations, St Anthony's fire (erysipelas, or 'red skin'), noli me tangere (lupus, an ulcerating face disease, often mistaken for leprosy), growths, worms, syphilis and other diseases, including frenacies (whatever they are). He treated madness by ritually 'ploughing' on the boundary between two

estates. He variously undertook love magic, transferred disease and removed bewitch-
ment. He performed an exorcism to save a boy's soul, and gave the lad a leather
pouch filled with rusty nails, bits of stick and roots. He used south running water
to dissolve certain powders to make curing drinks and washed a shirt in water over
which a 'Christian king' had ridden, and then used the shirt for healing and diagnosis of witchcraft. He kept a book of cures and had three healing stones called 'slake
stanes'. He employed amulets, bannocks and roots in his charms, called his healing
words 'holy orations' and favoured Barthills Day (St Bartholomew's Day, 25 August).
And, perhaps with some justification, he claimed he was more powerful than the
church ministers because he could actually give people health here and now. He was
clearly held in great respect in the area and five decades of professional work must
mean he produced results. It took five years' work for the church to take him down.
In October 1628 he was finally imprisoned while witness statements were taken all
over Perthshire and beyond. It was a massive legal undertaking; they must really have
wanted to get him. The Presbytery of Auchterarder could not make him confess so he
was transferred to Edinburgh Tolbooth, and executed on 11 July 1629. An unsuccessful
campaign was launched to posthumously clear his name, with letters being written
to the King. Alexander Drummond was one of the most extraordinary characters of
Scottish witchcraft; someone should write a play about him.

Auchterarder is awash with carvings:
Castleton Farm - broken (Pictish?) carving. Also possibly fake standing stone in a
garden (NN943133).
St Margaret's Hospital★, Townhead – GARGOYLES★.
Episcopal church, High Street – GARGOYLES★.
Old graveyard, GRAVESTONES.
Craigrossie Hotel – locomotive.
Former lodge of Coll-Earn House, and Greenbank, both in Hunter Street, - GAR-
GOYLES★.
Victorian doocot, The Doocot, off Hunter Street – GARGOYLES★★.
Ruthven Tower Nursing Home, Abbey Road – GARGOYLES★★.

The Lodge, Doocot and Ruthven Tower are all the work of William Leiper. His *pièce de
resistance* is Coll-Earn Castle Hotel★★★, off High Street, a riot of carved zoomorphery.
A raven sits above the motto *Deus Pascit Corvos* ('God Feeds The Ravens'), a reference
to Luke 12:24. An owl oversees the Shakespearean quote 'There I Couch When Owls
Do Cry', from *The Tempest* 5:1. The main circular tower proclaims 'A Fast Tower is Our
God' (based on Proverbs 18:10, 'The name of our Lord is a strong tower'). A panel showing Justice pointing to her scales (Lieper's client was a lawyer) exhorts us to 'Be Just And
Fear Not'. (Shakespeare again, *Henry VIII* 3:2.) Two other panels – a woman looking at
a mirror from a portable vanity table and another with a cup and two small children
– illustrate the motto 'Let Not Mercy and Truth Forsake Thee' (from Proverbs 3:3).

Right: Probable fake standing stone in the garden of Castleton Farm, Auchterarder. Note the suspiciously straight side and top.

Below: Broken (Pictish?) carving at Castleton Farm. Until recently it was attached to the small ruin of Auchterarder Castle.

Coll-Earn Hotel. For the price of a pot of tea you can enjoy the company of dozens of carved animals, birds, warriors and much more.

Easthill stone circle. The stone in the foreground has a groove at the waist. The one to the right has a carved handprint.

Ardoch Roman Camp. An old rhyme tells of a great treasure between the main camp and an outpost hill: 'Between Roman Camp of Ardoch and Grinnan Hill of Keir / Lies nine kings' rents for nine hundred year'.

St Kessog's church, ruined, GRAVESTONES★ (NN948140).
St. Mackessog's Well (NN950137).
Craig Banochy, blessing rock (NN962116).
Wester Biggs stone circle (NN863061).
Easthill stone circle★★ (NN929124).

BRACO/ARDOCH★★★
Huge Roman camps★★★ (HS) (NN839099), one of the sights of Scotland.

'There was near there a round opening like the mouth of a narrow well, of a great depth, into which my grandfather ordered a malefactor to go, who (glad of the opportunity to escape hanging) went and brought up a spur and buckle of brass'. So wrote James, Lord Drummond in 1672. The unnamed 'malefactor' was sent into the shaft for a second time – but he died in the 'foul air'. In 1690, a second condemned man was lowered on a rope, and brought up spears and helmets. He claimed to have seen gold and silver objects at a greater depth. Down the man went again…but he too died in the shaft. No further explorations took place (perhaps the supply of condemned criminals dried up) and all the items were apparently looted after the battle of Sheriffmuir in 1715, although an inscribed stone survives in the Hunterian Museum in Glasgow. Five years later, the elderly tenant of nearby Ardoch House lost a dog down the hole. He therefore had it covered up, and its site is now unknown. One wonders what happened to the two dead criminals? Were their lifeless bodies hauled up to the surface, or were they left to rot down there, their bones joining the mysterious, lost, and possibly mythical, Roman treasure of Ardoch? The remains of a medieval chapel and graveyard can be seen in the centre of the fort. Steggal, in *Picturesque Perthshire*, claims this was a burying-place for vagrants and suicides, although how he knows this is not clear. Further unfortunates are presumably buried at the spot marked 'Suicides Graves' (NN838130). Braco Castle (private) (NN824113), a wonderful mélange of architectural styles, has ghostly self-opening doors.

GREENLOANING

The Roundel Stone★ (aka The Greenloaning Stone) was ploughed up on the mound (NN832068) in 1822. Controversy has raged ever since about the lettering on the underside of the stone: BVAHQATTI IONATI (Bvahqattis son of Idonatos) and VERGAMEBO NOTVO (Vergamebos the Notian) presumably a clan or family name. We can't trust the inscription; after discovery the letters were deepened and re-cut by a herdsman, and others were added later by someone else, so what the inscription originally said is guesswork. The stone was dated to possibly the fifth or sixth century and now stands outside the front of the Smith Art Gallery and Museum in Stirling.

Innerpeffray chapel, GRAVESTONES★ (NN902184).

CRIEFF

Kate McNiven's alleged witch practices included turning herself into a bee, or at least a small winged insect. Even by the standards of the time this was an incredibly unlikely accusation, but nevertheless the Minister of Monzie sentenced her to death and she was burnt on the Knock of Crieff. Kate's master, the Laird of Inchbrakie, tried to save her but failed. In gratitude she bit a blue bead from her necklace, spat it at him, and, before the flames took hold, promised him that as long as the bead stayed in Inchbrakie, the Graeme's estates would never be sold. In the nineteenth century the ring accidentally left the great house, and, of course, the lands started to slip out of the family's control.

This, at least, is the story as told in the Revd George Blair's *The Holocaust; or the Witch of Monzie: a poem illustrative of the cruelties of superstition*, published in 1845, and elaborated by various writers since. But did Kate McNiven actually exist? There is no record of her trial. The year of her death is given as 1563, 1569, 1583, 1615, 1663, 1668, 1683 or 1715. Or probably any other year you like from the Reformation to the year the last witch was executed in Scotland (1727, in Dornoch). She was burned on top of the Knock, or below it, or rolled down it in a burning barrel. Or lightning struck her dead before the flames took hold (see PERTH MUSEUM for a painting of this). McNiven is variously spelt Neiving, Nik Neveing and NicNeven, 'Nic' being the female equivalent of the Gaelic patronymic 'Mac'. But several sources from this period show 'NicNiven' was the name of the Fairy Queen or Queen of the Witches. An example is at TULLIBARDINE. It may be derived from Neamhain, one of the Irish war goddesses or furies, better known as Badb. Neamhain and Badb may be different aspects of the same entity. The sense of the name is that of a terrifying death messenger, also 'deadly' or 'ill-fated'. A malignant variant of Badb turns up in GLENSHEE. So 'NicNiven' may be an honorific, or a title, or a generic name (like bad fairy or hobgoblin). John Brughe (see GLENDEVON) said he obtained his knowledge of witchcraft from Neane MacClerick. MacClerick was the widowed mother-in-law of John McIlvorie, who was tried for witchcraft in Crieff on 12th July 1643. We do not know what happened to McIlvorie, but Neane MacClerick claimed to be the niece of NikNeveing, the Witch of Monzie. This suggests Kate's name had 'celebrity status'. Of course it doesn't prove Kate McNiven did exist, but at least it shows any putative execution must have taken place before 1643.

In 1999 I wrote an article for the *Perthshire Advertiser* on Kate. The following week (16 August) Mr Thomas Brown of Bankfoot wrote in to say that many years earlier he had been contacted by a Devon resident who was a descendant of the Grahams of Inchbrakie. This gentleman claimed he possessed a ring containing the very bead bitten off by Kate McNiven. Unfortunately Mr Brown did not see the ring and over time forgot the name of his correspondent. Now, there was also another charm said to have belonged to Kate – an iron chain with a black heart and two crossbones of gold on the back, bearing the words 'cruell death' on it with an enamel death's head in the shape of a snake's head. Anyone know where this is?

Pictish stones, old town cross and stocks, Tourist Office, High Street★.
Former parish church of St Michael, GRAVESTONES.
Cradle Stone, a large glacial erratic split in two by lightning (NN865226).
Ferntower stone circle★, site of the murder of Patrick Graham, Earl Strathearn by his brother-in-law, Sir John Drummond of Concraig on 10 August 1413 (NN874226).

A number of paranormal episodes in and around Crieff are recorded in local ley-lines/black spirals researcher David Cowan's book *Ancient Energies of the Earth*.

MONZIEVAIRD

A coded supernatural tale about adultery and illicit sex was told about the laird of the former Monzievaird Castle, which used to be in the Hosh near Glenturret distillery. The laird brought back a fairy from somewhere abroad and used to visit her secretly at night. His suspicious wife fastened a piece of worsted yarn to a button on his coat and followed the thread along a secret tunnel to the bottom of the Turret Burn, and then down a precipitous ravine, where she found her man with the fairy. She accused the laird of infidelity and demanded he destroy the spirit. The fairy fled, and bad luck attended the castle ever after. The laird himself prompted a rebellion through his cruelties to the people, and he was forced to flee, and died abroad in obscurity.

Ochtertyre House Mausoleum★ (NN850235) GRAVESTONES★, the site of a notorious massacre in 1511 (the Drummonds burned over 100 Murrays alive). Dedicated to the dragon-killing St Serf (see Dunning); nearby, between the mausoleum and the small St Serf's Water, was Serf's Well (visited on Lammas Day and offered rags, spoons, and white stones). Bronze ritual deposits were found in the loch in the 1780s.

STROWAN is a corruption of St Ronan.
Ronan's dam-dike across the river, from where the saint fished (NN821213).
St Ronan's Well, a hole in the side of a steep bank (NN819213).
Tom a 'Chaisteil hill-fort, with an 1830s copy of Cleopatra's Needle (NN825217).
Samson's Stone★, glacial erratic (NN825220).

COMRIE★
'Shakey Town' is famously an earthquake zone; not weird in itself, you would think, but in *New Lands* Charles Fort, the unequalled researcher into the strange and unexplained (hence Fortean), dug up an entire strata of weirdness about a series of earthquakes in the eighteenth and nineteenth centuries. On February 15 1837, a black powder fell upon the Comrie region, echoing a previous fall of fine, black powder in 1788. Then on October 12, 1839 a quake at Comrie affected the sky – it was 'peculiarly strange and alarming, and appeared as if hung with sackcloth.' Throughout the month of October 1839, shocks continued to be felt, sometimes slight and sometimes severe; contemporary reports described accompanying sounds 'like distant thunder or reports of artillery'; 'the noise sometimes seemed to be high in the air, and was often heard without any sensible shock.' Then on October 23 came the climax - a violent 4.9 scale quake which seemed to be related to a whole series of aerial phenomena. Again and again, credible witnesses reported sounds in the sky that were separate and distinct from the underground noises. Rattling sounds or explosions were heard overhead, but these could not have been some bizarre echo because they occurred before the rumbles in the ground. In November a powder-like soot fell from the sky. On January 8, 1840 the air was filled with sounds like cannonading and crackling.. Altogether there were 247 such occurrences recorded between October 3, 1839, and February 14, 1841. On February 18 of the latter year a shock was accompanied by a fall of discoloured rain. What was going on in the air at Comrie? Why haven't similar phenomena been observed around other earthquakes? Back in the realm of human gullibility, a local writer called Gilfillan claimed the 70 earthquakes between 1792 and 1814 were associated with the French Revolution (as recorded in Korner, *Rambles Around Crieff*). Gilfillan's evidence? Mysterious noises were heard at the death of Caesar; fiery swords were seen to flash in the sky during the siege of Jerusalem under

Titus; and the Aurora Borealis presaged the 1715 Jacobite rebellion – 'kindled up as if to light the rebel lords to their unknown home'. Obviously, then, the Comrie earthquakes were Nature/God's protest at the fall of the French monarchy - the quakes of 1789 were especially strong, but significantly, they became more moderate with the fall of Napoleon. Sheesh.

The proprietor of Comrie House (NN773224) fell asleep in the local wood under an old oak and woke in a large fairy hall. Despite the music and dancing he was unhappy and managed to tell a servant what spells would free him. But when he returned home the house was shaken to its foundation. A female relative opened the door to see who or what was causing the noise and, of course, vanished.

Parish church, GRAVESTONES* (NN773220).
Wester Tullybannocher stone circle* (NN755225).
Balmuick stone circle* (NN784252).
Dalginross stone circle* (NN780213).
'Roman Stone' standing stone and cupmarked stone* (NN774206).
'Roman Stone' standing stone* (NN787196).
Clathick standing stone (NN812232).
Lawers standing stone* (NN801227).
Dunruchan Hill standing stones* (NN795174, NN792174, NN791171, NN790169, NN790168 and NN792179).
Kindrochat chambered cairn (NN723230).
Kinkhost whooping cough well (kinkhost – 'chincough') (NN765239).

The Straid well (NN779174) was also a renowned cure for whooping cough, but only if drunk before the sun rose or immediately it set, from a horn taken from a quick (live) cow, kept by an old woman who lived near the well. In 1845 a family came all the way from Edinburgh to use the well. Its lintel can still be found on a mound by the north side of the farm road to Middleton Farm, off the B827, but the well itself was filled in by a farmer who had lost a lamb in it. Another holy well with adjacent chapel at Blairinroar (now Blàr an Rodhar) was dedicated to St Patrick (NN c.794181 – note the proximity to one of the standing stones). By 1846 both chapel and well were gone.

North of Comrie (NN769236) is the Devil's (or De'il's) Cauldron, a spectacular waterfall. An imp who lived in the pool, kidnapping people for the Dev who lived at the upper fall, once wandered far from home and entered the house of an old woman. She persuaded him to sit by the fire, then 'accidentally' scattered the glowing embers over his naked limbs. He ran off and was never seen again.

Rock faces on the south slope of Uamh Mhór, GLEN ARTNEY (NN688110) are weathered into fantastic pinnacle shapes, like something out of the American West.

A giant made his home in a cave here; he must have been singularly diminutive, as the only possible candidates for a cave are a modest hollow in the rock face or a cavity below the boulders. On Meall Clachach to the north there is a massive boulder whose size cries out for an association with a giant/witch/the Devil/Samson/etc., but folklore is strangely silent on the subject.

Cupmarked stone (NN729173).
Ring-marked stone (NN762177); 10m west the Herd's Stone is engraved with the names of nineteenth-century shepherds: 'A {} DRUMMO{ND} 1809', 'JOHN () 1813', 'JOHN DRUMMOND 1848', 'JOHN McGREGOR 1855', and 'J K 1878'. ({} means damaged, () lost.)

ST FILLANS★★. Dundurn★★ (NN707233), also known as Dunfillan, Dun-Fhaolain and St Fillan's Hill, is an isolated rocky hill with a Pictish-era hillfort and St Fillan's Chair, a natural rock armchair on which the saint reputedly sat. Up until about 1800 rheumatism sufferers sat in it and then lay on their backs and were then pulled by their legs to the bottom of the hill. The slope is steep and littered with boulders and outcrops; I reckon if you could survive the descent, rheumatism was the least of your problems. Near the chair are two hollows in the rock (made by the saintly knees?). Then there is St Fillan's Well, once found on the top of the hill, but which suddenly relocated 400m to the south in apparent disgust at the Reformation. The well was visited on 1 May (Beltane) and 1 August (Lammas); seventy people were recorded making a pilgrimage to it in 1791. They walked, or were carried, three times around the well sunwise (deosil, from east to west), and drank and bathed in the water. The well was especially powerful in promoting fertility. The supplicants threw a white stone on the saint's cairn and left behind rags of linen or pieces of woollen cloth. At the foot of the hill there is a hollow on the top of a large stone, which was made by St Fillan; the water in the basin was said never to dry out, and washing three times in it cured sore eyes.

The circular graveyard of the ruined St Fillan's Chapel★★ (NN704236) indicates great antiquity (GRAVESTONES). The roofless ruins are of the sixteenth century but the first church on the site is said to have been erected by St Fillan. But which one? There were two St Fillans: the first, Fillan the leper, died *c.* 520. The second died in AD 649. Fillan's grave is claimed to be in the chapel, although there is an alternative story. At least two chapels claimed the body and when it was being carried up Glen Ogle a violent dispute about possession arose between two competing parties. The rammy was solved with the sudden appearance of a second, identical coffin, leaving both sets of good Christian folk with a saintly coffin apiece. Exactly the same story is told about the funeral of a man in GLENSHEE. Since 1586 the chapel has been the burial place of the Stewarts of Ardvorlich. Near the entrance is a small-shaped standing stone (or decayed headstone?) with two deep holes, in which you will almost certainly find coins. The chapel's pre-Reformation font is now in the Victorian Dundurn parish church in St Fillans village.

The 'blink-and-you-miss-it' painted Frog Stone lurks by the north side of a fast stretch of the A85 east of St Fillans. Further south is another painted stone, the toothy Crocodile or Serpent, in place by 1931, when the rock reptile was actually tethered by a rope. In legend it has been chained up since it chased Rob Roy across the hills one New Year's morning.

In 2005 local pressure forced builders Genesis Properties to abandon plans to move and carve on a large boulder associated with a battle and fairies. The developers relented and the stone will now remain untouched in the centre of the housing development. ('Builders rocked by history', *Perthshire Advertiser*, 21 October 2005).

Cupmarked boulder (NN714232).

LOCH EARN
As well as being claimed to be bottomless, the loch also has a monster, although this was actually a prop used in a television commercial filmed on the loch in the 1980s, with the fibreglass creature pursuing a water-skier. Needless to say, there was a spate of monster sightings at the time.

Late at night on 15 August 1995 David Hardy and Susan Underhill seemed to experience some kind of time slip as they were driving along the north side of the loch towards St Fillans: 'Everything looked strange. There were no cars, not even parked. There were no lights. The land and houses were there but not quite as they should be…it seemed to take forever, almost as if we were not moving forward at all, but someone was playing a film which was moving past us'. But the speedometer showed they were driving between 60-70mph. They passed under a railway bridge which had been demolished in 1965 and noticed that Loch Earn was bordered with old-fashioned white picket fencing for most of its length and that the road was very narrow with no white lines. It was not until they passed the sign for the Trout Farm near Comrie that things reverted to normal. (www.leyman.demon.co.uk/nmistim.htm)

Clach Mhor Na'h-Airighe Leithe (the Great Stone of Glen Tarken), natural, former rocking stone (?) (NN659273).

KINROSS-SHIRE AND AREA

KINROSS
Reports of ghostly footsteps and a crying baby in the Auld Manse, 8 Sandport, Kinross seem small fry compared to the poltergeist outbreak in an earlier building on the same site. In 1718 a Mr Sinclair published *Endorism, or a strange relation of dreams or spirits that*

troubled the minister's house of Kinross. 'Endorism' refers to the Witch of Endor, the only named witch in the Bible. Silver knives and spoons disappeared, only to turn up in the barn; pins and needles infested meat and boiled eggs; a cupboard fell, breaking the dishes; clothes on the line and in cupboards were torn; the minister's Bible was thrown on the fire, only to be found unburnt. The poltergeist vanished after several weeks.

In 1662 Janet Anderson was executed as a witch. She had named Christian Gray as a fellow witch, but then retracted the statement, which sounds like it was obtained under torture. Helen Balfour, Jonet Burrell and Cristian Steidman were also accused, although we have no record of their 'crimes'. Bessie Henderson became a servant of the Devil at Turfhills, just west of the town (NO105028) (See CROOK OF DEVON). In 1597 'the witches of Kinross were so numerous as to be household words' (Henderson and Haldane, *The Annals of Kinross-shire*). Refreshment can be taken at Carlin Maggie's restaurant, named after a local witch who was turned into a rock stack on the Lomond Hills.

In 1762 'The Wandering Jew' (John 21 v22) passed through Kinross and Milnathort, and as usual was followed by great crowds. 'Tall and gaunt, turban on his head, solemn aspect, eyes kept fixed on the ground, long flowing beard, and wrapt up in a worn-out cloak or gown, on his feet were heavy sandals, which made a clattering noise when he walked; all that he was ever heard to say, and that in a moaning voice, was "Jack alone, poor Jack alone'. David Beveridge of Kinross died at an advanced age in 1788. A weaver and cutler, he spent decades trying to invent a perpetual motion machine (an obsession of the age). Like every such machine ever attempted, breaking the physical laws of the universe was always just one pin or screw away.

Stately Kinross House is on one of the few unarguable alignments in Scotland, deliberately built on a direct line between Loch Leven Castle and the former Tolbooth of Kinross. An eighteenth-century plan shows the town was intended to integrate with this great axial avenue, but it never happened. GARGOYLES★. The area around Kinross was rich with hillocks named for fairies, elves and witches, but all have vanished under the plough.

St Pauls Episcopal Church, Muirs, GRAVESTONES★.
Kinross West Church, Station Road, GRAVESTONES★.
Fountain in centre of village, GARGOYLES★.
East Cemetery, GRAVESTONES★★.

MILNATHORT

Aubrey Burl, the doyen of standing stones experts, said of the Standing Stones of Orwell★★ (NO14940432): 'cremations close to the stones and the presence of cists and pockets of burnt bone in the ground nearby, show that the pair remained the focus of ritual activity for many years… with the stones acting as centres of funerary

Above: East Cemetery, Kinross
– the Worm Ouroborus
eating its tail, a symbol
of eternity much used in
alchemy and mysticism.

Right: Fat man's face,
simulacrum. Kinross Golf
Course.

Orwell Standing Stones. Excavation found evidence of four cremations, two of them in an unusual two-tier burial, and dog and pig bones, all buried before the stones were raised.

and fertility ceremonies'. Stone-spotters will notice the west stone has a quartz vein, while the larger, east stone has a v-shaped mark that looks natural but may be significant. The shapes of the stones may symbolise male and female.

Burleigh Castle (HS), haunted by 'Grey Maggie' (NO12890459).
Orwell Parish Church, GRAVESTONES★.
Blind Well (cured blindness or 'hidden' well?) (NO115058).
Rommante Well (from Ruam, Gaelic for Rome?) (NO158083).
Old Orwell Church★★ GRAVESTONES (NO14680386).

Reports of a persistent fireball phenomenon on Loch Leven are confusing it with other Loch Leven – in Argyll.

CARNBO
Witch Knowe (NO053047).
Jenny's Baking Stone, flat stone at the Washing Linn (NO0504).
Papist's Knowe (NO086060).

FOSSOWAY
Fossoway Church, GRAVESTONES ★ (NO1580192).

GLENDEVON

John Brughe, executed in Edinburgh in 1643, had been a well-paid folk healer for many years, and was possibly fifty-six at his death. He could cast elfin darts into animals and cure cattle by sprinkling them with water in which two enchanted stones had been placed. He learned the remedies and the spoken words from Neane VcClerich who claimed to be a niece of the famous Kate McNiven (see CRIEFF). He met the Devil at Glendevon church, and both there and in Muckhart graveyard he dug up bodies, including a servant called Johne Chyrystiesone, and put the flesh above the doors of byres and stables to harm cattle. This he did with Katherine Mitchell and Margaret Kinard. Mitchell, who had implicated Brughe, was executed at Culross in May 1642. Kinard seems to have fled and is mentioned as a fugitive in 1649. The Church, GRAVESTONES*, is at NN97950513. Plague victims were buried beside a laburnam tree. Just outside is a separate enclosure, where Jane Rutherford lies. Before her death she vowed that she would 'walk' if she was buried in the churchyard. 'Green Jean' now haunts the glen. At NO003050 is Bogle Burn. The gate of the Old Manse at (NN97990514) has one of the few Trysting Stones left in the country. The couple would put their hands through the opening in the stone.

An unhappy princess was imprisoned in Castle Gloom (later Castle Campbell, Dollar) because of her love for a commoner. The Burn of Care leads to Maiden's Well, (NO970014) haunted by her spirit; lovers who summon her here at night are found dead beside the well in the morning. One night a piper passing Maiden's Castle (NN971015) a hillside in Glen Quey, saw the castle ablaze with light. He was invited in, played for the company, and left well rewarded. On returning home he recognised no-one because 100 years had passed. There is no record of a castle here.

Standing stones NN96800567 (in a field-bank) and NN96750572.

CROOK OF DEVON.

In April 1662 Agnes Murie of Kilduff confessed to renouncing her baptism and entering into the service of the Devil at the back of Hillhead Yards. He gave her a witch name of Pepira, and she met him three more times, two of these being sabbats held at Gibson Craig. Among others present at these meetings were Robert Wilson, Agnes Allan, Gilles Hutton, Margaret Duncan and Agnes Brugh (possibly a relative of Johnne Brughe, executed nineteen years earlier?). Janet Millar of Craigton testified that when Agnes gave snuff to her husband Henry Anderson he was immediately struck dumb and was paralysed on one side (a stroke?) Further, Murie had cursed the animals of Adam Keltie. When Isabel Rutherford of Crook of Devon joined Satan (who appeared in the form of Samuel, a bearded man in grey clothes and blue bonnet) he gave her a new name of Viceroy. His hand was extremely cold.

Janet Hutton (a relative of Gilles Hutton?) testified that Isabel had spoke incomprehensible words to her sick husband, James Wilson, after which time his illness became much worse. She also charmed two other sick people, one of whom became much sicker after the act. Agnes Murie and Isabel Rutherford were present when Bessie Henderson submitted to Auld Horny (now called 'Charles') near KINROSS. Her new name was less glamorous than the others', merely changed to Bessie Irwall. At Lammas 1691 she and several fellow witches, including Janet Paton, joined together to trample down Thomas Whyte's crop of rye, which they did not with magic but with their own feet. The number executed at Crook of Devon is uncertain. Robert Wilson, Bessie Nult, Margaret Libster, Janet Paton and Agnes Brugh are named as burnt at a place called Lamblares west of the Crook Mill, but the total number may have been between ten and thirteen.

In the 1560s a blacksmith in Crook of Devon suspected his wife was sleeping with the priest, so he pretended to go on a journey, but returned and caught them *in flagrante*. He fastened the priest's penis to his anvil by a large staple, then set fire to the smithy, leaving a knife, giving the priest the choice of 'cut or burn'. The divine chose the former and was never seen again. The anvil was called the Reformation Clogg and was handed down from minister to minister.

A drinking contest took place between a trooper in the service of King James (it is not clear which one) and a man called Keltie, a vassal of the laird of Tullibole. They drank for two days and three nights; the trooper passed out and Keltie took a final drink and fell asleep; but when he awoke, the other man was dead. The small pool of water near his grave is called the Trooper's Dub. The soldier can still be seen sitting there at night.

Tullibole Castle, GARGOYLES (NO05260057).
Tullibole Church, GRAVESTONES (NO05450080).
Bull stone — witches' burning site, boundary marker or bull-baiting stone? (NT03329970).

ALDIE

Muckle Meg o' Aldie, a 'wise woman' who cured for both people and cattle, lived in a lone house near Aldie Castle. Her stone, about the size of pigeon's egg, could cure sores by being rubbed on them, but first had to be immersed in boiling water, at which point its surface strangely changed from smooth to rough. She claimed it was a toad-stone, a magical stone which she herself had extracted from the head of a toad. Meg seemed to have enjoyed the protection (and possibly the patronage) of the Laird of Aldie, which prevented her from being nabbed by the witch hunters. But that didn't mean she didn't make enemies and when the Laird was abroad his factor tried to evict Meg. Her response was that she would set out for France that night and return with a letter from the Laird. Her mode of transport would be an eggshell and a broom-cow (a bush used to 'sweep' in curling). The next morning she thrust a document at the factor, who was astonished to read an instruction from his master setting out Meg's lifetime lease. A huge ash tree on a knoll in the area of her cottage had for some years been observed to glow at night. No-one had dared visit the knoll when Meg was alive and only when she died was the luminescence investigated and found to come from the touchwood fungus.

A man was hanged at Aldie Castle (NT05009777) for stealing 'a caup fu' o' corn'. He cursed the family from the gallows, saying the estate of Aldie would not be inherited for nineteen generations. I've no idea if this happened but the castle was roofless by 1736. Workmen cutting drains in one of the low fields below the castle found a skull, teeth and ribs, lying face downward. The area was once a lake, so possibly this was an ancient drowning.

Cup-and-Ring-Markings (NT048997).
Cleish Church, GRAVESTONES (NT095981)
Cairn, in Dumglow hill-fort. When excavated in 1904 a 'hollowed-out tree-trunk of oak' was found, possibly a log-coffin or tree-burial (NT07599649).

By 1295 SCOTLANDWELL★ (NO18470165) or Fons Scotiae was already famed for curing leprosy and scrofula. Robert the Bruce famously visited the well, which is now covered by a Victorian canopy.

Portmoak Parish Church, GRAVESTONES★ (NO183019).

The Devil was on his way from Kirkcaldy to the Carse of Gowrie, carrying with him a lapful of boulders he intended to use as stepping-stones across the Tay. But he stumbled as he was stepping over Benarty Hill, south of Loch Leven, and dropped the stones. They can still be seen around the slopes (NT155980).

John Knox's Pulpit is a distinctive cave on the north side of Glen Vale, the deep valley which cuts into the LOMOND HILLS between West Lomond and Bishop Hill. A natural hollow in a honeycombed layer of sandstone, it resembles a pulpit, with the rock weathered into smooth pillars almost like a balcony. It was probably used during the Covenanting period; its connection with Knox is fictional.

Bibliography

Particularly useful works are marked ⋆.

NEWPAPERS, MAGAZINES AND JOURNALS:
Atholl and Breadalbane Community Comment
Dunning Parish Historical Society Magazine
Fortean Times
Perthshire Advertiser
Perthshire Courier
The Scotsman
The Society of Friends of Dunblane Cathedral
Strathearn Herald
West Highland Free Press

WEBSITES:
Survey of Scottish Witchcraft, www.arts.ed.ac.uk/witches.⋆
'Canmore', the Royal Commission on the Ancient and Historical Monuments of Scotland, www. rcahms.gov.uk.⋆
Andy Sweet, www.stravaiging.com/history/ancient/stones.⋆
The Modern Antiquarian, www.themodernantiquarian.com.⋆

PERTHSHIRE, KINROSS-SHIRE AND LOCAL HISTORY:
The Statistical Account of Scotland, 1799.⋆
The New Statistical Account of Scotland, 1845.⋆
The Third Statistical Account, 1979.⋆
Baxter, Peter *Perth and Sir Walter Scott*, Thomas Hunter & Sons, Perth, 1932.
Bowler, David P. et al *Perth The Archaeology and Development of a Scottish Burgh*, Tayside and Fife Archaeological Committee, Perth, 2004.
Breadalbane Historical Society, *Cupmarked Stones in Strathtay*, Scotland Magazine, Perth, 2005.⋆
Buchanan, Lachlan D. *Stories from Perth's History*, Melven Press, Perth, 1978.⋆
Campbell, Duncan *The Lairds of Glenlyon*, 1886 (New Ed.,Clunie Press, Strathtay, 1984).⋆
Cunningham, A.D. *A History of Rannoch*, (privately published, 1989)⋆
————— *Tales of Rannoch*, Perth and Kinross Libraries, Perth, 1989.⋆
Dorward, David *The Sidlaw Hills*, The Pinkfoot Press, Balgavies, 2004.⋆
Duncan, Jeremy *Perth and Kinross: The Big County*, John Donald Publishers, Edinburgh, 1997.
Findlay, W.H. *Heritage of Perth*, Perth and Kinross Libraries, Perth, 1996.
Fittis, Robert Scott *Historical and Traditionary Gleanings Concerning Perthshire*, The Constitutional Office, Perth, 1876.⋆
Fleming, Maurice *The Ghost o' Mause and Other Tales and Traditions of East Perthshire*, Mercat Press, Edinburgh, 1995.⋆
————— *The Sidlaws*, Mercat Press, Edinburgh, 2000.⋆
Forrester, The Revd David Marshall *Logiealmond*, Oliver and Boyd, Edinburgh and London, 1944.⋆
Fothergill, R and pupils of Primary VII, Caledonian Road School *Bridges of the Tay*, Perth and Kinross District Council, Perth, 1982.
Gillies, Revd William *In Famed Breadalbane*, 1938, Clunie Press, Old Ballechin, 2nd ed 1980.⋆
Graham-Campbell, David *Perth, The Fair City*, John Donald Publishers, Edinburgh, 1994.
Haldane, E. *Walks Around Auchterarder*, T. Nelson & Sons, London, Edinburgh and New York, 1896.
Haynes, Nick *Perth and Kinross: An Illustrated Architectural Guide*, Rutland Press, Edinburgh, 2000.
Henderson, Ebenezer, R.L. Wright and William Haldane, *The Annals of Kinross-shire*, Fossoway and District Community Council, Kinross, 1990.⋆
Hull, Robin *Ravens Over The Hill: Dùn Coillich Through The Ages*, Perth and Kinross Libraries, Perth, 2004.
Hunter, Thomas *St John's Kirk, Perth*, Thos. Hunter and Sons, Perth, 1932.
Hutcheson, Alexander *Old Stories in Stones and Other Papers*, William Kidd & Sons, Dundee, 1927.
Hutchison, William C. *Ardoch 2000: A brief history of Ardoch Parish to the end of the Second Millennium*, Ardoch 2000 Millennium Committee, Ardoch, 2000.
Huxley, Thomas *Exploring the Past In The Almond Valley*, (privately published) Pitcairngreen, 2005.
Kennedy, James *Folklore and Reminiscences of Strathtay and Grandtully*, The Munro Press, Perth, 1927.⋆

Kerr, John *The Robertson Heartland,* Highland Printers, Inverness, 1992.★

————— *Church and Social History of Atholl,* Perth and Kinross Libraries, Perth, 1998.★

Kettles, Sarah *Longforgan Architectural Heritage Trail,* (privately published) Longforgan, n.d.

Korner, Sinclair *Rambles Round Crieff and Excursions into The Highlands,* 1862.★

Liddell, Colin *Pitlochry Heritage of a Highland District,* Perth and Kinross District Libraries, Perth, 1993.★

Mackay, N.D. *Aberfeldy Past and Present,* Town Council of Aberfeldy, Aberfeldy, 1954.★

Maclagan, Robert Craig *The Perth Incident of 1396 From a Folk-Lore Point of View,* William Blackwood & Sons, Edinburgh & London, 1905.

MacMillan, Hugh *The Highland Tay: From Tyndrum to Dunkeld,* H.Virtue & Co., London, 1901.★

Marshall, William *Historic Scenes in Perthshire,* Edinburgh, 1881.★

Mayall, Colin *Around Crieff and Strathearn,* Tempus, Stroud, 2004.

Miller, Alastair Duncan *A Bit of Breadalbane,* Pentland Press, Durham, 1995.

Money, Bob *Strathearn Herald West Perthshire Hill Guide,* David Philips, Crieff, 1989.

Moody, D. (ed.) *Old Blairgowrie – Tours, History, Memories, Tales,* 1976.

T.(omar) M. [Revd Thomas Morris] *Perthshire Popular Rhymes and Ballad Fragments: Local Legends, Traditions and Histories,* compiled by R.S. Fittis from *The Perthshire Constitutional,* 9 August 1871 to 27 May 1872.

Ogilvy, Graham *The River Tay and its People,* Mainstream Publishing, Edinburgh, 1993.★

Penny, George *Traditions of Perth,* Dewar, Sidey, Morison, Peat and Drummond, Perth, 1836 (reprinted Wm Culross & Son, Coupar Angus 1986).★

Philip, Revd Adam *The Parish of Longforgan – A Sketch of Its Church and People,* Oliphant Anderson & Ferrier, Edinburgh and London, 1895.★

————— *Songs and Sayings of Gowrie,* Oliphant Anderson & Ferrier, Edinburgh and London, 1901.★

————— *Romance in Gowrie,* William Kidd & Sons, Dundee, 1923.★

Philip, Michael 'The Centre for Certain!' *Scots Magazine* Vol. 130 No.6 March, 1989.

Reid, A.G. *Strathardle its History and its People,* (privately published), Blairgowrie, 1986.★

Reid, A.G. and D.M. Lye, *Pitmiddle Village & Elcho Nunnery* Perthshire Society of Natural Science, Perth, 1988.

Ritchie, Anna *Meigle Museum Pictish Carved Stones,* Historic Scotland, Edinburgh, 1997.

Royal Commission on the Ancient and Historical Monuments of Scotland *North-East Perth an Archaeological Landscape,* HMSO, London, 1990.

————— *South-East Perth, an Archaeological Landscape,* HMSO, London 1994.★

————— *Pictish Symbol Stones, an Illustrated Gazetteer,* RCAHMS, Edinburgh, 1999.

Seath, J.W. and R.E. *Dunbarney A Parish With a Past,* Perth and Kinross District Libraries, Perth, 1991.

Sievwright, Martha Jane *The Abbey of Coupar Angus,* Culross & Sons, Coupar Angus, 1983.

Sinclair, Revd John *Schiehallion,* Eneas Mackay, Stirling, 1905.★

Smith, Anthony Mackenzie *Glenshee: Glen of the Fairies – 500 Years of Life and Legend in a Highland Glen,* Tuckwell Press, East Linton, 2000.★

Smith, D. Crawford *The Historians of Perth,* John Christie, Perth, 1906.

Stavert, Marion L. *Perth A Short History,* Urban Archaeological Unit, Perth, n.d.

Steggall, J.E.A. *Picturesque Perthshire,* Valentine & Sons, Dundee, 1906.

Steven, Campbell *Enjoying Perthshire,* Perth and Kinross District Libraries, Perth, 1994.

Stewart, Elizabeth *Dunkeld, an Ancient City* 1926 (new edition: Norman Burns, Dunkeld 1979).

Walker, Nancy H. *Historical Guide to the County of Kinross,* Kinross Antiquarian Society, Auchterarder, 1980.★

Watson, Angus *The Ochils – Placenames, History, Tradition* Perth and Kinross District Libraries, Perth, 1995.★

TRAVEL, HISTORY AND ARCHAEOLOGY – SCOTLAND:

Anon, *Scotland [An Historical Geography of Scotland, Printed 1610].*

Armit, Ian *Scotland's Hidden History,* Tempus, Stroud, 1998.

————— *Celtic Scotland: Iron Age Scotland in its European Context,* B.T. Batsford/Historic Scotland, London, 2005.

Breeze, David J. *Roman Scotland: Frontier Country,* B.T. Batsford/Historic Scotland, London, 1996.

Cruden, Stewart *Scottish Medieval Churches,* John Donald, Edinburgh, 1986.

Cuthbertson, D.C. *Highlands, Highways and Heroes,* Robert Grant and Son, Edinburgh 1931★

Dixon, Nicholas *The Crannogs of Scotland: an Underwater Archaeology,* Tempus, Stroud, 2004.

Driscoll, Stephen *Alba: The Gaelic Kingdom of Scotland AD 800-1124,* Birlinn, Edinburgh, 2002.

Drummond, Robert J. *Forgotten Scotland,* James Clarke & Co, London, 1936.

Fawcett, Richard *Scottish Abbeys and Priories,* B.T. Batsford/Historic Scotland, London, 1994.

——————— *Scottish Cathedrals,* B.T. Batsford/Historic Scotland, London, 1997.

Foster, Allan *The Literary Traveller in Edinburgh,* Mainstream Books, Edinburgh, 2005.

Gordon, Seton *Highways and Byways in the Central Highlands,* Macmillan, London, 1935 (reprinted Birlinn, Edinburgh 1995).

Jackson, Anthony *The Pictish Trail: A Travellers Guide to the Old Pictish Kingdoms,* The Orkney Press, Kirkwall, 1989.

Laing, Lloyd and Jenny *The Picts and the Scots,* Sutton, Stroud, 1998.

Mackinlay, James Murray *Influence of the Pre-Reformation Church on Scottish Place-Names,* William Blackwood and Sons, Edinburgh and London,1904.★

——————— *Ancient Church Dedications in Scotland: Non-Scriptural Dedications,* David Douglas, Edinburgh, 1914.★

New, Anthony *A Guide To The Abbeys of Scotland,* Constable, London, 1988.

Newton, Michael *A Handbook of the Scottish Gaelic World,* Four Courts Press, Dublin, 2000.

Oram, Richard *Scottish Prehistory,* Birlinn, Edinburgh, 1997.

Ritchie, Anna *Picts,* HMSO, Edinburgh, 1989.

Ritchie, Anna and Graham *Scotland: An Oxford Archaeological Guide,* Oxford University Press, Oxford, 1998.

Sadler, John *Scottish Battles: From Mons Graupius to Culloden,* Canongate Books, Edinburgh, 1996.

Scotland's Churches Scheme, *Churches to Visit in Scotland,* NMS Enterprises/Scottish Christian Press, Edinburgh, 2003.

Scott, Andrew Murray *Bonnie Dundee: John Graham of Claverhouse,* John Donald Publishers, Edinburgh, 2000.★

Wainwright, F.T. *The Souterrains of Southern Pictland,* Routledge and Kegan Paul, London, 1963.

Watson, W.G. *Celtic Place Names of Scotland,* 1926.★

TRAVEL, HISTORY AND ARCHAEOLOGY – BRITAIN:

Anderson, William *Holy Places of the British Isles: A Guide to the Legendary and Sacred Sites,* Ebury Press, London, 1983.

Burl, Aubrey *From Carnac to Callanish: The Prehistoric Stone Rows and Avenues of Britain, Ireland and Brittany,* Yale University Press, New Haven and London, 1993.★

Ellis, Peter Berresford *A Guide To Early Celtic Remains in Britain,* Constable, London, 1991.

Hayman, Richard *Riddles in Stone: Myths, Archaeology and the Ancient Britons,* The Hambledon Press, London, 1997.

Merrifield, Ralph *The Archaeology of Ritual and Magic,* B.T. Batsford, London, 1987.★

Ross, Anne *Pagan Celtic Britain,* Academy Chicago Publishers, Chicago, 1996.★

MYSTERIOUSNESS:

Adams, Norman *Haunted Scotland* Mainstream, Edinburgh, 1998.★

Archibald, Malcolm *Scottish Animal and Bird Folklore,* Saint Andrew Press, Edinburgh, 1996.

Ashe, Geoffrey *Mythology of the British Isles,* Methuen, London, 1990.

Black, George F *A Calendar of Cases of Witchcraft in Scotland 1510-1727,* New York Public Library, New York, 1938.★

Brazil, Nick *A Journey With Ghosts,* The Book Guild, Lewes, 1999.

Buczacki, Stefan *Fauna Britannica,* Hamlyn, London, 2002.

Cameron, Charles W. *Scottish Witches,* Jarrold, Norwich, 1990.

Campbell, John Gregerson (ed. Ronald Black), *The Gaelic Otherworld: John Gregerson Campbell's Superstitions of the Highlands and Islands of Scotland* and *Witchcraft and Second Sight in the Highlands and Islands,* Birlinn, Edinburgh, new edition, 2005.★

Campbell, John Gregerson (ed.) *A Collection of Highland Rites and Customes, copied by Edward Lhuyd from the manuscript of the Revd James Kirkwood (1650-1709) and annotated by him with the aid of the Revd John Beaton,* D.S. Brewer/The Folklore Society, Cambridge, 1975.

Campbell, John Lorne and Trevor Hall *Strange Things: The story of Fr Allan McDonald, Ada Goodrich Freer, and the Society for Psychical Research's enquiry into Highland second sight,* Routledge & Kegan, London, 1968.★

Christie, John *Witchcraft in Kenmore 1730-57 – Extracts From The Kirk Session of the Parish,* Duncan Cameron & Son, Aberfeldy, 1893.★

Cowan, David, with Anne Silk *Ancient Energies of the Earth,* Thorsons, London, 1999.

Coxe, Anthony D. Hippisley *Haunted Britain,* Hutchinson, London, 1973.

Dalyell, James G. *The Darker Superstitions of Scotland,* Richard Griffin, Glasgow, 1835.

Fittis, Robert Scott *The Witches and Warlocks of Perthshire, (*no date or publisher; photocopy at A.K. Bell Library, Perth).★

Fort, Charles *New Lands,* John Brown Publishing, London, 1996.

Frazer, Sir James George *The Golden Bough*, London, 1922.

Green, Andrew *Our Haunted Kingdom,* Fontana/Collins, Glasgow, 1974.

Grey, Affleck *Legends of the Cairngorms,* Mainstream Publishing, Edinburgh, 1992.★

Hall, Trevor *The Strange Story of Ada Goodrich-Freer,* Duckworth, London, 1980.

Halliday, Ron *UFO Scotland,* B&W Publishing, Edinburgh, 1998.

———— *Evil Scotland,* Fort Publishing, Ayr, 2003.

Harpur, Charles G. *Haunted Houses,* Cecil Palmer, London 1907 (new edition Senate, Twickenham 1994).

Harries, John *The Ghost Hunter's Road Book,* Frederick Muller, London, 1968.

Henderson, Lizanne and Edward J. Cowan *Scottish Fairy Belief: A History,* Tuckwell Press, East Linton, 2001.★

Holiday, F.W. *The Goblin Universe,* Xanadu Publications, London, 1986.

Hutton, Ronald *The Pagan Religions of the Ancient British Isles – Their Nature and Legacy,* Basil Blackwell, Oxford, 1991.

———— *The Stations of the Sun: A History of the Ritual Year in Britain,* Oxford University Press, Oxford, 1996.

Lamont-Brown, Raymond *Scottish Witchcraft,* Chambers, Edinburgh 1994

Love, Dane *Scottish Spectres,* Robert Hale, London, 2001.★

MacDonald, Stuart *The Witches of Fife: Witch-hunting in a Scottish Shire 1560-1710,* Tuckwell Press, East Linton, 2002.

MacGregor, Alasdair Alpin *Phantom Footsteps,* Robert Hale, London, 1958.★

———— *Strange Tales of the Highlands and Islands,* Lang Syne, Newtongrange, n.d.★

MacGregor, Alexander *Highland Superstitions,* Enneas Mackay, Stirling, 1946.

McHardy, Stuart *Scotland: Myth, Legend and Folklore,* Luath Press, Edinburgh, 1999.

———— *The Quest for The Nine Maidens,* Luath Press, Edinburgh, 2003.

McOwan, Rennie *Magic Mountains,* Mainstream Publishing, Edinburgh, 1996.★

Martine, Roddy *Supernatural Scotland,* Robert Hale, London, 2003.★

Maxwell-Stuart, P.G. *Satan's Conspiracy: Magic and Witchcraft in Sixteenth-Century Scotland,* Tuckwell Press, East Linton, 2001.★

———— *An Abundance of Witches: The Great Scottish Witch-Hunt,* Tempus, Stroud, 2005.★

Melville, Lawrence *Errol: Its Legends, Lands and People,* Thomas Hunter & Sons, Perth, 1935.★

Miller, Joyce *Magic and Witchcraft in Scotland,* Goblinshead, Musselburgh, 2004.

Mitchell, Ann Lindsay *Mystical Scotland* Thomas & Lochar, Nairn, 1994.

O'Donnell, Elliott *Casebook of Ghosts – True Stories From The Files of the World's Greatest Ghost-Hunter,* Foulsham, Slough, 1969.★

———— *Scottish Ghost Stories,* Jarrold, Norwich, 1975.

Parsons, Coleman O. *Witchcraft and Demonology in Scott's Fiction,* Oliver & Boyd, Edinburgh & London, 1964.

Pennick, Nigel *Celtic Sacred Landscapes,* Thames and Hudson, London, 1996.

Pickering, David *Dictionary of Witchcraft,* Cassell, London, 1996.

Pugh, Roy J.M. *The De'il's Ain,* Harlaw Heritage, Balerno, 2001.

Richardson, Alan *Spirits of the Stones: Visions of Sacred Britain,* Virgin, London, 2001.

Robertson, R MacDonald *Selected Highland Folk Tales,* Oliver and Boyd, Edinburgh and London, 1961.★

Ross, Anne *Folklore of the Scottish Highlands,* Tempus Publishing, Stroud, 2nd Edition, 2000.★

Seafield, Lily *Scottish Ghosts,* Lomond Books, New Lanark, 1999.

Sharpe, C.K *Witchcraft in Scotland,* London, 1884.

Shuker, Karl P.N. *In Search of Prehistoric Survivors,* Blandford, London, 1995.

Spence, Lewis *The Magic Arts in Celtic Britain,* Constable, London, 1995 (original edition 1945).

———— *The Fairy Tradition in Britain*, Rider, London, 1948.

Sutherland, Elizabeth *Ravens and Black Rain: The Story of Highland Second Sight,* Constable and Co., London, 1985.★

Thomas, Keith *Religion and the Decline of Magic,* Peregrine, Harmondsworth, 1978.

Toulson, Shirley *Celtic Journeys: Scotland and the North of England,* Hutchinson, London, 1985.

Underwood, Peter *No Common Task: The Autobiography of a Ghost-Hunter,* Harrap, London, 1983.

———— *This Haunted Isle,* Harrap, London, 1984.

———— *The Ghosthunters Almanac,* Eric Dolby Publishing, Orpington, 1993.

———— *Guide to Ghosts and Haunted Places,* Piatkus, London, 1996.

Wilson, Stephen *The Magical Universe: Everyday Ritual and Magic in Pre-Modern Europe,* Hambledon, London and New York, 2000.

Index